THE NĀGA TRIBES OF MANIPUR

THE NĀGA TRIBES OF MANIPUR

By

T. C. HODSON

LATE ASSISTANT POLITICAL AGENT IN MANIPUR AND
SUPERINTENDENT OF THE STATE. FELLOW OF THE ROYAL ANTHROPOLOGICAL
INSTITUTE AND MEMBER OF THE FOLKLORE SOCIETY

GYAN

Published by

Gyan Publishing House
5, Ansari Road
Daryaganj, New Delhi-110002
Phone: 011-47034999, 9811692060
E-mail: books@gyanbooks.com

Distribution Network
gyanbooks.com
India, USA, Canada, UK, Australia, France

ISBN : 978-81-212-6282-8 (PB)
First Published, 1911

2nd Impression 2022

Printed at: Gyan Press, Delhi.

THE NĀGA TRIBES OF MANIPUR
Author: T. C. HODSON

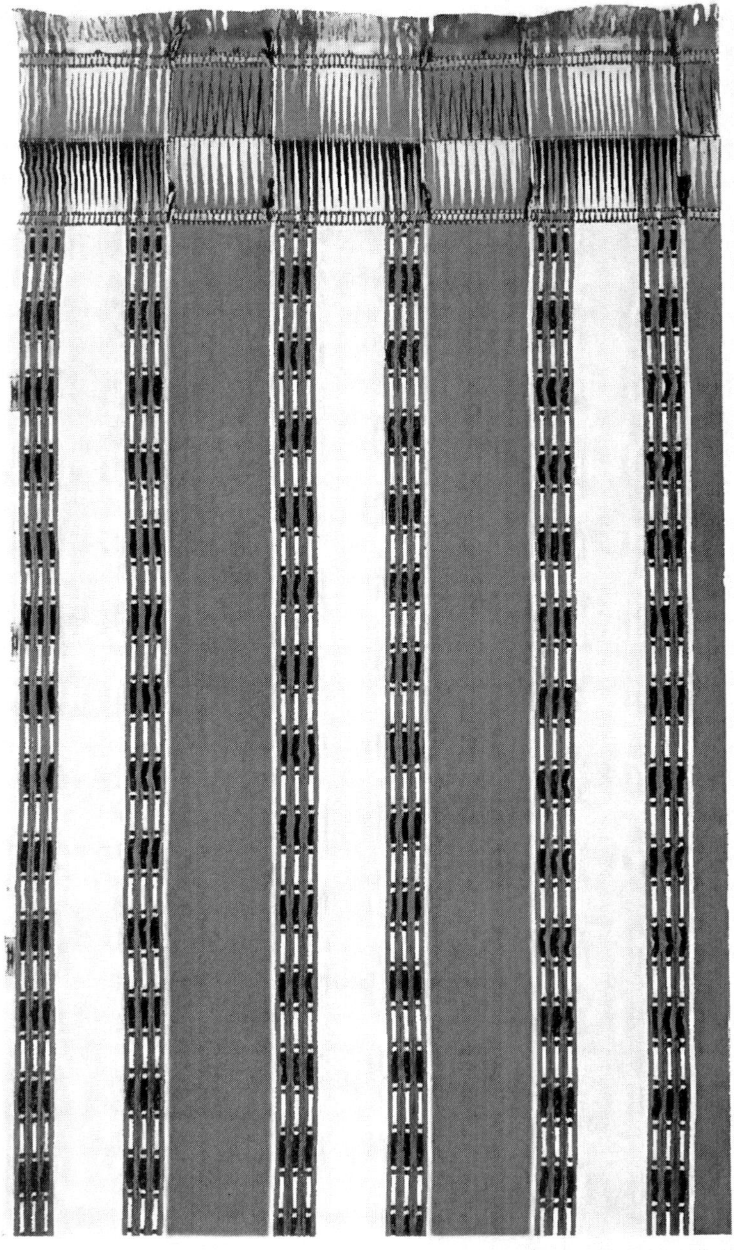

TANGKHUL KHULLAKPA'S CLOTH. See p. 22.

Frontispiece

THE NĀGA TRIBES OF MANIPUR

BY

T. C. HODSON

Late Assistant Political Agent in Manipur and Superintendent of the State. Fellow of the Royal Anthropological Institute and Member of the Folklore Society

PUBLISHED UNDER THE AUTHORITY OF THE GOVERNMENT OF EASTERN BENGAL AND ASSAM BY

1911

PREFACE

I DESIRE to tender my sincere thanks to the President and Council of the Folklore Society for their courtesy in lending me the blocks from which the illustrations on pages 64, 120, 126, and 186 have been reproduced and in permitting me to make copious extracts from the paper on Head-hunting, published in *Folklore* for June, 1909.

I should also like to express my gratitude to Lieut.-Colonel J. Shakespear, C.I.E., D.S.O., Political Agent in Manipur, who read the manuscript through and made many valuable suggestions to me. The notes to which the initials J. S. are appended are by Colonel Shakespear, and form a remarkable addition to the book, the material for which was collected —without any idea of publication—ten years ago.

T. C. HODSON.

EAST LONDON COLLEGE,
UNIVERSITY OF LONDON.

CONTENTS

SECTION IV.—RELIGION.

LIST OF ILLUSTRATIONS

LIST OF AUTHORITIES CITED

Allen, Grant, "The Attis of Caius Valerius Catullus." 1892.

"L'Année Sociologique." Vols. I–X. Edited by M. E. Durkheim. 1898–1907.

Banerji, Babu Nithor Nath, MSS. Notes.

Boulger, D., "Short History of China." 1893.

Brown, Dr. R. (*Political Agent in Manipur*), "Selections from the Records of the Government of India, Foreign Department," No. LXXVIII. 1870.

Burne, Miss C. S., Presidential Address, *Folklore*, XXI. 1. 1910.

Butler, Major J., "Travels and Adventures in the Province of Assam." 1855.

Clodd, E., "Tom Tit Tot." 1898.

Crawley, E. A., "The Mystic Rose." 1902. "The Idea of the Soul." 1909.

Dalton, Capt. E. T. (*Principal Assistant Agent to the Governor General*), "Selections from the Records of the Bengal Government," No. XXIII. 1855.

Das, Sarat Chandra, C.I.E., "Journey to Lhasa and Central Tibet." 1904.

Davis, A. W., "Assam Census Report," Vol. I., pp. 237–251. 1891.

Durkheim, E., "La Prohibition de L'Inceste." *L. A. S.*, Vol. I. 1898.

Elias, N., "History of the Shans." 1876.

Farnell, Dr. L. R., "Transactions of the Third International Congress on the History of Religions." Vol. II. 1908. "Cults of the Greek States," Vol. V. 1909.

Forbes, Capt. C. J. F. S., "British Burma." 1878.

Frazer, Dr. James, "The Golden Bough." 2nd ed. 1900. "The Early History of the Kingship." 1905. "Totemism and Exogamy." 1910.

Fuller, Sir Bampfylde, K.C.S.I. (*late Lieutenant-Governor of Eastern Bengal and Assam*), "Studies of Indian Life and Sentiment." 1910.

Gait, E. A., C.I.E. (*late Chief Secretary to the Government of Assam*), "History of Assam." 1906.

Gomme, Sir G. L., "The Village Community." 1890. "Folklore as a Historical Science." 1908.

Grierson, Dr. A., C.I.E. (*Director of the Linguistic Survey of India*), "Report of the Linguistic Survey of India." Vol. III. Parts ii. and iii. 1903.

Gurdon, Colonel P. R. T. (*Commissioner of the Assam Valley and Superintendent of Ethnography, Assam*), "The Khasis." 1907.

Harrison, Miss J., "Prolegomena to Greek Religion." 1903.

Hartland, S., "Primitive Paternity." 1909. "The Cult of Executed Criminals at Palermo," *Folklore*, XXI., 2., pp. 168 *et seq.*

Henderson, Colonel G. F. R., C.B., "The Science of War." 1908.

Henry, V., "La Magie dans L'Inde Antique." 1909.

Hertz, R., "La representation collective de la Mort." *L. A. S.*, Vol. X. 1907.

Hobhouse, L. T., "Morals in Evolution." 1906.

Hodson, T. C., "Thado Grammar." 1906. "Genna Amongst the Tribes of Assam." *J. A. I.*, Vol. XXXVI. "The Meitheis." 1908. "Mortuary Ritual and Eschatological Beliefs among the Hill Tribes of Assam." *Archiv für Religionswissenschaft*, Vol. XII. 1909. "Head-hunting among the Hill Tribes of Assam," *Folklore*, Vol. XX., 2. 1909.

Jevons, Dr. F. B., "Plutarch's Romane Questions." 1892. "Introduction to the History of Religion," 3rd ed. 1904.

Johnstone, Major-General Sir James, K.C.S.I. (*Political Agent in Manipur*), "My Experiences in Manipur and the Nāga Hills." 1896.

King, I., "The Development of Religion." 1910.

Lang, A., "Custom and Myth." Edition 1901. "Myth, Ritual, and Religion." 1899.

Lewin, Colonel T. H. (*Political Officer*), "The Hill Tracts of Chittagong." 1869. "Wild Races of South-Eastern India." 1870.

Ling-Roth, H., "Significance of the Couvade," *J. A. I.*, Vol. XXII., pp. 204-241.

Logan, J. N., "Journal of the Indian Archipelago," N.S., Vol. II., p. 82.

Lorrain and Savidge, "A Grammar and Dictionary of the Lushai Language." 1898.

Lyall, Sir Charles J., K.C.S.I., C.I.E. (*formerly Chief Commissioner of Assam*), "The Mikirs." 1908.

Maine, Sir Henry S., K.C.S.I., "Ancient Law." 1861. "Early Law and Custom." 1883.

Marett, R. R., "The Threshold of Religion." 1909.

McCulloch, Colonel W. (*Political Agent at Manipur*), "Account of the Valley of Munnipore. Selections from the Records of the Government of India, Foreign Department," No. XXVII. 1859.

McLennan, J. F., "Primitive Marriage." 1865.

Neufville, Capt. J. B. (*D.A.Q.M.G.*), "Selections from the Records of the Bengal Government," No. XXIII. 1855.

Owen, J., "Notes on the Nāga Tribes in Communication with Assam." 1844.

Payne, E. J., "History of the New World called America." 1892.

Peal, S. E., "On the Morong as possibly a Relic of Pre-marriage Communism," *J. A. I.*, Vol. XXII., pp. 244–261. Illustrated.

Pettigrew, Rev. W., "Kathi Kashām, the Soul Departure Feast, as Practised by the Tangkhul Nāgas, Manipur, Assam," *J. A. S. B.* (N. S.), Vol. V., No. 2, pp. 37-46, 1909.

Playfair, Major A. (*Deputy Commissioner, Garo Hills*), "The Garos." 1909.

Risley, Sir Herbert, K.C.I.E., C.S.I. (*Director of the Census of India*), "Ethnography of India." 1903.

Rivers, Dr. W. H. R., F.R.S., "The Father's Sister in Oceania," *Folklore*, XXI., 42–59. 1910.

Seligmann, Dr. C. G., "The Vedda Cult of the Dead." *Transactions of the Third International Congress of the History of Religions.* Oxford, 1908.

Soppitt, C. A., "Account of the Kachcha Nāgas." 1885.

Shakespear, Colonel J., C.I.E., D.S.O. (*Political Agent in Manipur*), "The Kuki-Lushai Clans," *J.R.A.I.*, Vol. XXXIX., pp. 371–385. "Journal of the Society of Arts," Vol. XLIII.

Tylor, Dr. E. B., "Early History of Mankind." 1865. "Primitive Culture," 4th ed. 1903.

"Upper Burma Gazetteer." Edited by Sir George Scott, K.C.I.E., and J. P. Hardiman. 1900.

Van Gennep, A., "Rites de Passage." 1909. "La Formation des Légendes." 1910.

Vetch, Major H. (*Political Agent, Upper Assam*), "Selections from the Records of the Bengal Government," No. XXIII. 1855.

Webster, Dr. H., "Primitive Secret Societies." 1908.

Westermarck, Dr. E. A., "The History of Human Marriage." 1901. "The Origin and Development of the Moral Ideas." 1906 and 1908.

Wilcox, Lieut. R., "Survey of Assam and the Neighbouring Countries." 1825–6–7–8. "Selections from the Records of the Bengal Government," XXXII. 1855.

THE NĀGA TRIBES OF MANIPUR

ASSAM SHOWING AREA OCCUPIED BY HILL TRIBES NAGA & KUKI IN THE MANIPUR STATE

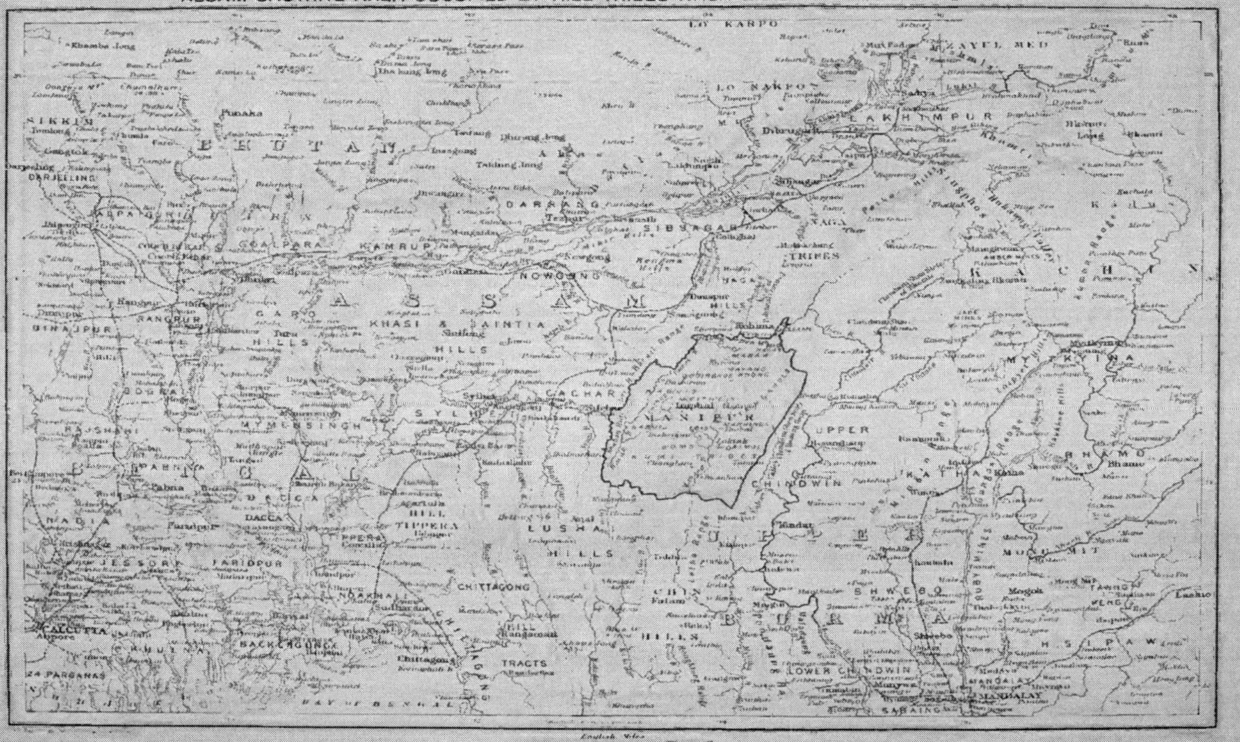

THE NĀGA TRIBES OF MANIPUR

SECTION I.

HABITAT AND GEOGRAPHICAL DISTRIBUTION.

In this volume it is proposed to describe the ethnology of the tribes inhabiting the hills which in point of area form the greater part of the State of Manipur. The State lies between latitude 23°50′ and 25°30′ North and longitude 93°10′ and 94°30′ East and contains about 8,000 square miles of which 7,000 square miles are hill territory as opposed to the valley territory and are inhabited by Nāga and Kuki tribes, hill people, who number slightly more than 100,000. While accepting with due reserve the familiar distinction between Nāgas[1] and Kukis, it may be pointed out that the tribes commonly classed together as Nāga and Kuki occupy definite areas in these hills. A line drawn across the map following the Kubo valley road *viâ* Aimole and joined to the Cachar road which traverses the western hills from Bisnupur in Manipur to Jiri Ghat on the western boundary of the State separates the Nāga area from the Kuki area without excluding more than a few small Kabui villages which lie to the south of Nongba. North of that line we find Nāga villages and to the south of it Kuki settlements, although for various reasons, economic and political, Kuki settlements exist not only in the British District of the Nāga Hills in the vicinity of Henema but also far away on the north-east of the

[1] The term Nāga is said to be derived from the Assamese, Nogā—applied by them to the hill-tribes in the Hinterland of the Lakhimpur and Sibsagar Districts. (Grierson, L.S.I. Vol. iii. Part ii. p, 194.) The term Kuki is of Assamese or Bengali origin and of some antiquity. (Grierson, L.S.I. Vol. iii. Part. iii., p. 1.)

Manipur State, in the neighbourhood of Melome and Lapvome where the frontier has been delimitated and ascertained only within the last few years. Indeed the Kuki is to be found almost everywhere in the State except in the territory occupied by the Mao confederacy. "We are like the birds of the air," said a Kuki to me once, "we make our nests here this year, and who knows where we shall build next year." Yet inasmuch as their affinities are with the Lushai tribes of the hills south of the Manipur State rather than with the Nāga tribes of the north, it has been considered desirable to separate the Kukis from the scope of the present volume in order that they may be dealt with along with their congeners.

The Nāga tribes in Manipur with whom this olume is concerned, are (1) the Tangkhuls who inhabit the hills immediately to the east and north-east of the valley of Manipur; (2) the Mao and Marām Nāgas who inhabit the hills north of the valley and to whom the title quasi-Angāmi Nāgas has been given by some writers on the ground that they are more closely connected with the Angāmis than with their fellow subjects the Tangkhuls and the Kabuis; (3) the Kolyā, Khoirao or Māyang Khong group in the hills south of Mao and Marām; (4) the Kabuis who inhabit the hills to the west and north-west of the valley and (5, 6 and 7) Quoirongs, Chirus, Marrings, smaller tribes, who are to be found in the hills bordering the valley.

The Tangkhuls are found over a large area which has for its western limit the line of the river Iril. The most northerly villages are Kharasom, Chatlao and Tussum, close to the Eastern Angāmi Political Control Area of the Nāga Hills District with which, when the frontier was rectified, they were incorporated, although for long years tributary to Manipur. On the east they touch the frontier of Upper Burma (Upper Chindwin District) and the Somra group of villages, which is outside the territory of the State of Manipur, is of Tangkhul origin and is in contact with Singpho tribes on the east and north-east. The most southern Tangkhul villages are Sagōk-lang and Tangkhul Hundung. Mapao, to the immediate north of Imphāl, is their most westerly settlement and there are some stray settlers in the valley itself at Thobāl. We may fix the peak, Sirōhifurar, as the centre of their distribution and note incidentally that it dominates the landscape of nearly every Tangkhul village and plays an important part in their eschatology.

The Mao and Māram Nāgas derive their name from the two most important villages in their area. While they are often associated, they are in all probability as different *inter se* as any two Nāga tribes in such close proximity can be. The peak Kopamedza, marks the centre of the maximum density of the Mao group fairly well, and we may here observe that this and Sirohifurar form part of the watershed which separates the river system of Burma from that of Bengal. The Lanier rises below Sirohifurar, flows thence northward, bends east by Saramettį and joins the Chindwin, ultimately discharging its waters into the Irrawaddy. The Barāk river rises in the folds of Kopamedza, flows thence southward, bends north at Kairong,[1] and below Marām takes a second bend to the south right through the hills, receives tributaries from the western face of the hills that guard the western side of the valley of Manipur and from the Lushai Hills, turns westwards through Cachar and Sylhet, whose plains owe much to its fertilising floods, and at last reaches the river system of the Ganges and the Brahmaputra. Whether the geographical formation has played any and, if so, what part in the distribution and evolution as regards social structure of these tribes, are questions, large questions, to which at the present time and in the present volume no reply can be offered. It is certain that the settlement of permanent villages with permanent rice fields is only possible in those portions of the hills where the slopes are lenient and the soil suitable.

The village of Mao, a Meithei name, or Sopvoma as it is called by the Nāgas themselves, lies on the western spurs of Kopamedza, on the cart road from Dimapur to Imphal. Close to it and almost contiguous are the villages of Robugnāmei and Pūdugnāmei which form part of the Mao leaguer. Its kindred villages stretch to the east as far as Jessami (Phundrak in Meithei), which is built on an apex of land between the Lanier and the river which rises below Mao, and looks towards Melome and Lapvome. Svemi (Chinjaroy in Meithei), the

[1] "Ong" in Meithei in place-names means a place where waters meet.—T. C. H.

scene of one of the most bloodthirsty raids which we have to place to the credit of the Kukis, is an interesting village since it is now inhabited by Mao people and by Tangkhuls with the result that the typical customs of both tribes are here being subjected to modification owing to the synœcism that has taken place. Oinām and Purum belong to the Mao group but are so far removed from the direct influence of Mao that they present many features of interest, enough to differentiate them from Mao. On the west of the Manipur-Kohima road the group extends to Uilong, the village in whose vicinity is a collection of stone monoliths of rare symmetry, and to Yang and Bakema, villages more nearly connected with Mao or Marām than with the Kabui Nāgas or with the Katcha Nāgas. West of the Barāk are villages which told Colonel Shakespear that they took their origin from Marām.

The Kolyā Nāgas[1] or Khoirao Nāgas,[2] or, as I prefer to call them, the Māyang Khong, inhabit nine villages in the hills south of Marām and Kairong. They are now almost indistinguishable, in so far as customs and appearance are concerned, from Mao and Marām, and I was informed that they were descended from Marām. The specimens given in the Linguistic Survey report[3] show clearly that they belong to a different linguistic group, designated by Dr. Grierson the Nāga Bodo Sub-group, from the Mao or Sopvoma Nāgas, who on linguistic grounds are connected with the Angāmis, especially with Kezhāma.[4] Colonel McCulloch,[5] however, says of the group that "It partakes more of the character of Koupooees than of its northern neighbours"—thus bringing them into the same linguistic group to which, on philological grounds, they are assigned by Dr. Grierson.

The Kabui Nāgas are now restricted to the hills immediately north of the Cachar road. There is ample evidence, historical and traditional, to show that their expulsion from the hills to the south is comparatively recent. I have stumbled across ruins of large villages in the jungles south of Nongba, and learnt that they were the ruins of Kabui villages that had

[1] Brown, *Report*, p. 121.
[2] Grierson, *L.S.I.*, Vol. iii. Part ii. p. 424.
[3] *Loc. cit.*
[4] *Op. cit.* p. 451.
[5] *Op. cit.* p. 70.

been destroyed either by Kukis or by Manipuris in the early part of the last century. There are small villages of Kabuis in the valley of Manipur which are in a semi-servile condition.

The Quoirengs now consist of but nine small villages in the country just south of the great Bar'ail range, which forms the north-western boundary of the State.

The Chirus inhabit some thirteen villages situated on the slopes of the hills on the western side of the Manipur valley, and are not numerous.

The Marrings have a few villages in the Hirok range of Hills, in the south-west of the valley.

Appearance.

Differences of stature, dress, coiffure and weapons make it easy to distinguish between the members of these tribes. In colour they are all brown with but little variety, though some of the Tangkhuls who earn their living by salt making seem to be darker. Among them all, as among the Manipuris, there are persons who have a tinge of colour in their cheeks when still young. The nose also varies, for there are cases where it is almost straight, while in the majority of individuals it is flattened at the nostril.[1] No information is at present available as to the measurements of the skull. The eyes are usually brown, though black eyes are sometimes found to occur. The jaw is generally clean, not heavy, and the hair is of some variety, as there are many persons whose hair is decidedly curly, and in most there is a wave. Beards are very uncommon, and hair on the face is very rare, so much so that the few who possess a moustache are known as *khoi-hao-bas* (Meithei words, meaning moustache grower). I am informed that the ladies do not like hirsute men, and that the men therefore pull out any stray hairs. The cheek-bones are often prominent, and the slope of the eye is not very marked. Two excellent accounts of the Kabuis, the earlier by Colonel McCulloch and the later by Dr. Brown, have been preserved, and from them I have drawn freely. Dr. Brown states[2] that "The facial characteristics of the Kowpoee

[1] Here and there one may see noses which in profile are almost Roman.
[2] *Op. cit.* p. 101.

tribe are as various as amongst the other hill clans: occasionally an almost purely Mongolian cast of countenance will be observed, to be succeeded by one closely approaching the Aryan type. The stature is moderate, and sometimes very short men are seen; tall men are rare; they generally have well-shaped slender figures, but no prominent muscular development. Some of them have good looks, and not infrequently the younger girls are prepossessing in appearance." "The features of the Murrings approximate to those of the Burmese; some of them have flat and others well-shaped noses, and their general expression is mild and intelligent."[1]

Physical and General Characteristics.

The height of the men of these tribes varies from the slender, lightly built Marrings to the tall, sturdy, finely proportioned Maos. The range of variety must be from about five feet three inches to six feet, and although it is difficult without data to speak with the accuracy that is essential, yet the impression upon my mind is that the men of the large, permanently settled villages which possess terraced cultivation are bigger, stronger, finer creatures in all respects than those of the small villages, where living is scanty, where all depend upon the precarious produce of the jhumed fields, and where of necessity there is still a tendency to move in search of better lands.

The women are all much shorter than the men, but strongly built, with a muscular development of which the men would not be ashamed. Before aged by the cares and troubles of motherhood and matrimony, they are often very comely, with handsome figures. The habit of suckling children until they are four years of age or even more soon destroys the soft fulness of the bosom, and women of thirty are to all appearance aged hags, worn and wrinkled.

Both men and women carry heavy loads, and when impressed as coolies are not authorised to carry more than thirty seers, or about sixty pounds. On their own account they will carry twice that amount. The loads are fastened by means of a browband made of plaited cane, which is tied to the basket or

[1] *Op. cit.* p. 125.

A MARRING NĀGA. [*To face p.* 20]

From a photograph by the Author.

MAO NĀGAS.

From a photograph by E. J. Mitchell, Esq., P.W.D.

[*To face p. 6*

box and keeps it in position. The Kabuis have taken to the yoke over the shoulders. I suspect that this has been borrowed from the Meitheis,[1] who have now taken to disapprove of even this method of carrying a load, as it makes them look like Nāgas. In preference the Nāgas use the short cuts,[2] but the roads through the hills are coming into increasing favour, and as the traveller finds it more satisfactory to employ a bullock cart on the Kohima-Manipur road, the villages near the road do very little service in transport.

There is more cheerfulness among the people who live in the large permanent villages than among those who have to lead the wearisome, precarious life of the small villages. Yet laughter is not stilled even there, and some of the heartiest audiences I have ever talked to with the aid of a magic lantern have been gathered from quite small villages to which the European is an utter stranger. One source of amusement to them is their love of a joke, and peals of laughter used to greet the boastful youth who tried to snatch a four anna piece from a pail of water which was connected with a galvanic battery. The women do not take much part in amusements of this nature, for on them falls most of the burden of life; but they are not unnaturally shy, and become talkative when they are certain that their remarks will be listened to. I do not remember any case of cruelty to women or children in these tribes, and it has often seemed to me that the neglect of Solomon's maxim, "Spare the rod and spoil the child," accounted for the waywardness of the young men, who had not learnt the saving grace of peacefulness in sorrow and tribulation as had their fathers. Children are scolded, but seldom chastised. They are industrious, but the unpleasant tasks which make up the daily round all fall to the women, who take at least their fair share in the work of cultivation.

A large amount of rice beer is consumed in a village during the festivals and is soporific rather than intoxicating in its effects. The raw spirit manufactured at Sengmai is purchased

[1] The yoke is used all over the Lushai hills, but I think gets a little rarer as you go south.—J. S.

[2] I found that a Government road was sufficient to deflect the trade from Demagiri to Aijal. The Lushais said that the bridges and clear road more than compensated for an extra day's journey.—J. S. *See* McCulloch, *op. cit.* p. 44.

by Nāgas, especially those of the Mao and Marām villages, who visit the valley for trade. Special permission is necessary, as the spirit is ardent and not as good as rice beer when consumed in quantities. It is seldom easy to get a clear understanding of what these people regard as virtuous and vicious in conduct.

Hostility to outsiders is not uncommon among tribes organised as are these in small communities which tend to become endogamous as regards other similar communities, but which are internally composed of exogamous divisions. They lived in a constant state of feud—village with village, clan with clan. "Even now," said Colonel McCulloch,[1] "the inhabitants of one village will not drink of the running stream which supplies the wants of another village with which they were formerly at feud. Perhaps in either village, no one has personal knowledge of the cause of the feud, but it is preserved by tradition, and descends from generation to generation, a heritage of hate." The great solvent of these feelings is trade, and it is intelligible that the most enterprising among them, whether individuals or whole villages, now take to commercial instead of bellicose activities.

They display no mean skill in minor manufactures, but their tools are as yet unspecialised. The manufacture of earthen pots is a good example of a localised industry. It is characteristic of their "mentality" that all these valuable but subsidiary industries are "tabued" when they might conflict with the staple, the cultivation of rice. When and how did the Mao Nāgas learn the art of "polling" trees?

ORIGIN.

In the case of the Tangkhuls the traditions as to their origin resolve themselves into at least three groups. In the first group are the traditions which connect them with the valley and derive them thence as emigrants on account of the heat and mosquitoes. According to the second group of traditions, the village of Hundung (which must be distinguished from Tangkhul Hundung) is the centre of their dispersion, and the stories declare that they sprang from immigrants from the village of Maikel Tunggām (a village which is also the

[1] *Op. cit.* p. 43.

traditional home of the common ancestors of the Quasi Angāmi tribes in the Mao group). The third set of traditions refers to a period rather later and mainly deals with the growth of new villages and their establishment by emigrants from older villages which suffered from an excess of population. The second group of tradition affords a link with the general tradition which makes the Nāgas, Kukis, and Manipuris descended from a common ancestor, who had three sons who became the progenitors of those tribes. This tradition, which is widely spread, agrees in its many versions in assigning the primacy of descent to the Kukis, the next place being given to the Nāgas, while the Manipuris are said to be the children of the youngest of these three brothers. The Tangkhul legend is to the effect that one day a sow heavy with young wandered from the village of Hundung and was tracked to the valley by the younger of the two brothers who had migrated from the village of Maikel Tunggām, where their parents lived, and had founded the village of Hundung. Oknung, the pig's stone, the place where the sow was eventually found, is situated on the banks of the Iril river. The sow littered there and the young man stayed to look after her, and as he found the country to his liking he made up his mind to settle there. For a time he kept up friendly relations with his brother in the hills, who made a practice of sending him every year gifts of the produce of the hills and in turn received presents of the manufactures of the plains. The younger brother waxed fat and proud, and abandoned the custom of sending presents to his brother in the hills, who promptly came down and took what he had been in the habit of getting. In this story, therefore, is found an explanation of the curious custom which allowed the Tangkhuls to loot the women vendors at the *Sena Kaithel* of certain articles on the day of the *Hao chongba*,[1] or the Nāga sports. Others find in it a reminiscence of the frequent Tangkhul raids on the valley or of their pilfering habits. The Manipuris got round the difficulty by ordering the women who sold the produce that custom made liable to this undesirable impost to stay away from the market on that occasion. It is probable that the legend was invented to explain the custom.

[1] Hao—Meithei for Nāga. Chōngba = to jump.

If so, the custom is derived from a time when the rights of the youngest son were prepotent; in fact, this position of affairs actually obtains among some Kuki clans and in part among the Meitheis.[1]

The common feature in all these legends about their origin is the absence of any claim to be the original inhabitants of the country they now occupy.

The legend which connects them with the valley declares that they sprang from a stone in the police lines, which, curiously enough, is also claimed [2] by a section of the Marring Nāgas, the southern neighbours of the Tangkhuls, as their place of origin. They left the valley because the heat and the mosquitoes made life there impossible, and migrated to the hills, taking with them fire which became extinguished when they were on the ridge between Hundung and Ukrul. This misfortune was set straight by the timely intervention of the Deity, who taught them to get fire from a stone, and to this day the sacred stone from which they first struck fire is still standing and is worshipped. The *maibung*, or fire-stone, is the abode of, but not, the Deity himself, and is well known as a *laiphain*.[3] They struck the stone with a dao and thus got fire. In general, they kindle fire by means of the friction of a piece of cane twirled in the hands against a piece of dry wood, on which dry thatch is piled. They do not use a drill or bow.

They preserve the memory of migrations to the area occupied by the Somra group, among whom are current traditions acknowledging the connection. These as well as the inter-village migrations are definitely stated to have been due to the pressure of population on the available land near the parent village.

Dr. Brown [4] states that the origin of the Tangkhuls is thus given by themselves. They say they came out of a cave in the earth at a place called Murringphy in the hills, about four days' journey north-east of the Munnipore valley. They attempted to leave this cave one by one, but a large tiger, who was on the watch, devoured them successively as they emerged. Seeing this the occupiers of the cave by a stratagem—throwing

[1] *Vide The Meitheis*, p. 77. *See below*, p. 12.
[2] *See below*, p. 15.
[3] *I.e.*, abode of or place of a Deity.
[4] *Report for* 1868–9, p. 118.

out the effigy of a man they had dressed up—distracted the attention of the tiger, and took the opportunity of leaving the cave in a body: the tiger, on seeing the numbers before him, fled. They placed a large stone on the top of a high hill near this spot (which still remains) as a mark, from which situation they spread in the hills around."

An identical story is current among the Marrings and I have never met it among the Tangkhuls. Murringphy is in the Marring area, and it is quite possible that Dr. Brown, in many respects a very careful observer, was misled in this matter. We may conclude that the pedigree of this, the one and only legend of their origin which describes them as autochthonous, is not sufficiently authenticated for general acceptance.

From the records of Manipur we gather some rather important facts regarding the antiquity of the Tangkhuls. One of the earliest raids mentioned in the chronicles of Manipur is dated 1435, and is said to have been the work of Tangkhuls who then, as on subsequent occasions, availed themselves of the opportunity afforded them by the temporary absence of the forces of Manipur on what the local historian calls a march of conquest in the direction of Thaungdut, to make a raid on the valley. Frequent mention is made of the Tangkhuls in connection with attacks on Manipuri settlements on the edge of the valley, and it may be argued with plausibility that, as Dr. Tylor says of primitive poetry,[1] while what they relate may be fiction, what they mention is apt to be history. In fact, I might go further and say that we may regard as very largely true anything that tells against their pretensions. There can be no doubt that much of what we find in the chronicles is hopelessly exaggerated, but it is quite clear that these tribes, especially the Tangkhuls, were settled in the areas they now occupy at an early date, when the Meitheis, now their masters, were yet wild and untouched by the finer arts of life.

Among the Mao Nāgas we find a variant of the legend which connects the hill tribes Nāga as well as Kuki with the Manipuris. Once upon a time there was a jumping match between the three sons of the common ancestor. The Kuki leapt from the top of one range of hills to the crest of the next, while the

[1] *Primitive Culture*, Vol. I. p. 416.

Nāga, nearly as good, cleared the intervening valley, but his foot slipped and touched the river. Hence the limit on his ablutions, while the stronger Kuki to this day avoids all use of water. The Manipuri tumbled headlong, which explains his fondness for bathing. Another variant says that the father of them all was a Deity named Asu who had three sons, Māmo, Alapa, and Tuto. From Māmo are descended the Kukis and the Nāgas, while the Gurkhalis[1] are sprung from the loins of Alapa and the sons of Tuto are the Manipuris. Asked why they paid revenue to the Manipuris, they said that they grew the cotton on the hills (which is not specially true because the Kukis grow rather more) and sent it down to the Manipuris, who had learnt the art of weaving. In course of time the finished cloth was returned to them, and, not knowing what to do with such long pieces of cloth, the Nāgas gave back the greater part to the Manipuris, who wear more clothes than they do.[2] The Manipuris were the Benjamin of the tribes who supported them and have gone on doing so ever since.

A Thādo variant of this legend is recorded by Dr. Grierson:[3] "Our forefathers have told us that man formerly lived in the bowels of the earth. The Khongzais and the Mēthēs were then friends. One day they quarrelled about a cloth, and their mother took a dao and cut it in two pieces. The Mēthēs began to cut haimang trees and, finding their footprints fresh, many people followed them. That is the reason why the Mēthēs are so numerous. The Khongzais went to cut plantain trees and then ascended into the earth. These footprints looked rather old and therefore only few people followed. The Khongzais are, therefore, few." As I have pointed out in my Thādo Grammar,[4] the story is not complete in its present shape, as the point of the quarrel is not brought out. The Manipuris

[1] *See below*, p. 25.

[2] The common feature on all these tales is the insistence on the fact that the Benjamin's share is the largest. The custom of "Borough English" has been variously explained, but its real nature may be elucidated by a comparative study of the customs of inheritance as found among people in this stage of culture, provided always that economic environment be, if not identical, at any rate not too widely dissimilar. *See Upper Burma Gazetteer*, Vol. i. Part i. p. 373. Davis, *A.C.R.*, 1891, p. 240. Gomme, *Folklore as a Historical Science*, p. 171. *Folklore*, xxi. i. p. 20.

[3] *Linguistic Survey of India*, Vol. iii. Part iii. p. 71.

[4] P. 59.

THE MAIKEL STONE. [To face p. 12

From a photograph by the Author.

got the larger share, and for that reason they now use more cloth in dressing themselves than the Kukis, and they, the Manipuris, being the younger, were helped by their mother in the quarrel.

At Maikel is to be seen a stone, now erect, which marks the place from which the common ancestors emerged from the earth. Maikel is regarded as the centre from which migrations took place, and at the present time there are two distinct groups, each denouncing the other as schismatic, the one headed by the gennabura of Mao and the other by the khullākpa of Maikel. So far as the temporalities are concerned, the gennabura of Mao enjoys the spoils of victory, for he gets two baskets of paddy from the villages specially leagued with Maikel in addition to the tribute of his own particular villages.

The legend of the origin of Marām presents several features of interest. In the first place the ancestors of the village came from the west. They were a couple named Medungasi and Simoting, and it fell out that a great flood came and destroyed all mankind but these two. Finding themselves alone they did not know if they might properly marry and therefore went out into the jungle together. There what befell them showed that there was some hindrance to their union, and they dreamed that night, and in their dreams a god came to the man and told him that they might marry, but on the condition that henceforth none of their descendants should eat the flesh of the pig. Thus is it that to this day the pig is forbidden to the men of Marām and to all the villages that follow Marām. We may notice the importance of dreams and of the divine messages revealed in them. Next that the exogamous principle is founded on a divine ordinance.[1] Then we have the almost totemistic connection of an animal ancestor with the prohibition against the flesh of the animal. Then, as a small matter of sociological importance, the consummation of the marriage occurs, not in the house or in the village, but outside, in the jungle, a fact which is intimately connected with the marital genna.

From the couple to whose union divine consent had thus been obtained, sprang two brothers, Kela Sangmuk and Marām

[1] *Cf. The Meitheis*, p. 132.

Pungsa. The elder went to Cachar and the younger, as his name shows, founded the village of Marām. Then from him sprang four sons, who gave their names to the four clans of Marām. Thus we have another instance of exogamous divisions arising in times when apparently endogamous unions were sanctioned. It is clear that the obstacle to the union of the ancestors of the founder of the village was the doubt in their minds as to their kinship when all their fellows had been swept away by the flood. It is also instructive to observe that the prohibition rests on the physical peculiarity of the ancestress of the village. I was solemnly assured that the bones of the lady, an examination of which would have proved the existence of this very remarkable malformation, had been preserved in the village for centuries, and were only destroyed when the village was burnt as a punitive measure soon after the occupation of the Manipur State in 1891.

As regards the Kabuis, Colonel McCulloch states that "Songboo tradition gives, as the place of their origin, the mountain towards the south of the valley named Thungching. They state themselves to be at present located on the sites of villages at one time occupied by the southern tribes, who are, they say, the elder branch of the family of which they themselves are the middle and the Munniporees the younger branch." Dr. Brown adds that "the Munniporees place their origin at Kayboching, near the Aquee route, north of the Government road, from whence they spread to the south." I myself was informed at the village of Aqui that there is a split stone in the north from which they came. Long-ding-yong is the name of the place, and the meaning of this is the place where the thick jungle weed grows.[1]

The Quoirengs state that they were driven from their homes in the north-east by the people of Marām. Now the legend current among the folk of Marām brings them from the west and in certain of the Quoireng villages it is definitely stated that at one time they lived in a spot called Nohemi, near the sources of the river Barāk. This area is now held by the

[1] Long, a jungle weed, grows like a tree. Ding seems to be a tree of Thādo thing, and yong is connected with the root yung, to stand straight.—T. C. H. Nong or Long-dieng-iong in Khasi would mean the village of the black tree; dieng=tree, iong=black, nong=shnong=village.—P. R. G.

Nāgas, who are associated with the Maikel group which includes the people of Sopvoma or Mao.

The authorities differ as to the origin of the Marrings. Colonel McCulloch[1] states that "the Marrings say the place of the origin of a portion of their tribe is the part of the Munnipore capital at present called 'Haubum Maruk,'[2] and that another portion took their origin at Leisang Kong, a village in the valley some seven or eight miles south of the capital." Dr. Brown, however, gives the following account.[3] "The origin of the Murring is thus given by themselves. 'We originally came out of the earth near the eastern foot of the eastern Heerok range, but in the Kubbo valley, in the higher ground immediately under the hills at a place named Mungsa.[4] Seven men and seven women thus emerged. At this time women and men wore the same clothes (the dhotie or cloth round the loins is to this day identical in both sexes, though worn differently). By way of making a distinction the man made his hair into a knot or horn in front; the woman behind. The woman also lengthened her waistcloth, while the man shortened his.' Not being satisfied with their location in the plain, they migrated in a body to the hills lying close by, where they have since remained; the tradition among them is that the Kubbo valley was then almost entirely a vast lake. The nature of the ground at the foot of the Heerok range at Mungsa bears out this tradition, as under the hills there is a strip of forest land of no great breadth, which is much higher than the plain to the east below it. . . . Murrings of intelligence state with reference to the account given by Colonel McCulloch as quoted above, that their origin, according to all their traditions, is as given above and that the two places mentioned by McCulloch were settled by Koiboo Murrings from the Heerok hills. The sites mentioned were evacuated, they say, on account of water then in the valley, after an occupation, the length of which is unknown." According to the information which I collected,

[1] *Op. cit.*, p. 65.

[2] This means Source of the Nāgas: *Hao* means Nāga, bum is the old form of the adjectival suffix, and *Maruk*, is identical with *maru*, seed, source or origin.—T. C. H.

[3] *Op. cit.*, p. 124.

[4] There is a place of that name in the Kubo valley.—T. C. H.

there is no doubt that the people themselves believe that they came from the vicinity of the Angoching range, which was their original home. Haubum Maruk is claimed by the Tangkhuls as the place of their origin.

Among the Chirus we find the legend of the three brothers who became in time the progenitors of the Kukis, Nāgas, and Manipuris, coupled with the fact that in comparatively recent times they migrated, under pressure of the advance of tribes from the south, to their present homes from sites in the south-east of the valley beyond Moirang.

Interesting stories are preserved in one or two of the smaller villages which form connecting links with larger groups. At Hiroi Lamgang, a village in the south-east corner of the valley, we have a legend similar to that in vogue among the Marrings, their neighbours, which presents us with ancestors dwelling inside the earth, a feature of the Thādo legend, and their horrible enemy who devoured them as they emerged from the cavern. A Deity armed with two horns then slew the beast, thus affording them safe exit from the cave, to which he returned. The site of this cave is the hill called Kang Mang Ching, south of their present home. The people of Anāl Namfu, a village close to Shuganu, also assert that they came from the south and that they are the sons of one of two brothers and that from the younger are descended the Manipuris. They too took their origin from a cave on the slopes of Haobiching. A similar place of origin is claimed by the people of Sadu Koireng. At Aimole, a small village on the first ridge of the Hirok range, is preserved a legend of their origin which declares them to have migrated from the Takkel lam (Tippera Hills).[1] The Thādos are among the earthborn tribes[2] and Dr. Brown quotes a legend of the origin of the Angāmi Nāgas much to the same effect.[3] Of the origin of the Vuites, a small clan in subjection to the Thādos, the following tale is told. One day Aisan[4] Ningthou the head of the Thādos, found two eggs in a paddy-basket and ate one, which he found bitter,

[1] Till fairly recent times the Tippera rāj claimed everything between them and Manipur.—J. S.

[2] McCulloch, *op. cit.*, p. 55.

[3] *Op. cit.*, p. 113.

[4] Aisan, a territorial title, because their village was a long time on a hill of that name.—J. S.

so he laid the other aside, possibly in order that it might reach that maturity which tickles the palate of a Kuki in good health But from it there sprang a lad who became the piba or chief of the Vuites.

Relationship with the Kukis is directly claimed by the people of Yāng, a village which is in the hinterland of Marām and which at the time of my visit to it I observed to be on the point of abandoning some of the customs which filiate them with Marām.

The fact is that all these legends are ætiological, invented to explain a state of affairs which was recognised as needing some sort of an explanation. Colonel Shakespear [1] has shown how at the close of the seventeenth century the expansion of the Lushei clan supplied the motive force which drove hordes of savages into British territory in the eighteenth century.

We know from the chronicles of Manipur that raids and reprisals marked the relations of the hill villages with the people of the valley from the earliest times. We know too that great popular movements were started by the conquest of China by the Mongols. Kabul Khan attacked the Kin Emperor Hola in 1135 A.D. Gengis Khan, who died in 1226 A.D., carried the Mongol arms right into the heart of China, and the task was completed by Kublai Khan, who in the person of Uriangkadai secured a great general who captured Talifu, the capital of Yunnan, and dealt with the Shans in 1263.[2] The Shan invasion of Assam is dated by Ney Elias [3] some time after 1220. We cannot now estimate the effect, if any, of these great movements upon the inhabitants of the hills of Assam. The cruelties perpetrated by the Shan leaders upon Nāga villages [4] who attempted to resist their advance are perhaps enough to enable us to understand that these movements did exercise—in the long run—a very profound influence upon the hill people.

AFFINITIES.

To each of the tribes now under discussion a definite place in the family of Tibeto-Burman languages has been assigned by

[1] *J.R.A.I.*, xxxix., p. 372.
[2] See Boulger, *Short History of China*. pp. 47–60.
[3] *History of the Shans*, p. 18.
[4] Gait, *History of Assam*, p. 74.

Dr. Grierson in the Report of the Linguistic Survey of India.[1]

"Between Angami Nāga and the Bodo languages there is a group, which I call the Nāga-Bodo group, bridging over the difference between the characteristic features of the two forms of speech, and similarly between Angāmi Nāga and the Kuki languages there is another group which I call the Nāga-Kuki. . . . The Nāga-Bodo group . . . consists of two main languages, viz., Mikir . . . and Kachcha Nāga. . . . Subordinate languages, closely akin to but not dialects, of, Kachcha Nāga, are Kabui Nāga and Khoirao Nāga. . . . As might be expected, the Bodo language with which they show the most important points of kinship is the eastern one—Chutiya; while Angāmi and Lhōta are the two Nāga tongues to which they are most closely allied. It must, however, be confessed that in regard to Kabui and Khoirao the classification is somewhat arbitrary, for, though they have undoubted connection with the Bodo languages, they also show many points of contact with the Kuki ones."[2] Sir Charles Lyall has shown good reasons for declining to accept the inclusion of Mikir in this group and finds evidence for grouping it with the Kuki-Chin languages.[3] "The Nāga-Kuki sub-group includes Sopvoma or Mao Nāga, Marām, Miyangkhang, Kwoireng or Liyāng, Luhupa or Luppa language, viz., Tangkhul and Maring.[4] The language of the Mao Nāgas most nearly approaches the true Nāga languages. Of these it possesses the closest resemblance to Kezhāma. . . . Indeed, Sopvoma is so closely connected with all the languages of the Western sub-group (in which are included Angāmi, Sema, Rengma and Kezhāma,[5] that it might with equal propriety be classed as belonging to it as to the Nāga-Kuki one. These three languages (Sopvoma, Tangkhul and Maring) exhibit a regular gradation in the change of speech. Sopvoma is most nearly connected with the Western Nāga languages, and Maring with the Kuki ones, while Tangkhul occupies an intermediate position." The Chirus speak a language which belongs to the old Kuki sub-group of the Kuki-

[1] Grierson, *op. cit.*

[2] *L.S.I.*, Vol. III., Part ii., p. 379.

[3] *The Mikirs*, pp. 151–172.

[4] *L.S.I.*, Vol. III., Part ii., p. 451.

[5] *See L.S.I.*, p. 193.

Chin languages, in which its fellows are Rangkhol, Bete, Hallam, Langrong, Aimol, Kolren, Kom, Cha, Mhar, Anāl, Hiroi-Lamgang and Purum. This last must not be confused with the Nāga village of the same name, which belongs to the Marām group.[1]

We have languages connected with typical Nāga dialects, with Kuki elements, the influence of which gradually diminishes as we recede from the area occupied by Kuki tribes. We have languages related in part to Bodo dialects, in part to Nāga languages, while containing Kuki elements. It is clear that we have in this area a rich variety of dialects due to the effect of the confluence of two, if not of three, streams of language. And in regard to custom the same holds true. The more detailed our examination, the more would it be possible to augment our display of variety, and to emphasise the remarkable graduation and series of development.

The truth is that the village,[2] rather than a group of villages or tribe, is the natural unit of organisation, and therefore the proper basis of investigation. But were we to make a comprehensive survey of each village on the Domesday principle, we should be in jeopardy of losing sight of the essential unities underlying this wealth of variety. In certain areas the natural environment prevents the growth of large communities, necessitating migration when the available land has all been taken into cultivation. Thus the centripetal tendency is continually in process of modification, and thus we have permanent villages with shifting cultivation and the formation of colonies from a centre whose land is exhausted. There is, however, enough evidence to show that the Nāga population is slowly diminishing. A village like Marām had 900 houses in 1859, 200 in 1891, and 120 in 1900. There is therefore less pressure of population on the land, and the formation of colonies is for the moment checked.

The affinities of the tribes with their proximate neighbours are great, and they are very similar in political construction, in economic development, in the essence of their religious beliefs,

[1] *L.S.I.*, Vol. III., Part iii., pp. 9 and 226.

[2] I take this description to only apply to the Nāgas, and it constitutes one of the main differences between them and the Kukis.—J. S.

and in their general habit of thought. There is undoubtedly some borrowing and conscious imitation one of another. With the increased opportunities for commercial intercourse and pacific penetration which are ensured by the Pax Britannica, it is legitimate to anticipate that a tendency to unification will supplant the habit of variation which has preserved tribal individuality, and accentuated their points of difference.[1] The detrition of custom cannot but be accelerated when political circumstances enlarge their experience.

From the materials made available by the pioneers of linguistic and ethnological investigation, it is evident that the area of "adjacent anthropology" must be in this case of very wide extent, for the labours of Brian Hodgson show that the languages of sub-Himalayan tribes possess affinities of structure and vocabulary with the dialects of this area.[2] The discoveries of those splendid explorers in the early years of British rule in Assam in the last century revealed the existence of tribes on the hills beyond Sadiya, Abors, Mishmis, Singphos, whose customs closely resemble those of our tribes. The genna is found among the Mishmis.

Captain Dalton found what we now recognise as the same system among the Abors in 1855.[3] We find many points of resemblance both in regard to custom, to religion and organisation among the tribes in the southern hills, whose ethnography has been so well described by Colonel Lewin.[4] It is impossible to read the Gazetteer of Upper Burma without recognising the identity of many of the customs therein described with those set forth in this volume. So too, did space permit, we might enlarge our borders by extending our comparisons to the peoples of Borneo and the Celebes. As it is, we base our differentiation of those tribes rather upon external variations of dress and coiffure, which are liable to change in the standard of fashion, than upon the more important matters of structure and customs which are less capable of rapid modifi-

[1] *Vide* Lyall, *The Mikirs*, p. 151. *Cf.* Logan, *Journ. Ind. Arch. N.S.*, Vol. II., p. 82.

[2] J.A.S.B., Vol. XVIII., p. 451 *et seq.*

[3] *Memoir of a Survey of Assam and the Neighbouring Countries executed in 1825-6-7-8 by Lieut. Wilcox*, p. 64; Selections from the *Records of the Bengal Government.* No. xxiii. Calcutta, 1855.

[4] *The Hill Tracts of Chittagong.* Calcutta, 1869.

cation. All the villages consist of a number of "clans," which are groups of agnatic kindred who must marry outside the clan. Kinship is not reckoned through females, and rights of succession, both to village office and to movable or personal property, are vested in males. The tenure of immovable property is complicated by the reversionary rights of the clan which accrue in the event of a failure of direct male heirs. Among tribes which, whether by inclination or by necessity, subsist by temporary cultivation and therefore migrate, if not annually, at any rate with frequency, there is not the same reason for evolving definite customs in regard to the ownership of land. We are sometimes able to distinguish a Kuki from a Nāga clan by the development of the chieftain in the former instance into a secular leader who takes only a ceremonial part in the tribal rites, and in the latter case by the diminution of the secular authority of the gennabura, who remains the religious head of his village. Perhaps the evolution of the secular authority of the Kuki chief is due to the urgency of the need among such communities of strong administration unimpeded by "turbulent priests."

In conclusion, while the first impression to be derived from a study of these tribes is of luxuriant variety in every detail, the final result is to deepen the sense of an underlying unity; to realise that all these variations mark experiments in social evolution and development, some of which are doubtless intentional, and to perceive that here, as elsewhere, man is adapting himself to the conditions rigorously imposed upon him by his physical environment, which he is intelligently handling so as to enjoy its advantages and to mitigate the rigour of its domination.[1]

Tribes such as the Chiru on the western side of the valley and the Marring on the eastern side, form connecting links with the true Nāga tribes and the numerous Kuki tribes then living in the south.[2]

DRESS.

The dress of Tangkhul men consists of a simple cloth worn round the waist and tied in a knot in front leaving the ends

[1] *Cf.* Frazer, *Totemism and Exogamy*, Vol. I., p. 281 and Vol. IV., p. 271.
[2] McCulloch, *op. cit.*, p. 65.

hanging down. These ends are fringed with straw pendants. The waist cloths are made of stout cotton woven in red and blue stripes two inches wide and horizontal. Over the body they wear in cold weather a long cloth in red and blue stripes to which in the case of chiefs custom permits the addition of a handsome border. Another pattern is in white stripes with terra cotta stripes and a black and white checker pattern, the plain variety being worn by the common people and the variety with the fringed border twelve to eighteen inches deep with white orange, green and red stripes being restricted to chiefs. They often dispense with the not very ample clothing above described and consider themselves properly garbed if only they have the ring on.[1]

On high days and holidays the men wear a much more elaborate costume than that described above. It consists of a handsome kilt embroidered with ornaments like sequins and the headdress is the luhup with decorations of toucan feathers and tresses of hair.

The women wear small caps of blue cloth when working in the fields. Their petticoats reach from the waist to the knee and are made of cotton cloth manufactured in the weaving villages with red and white or black and white stripes two inches in width. Occasionally those who have some pretence to wealth or position wear petticoats of red with small stripes of white and black. A small jacket of the style worn by Manipuri women or a single cloth of the kind worn by the men completes the costume.

The ordinary dress of a Mao Nāga[2] consists of a short black cotton kilt about eighteen inches deep which is ornamented by three or four rows of white cowries, or in these degenerate days of white trouser buttons. Tradition and the statements of the older officers who knew these people in their unreformed period, declare that no man put these rows of cowries on his kilt until he had slain two men. A dirty white cotton rug thrown over the shoulders completes the costume. Headmen and "lung-chingbas," men who have erected a stone, are privileged to wear a dark blue cloth woven in Manipur on which are embroidered in red thread quaint figures of animals

[1] *See* Appendix I. *below*. [2] Of Marām and Mayang Khong Nāgas also.

and conventional patterns which I have often thought were remotely like some fantastic animals. On gala days the costume of a warrior is most handsome. The cane helmet which is sometimes covered with tiger or leopard skin, bears a brass disc in front, and thin crescents of buffalo horn tipped with red hair are fastened to it in front. I have seen a red and yellow painted structure made of thin lath worn on the helmet rising at least two feet above the peak of the cane helmet. This looks like a pair of horns which it may be intended to imitate. From the sides hang solid wooden discs decorated with red seeds, with the wings of the green beetle and with pendants of hair which also fringe the helmet at the back. In the bad old days before the Sircar stopped all raids, these tresses were shorn from the heads of the slain in battle. On these days men wear their decorations from bravery in fights. Here as with us there are various degrees of merit each with their appropriate badge. An article like a sporran but fringed with red and yellow hair and ornamented with bands of cowries is hung round the neck of the valiant. The next higher degree is marked by a badge from shoulder to shoulder made of the same material and of the same colours, which may be called their "colours" as much as red and blue are the "colours" of the Tangkhuls. The most curious ornament on these occasions is the caudal appendage with its curve upwards and a long hair fringe of the usual colours. Is this indeed a tail, is the curved horn attachment to the helmet intended to resemble horns of some animal, is there a conscious therio-mimesis in all this scheme of decoration? Indeed, three tails are sometimes worn. One may be a totemic survival, but three are surely only swagger. The "tail" serves a useful purpose, for it has a space hollowed out in which panjis (sharpened bamboo spikes) are kept by the warriors. Handsome white plumes are worn and attached to the shield. Of the weapons, the shield, the spear, and the dao that are brandished by the gay warrior with this dress, more will be said in the section dealing with weapons. The ample calves are covered by leggings of the usual combination of colours which hide the black rings of cane which all wear round the knee, perhaps, as some say, to give them strength when climbing.

The memory of other days is preserved by the substitution of a gourd image for the enemy's head which they say was once the usual accompaniment of a gentleman's full dress.

That the kilt is not assumed until the approach of puberty is evident.

Girls wear two garments, one of which may be regarded as worn for effect only as it consists of a plain square of cloth, often dark blue with a red border, hung round the neck over the bosom. The skirt descends to the knee which it barely covers. Older women wrap themselves up in a white rug which is thrown apparently without any method over the shoulders. At one village I noticed women wearing petticoats of white with black horizontal stripes, while in another the ground was white with red and blue horizontal stripes. Small geometrical patterns which constitute the "signature or trade mark" of the weaver, or which may be "luck" marks, and magical in origin and intent, ornament the borders of the better cloths.

Special cloths are worn by the headman and by those who have erected a stone. One has been mentioned above. Another is of stout plain white cotton woven in sections which are narrower than usual and the seams are joined in such a manner as to make a thick roll which stands up about half an inch. This cloth is particularly strong and lasting.

A cloth in my possession is made of stout cotton, and consists of four breadths or pieces from the loom which are neatly stitched together. The colours are red and black, arranged in stripes. The two edge breadths have stripes about an inch wide, while the centre breadths have a different arrangement of the stripes; the black stripes have faint white stripes, and the red stripes are about four inches wide, with black lines down them. I bought this cloth at Mao.

Many of the cloths are obtained by barter from the Angāmis, and in this way the fashions of that enterprising group are spread among their neighbours.

An interesting proof of the effect upon general appearance [1] which is produced by different dress was afforded by the case

[1] A Lushai bugler in uniform was taken for a Damai by an officer well competent to speak on Gurkhas.—J. S.

of two lads from Mao, who came to Manipur as scholars and there adopted the dhoti. It was nearly impossible to distinguish them from Manipuri lads of their age. The rapidity with which Nāgas, Kukis, and Gurkhas are absorbed by and disappear in the Meithei population may afford an explanation of the ætiological legends of origin cited above. These people are all of the Tibeto-Burman stock.

Dr. Brown states[1] that "the dress of the male (Kabui) is scanty: those living in the jungles only wear a small square piece of cloth in front, hanging below and covering the privates, and confined to the waist by a string. In the valley of Munnipore and in Cachar a more decent costume is adopted—either a kilt like a piece of cloth round the waist or a short dhotie put on Bengalli fashion. The only other article of clothing worn by the men is a thick sheet of cotton cloth, and this only when the weather is cold. The women wear a piece of cotton cloth of thick texture, which is put on in the same way as the Munniporie fanek, and reaches to a little below the knee: this garment is confined round the waist by a coloured scarf with fringed ends. The colour for ordinary wear is usually of a muddy hue, with coloured stripes of various widths: on holiday occasions the blue with red stripes is the favourite colour. Over the shoulders is worn a scarf-shaped piece of cloth, generally of blue, with a border and fringe of other colours. In the cold season a jacket is sometimes worn resembling the Munnipore furit or woman's jacket."

Very little need be added to this account, but it may be of interest to note that the fanek or long petticoat is fastened under the right breast, while Manipuri women fasten it under the left breast. On gala days and on other festive occasions, the ordinary plain fashions are supplanted by elaborate costumes, the men wearing coats embroidered with a fringe of green beetles' wings and a headdress ornamented with feathers of the toucan, or horn-bill, and silk dhoties, which may be purchased in Manipur. The girls often wear small caps made of blue cloth, especially when working in the fields. The petticoats are often of red, black and white stripes, with small geometrical patterns worked in. The value of the cloth is enhanced by these patterns,

[1] *Op. cit.*, p. 101.

and they also seem to serve as private marks,[1] and it is interesting to observe that such private marks may be the very earliest beginning of a rude system of writing. The loin-cloths worn by the men are dark in colour, and have the ends fringed with cane work. It should also be noted that some of the faneks worn by the women are made in narrow stripes as well as in broad patterns, one remarkable cloth being made of khaki-coloured bands about eight inches in width, with narrow stripes of red in between.

The loin-cloths worn by the men are dark in colour, and the upper cloth is surrounded by red, blue and white lines about one inch in width, and the centre is white.

Quoireng men wear the short black kilt that is the costume of their neighbours the Angāmis, with whom they have trade relations. On the occasion of the Mang-la-thā, or festival of the dead, which I once witnessed, the young men wore their hair frizzed up in front, and round the knot at the back of the head they tightly coiled strips of cotton, and over all this placed an article of attire which I can only liken to a "glory" such as is worn by the anæmic Saints of mediæval art. This "glory" consisted of bands of yellow and red thread about an inch and a half wide. Rays of bamboo decorated with jays' wings and cocks' feathers stuck out from this. The height of the whole thing was about eighteen inches, and its weight inconsiderable. They wear jays' wings as an ear ornament, and armlets of white wood which at a distance look like the ivory armlets of the true Angāmi buck. They smear the legs with white earth, making a criss-cross pattern with a pointed stick.[2] I learnt that the hair is curled by the use of round bamboo splints. The small boys have a stout wisp of cotton twisted round their lock at the back of the head.

The women wear several kinds of petticoats, all of which are made at home. The general colouring is white background with red and blue stripes, while in a southern village I noticed

[1] *See above*, p. 24.

[2] For the use of earth as a decorative disguise, then as a means of purification, see Miss Harrison's *Prolegomena to Greek Religion*, pp. 492–493. See also Andrew Lang, *Custom and Myth*, p. 41; Jevons' *Introduction to the History of Religion*, pp. 348–349. It is used in connection with initiation rites. *See Primitive Secret Societies*, p. 44.

a variety with broad khaki bands between which there were narrow red bands. The method of coiffure usual among the Quoirengs is similar to that practised by the Kabuis both before and after marriage.

Dr. Brown's account of the Marrings is interesting,[1] and in the years which have passed since that account was written there has been no change in the habits of the people in this matter. "Their dress consists, amongst both men and women, of a sheet, white with a striped border, or striped throughout; this is folded across the waist and twisted or tucked in at the side; the men fasten one end behind, dhotie-wise; in the women this is allowed to hang down, so as to form a petticoat. For the men the only other article of clothing worn is a sheet for the upper part of the body of thick cotton, either striped or checked, and sometimes a woollen blanket. The women's dress, besides the waist-cloth common to both sexes, consists of a white sheet with striped borders, worn like the Munnipore farak (fanck), and reaching from over the bust to a little way below the knee. A sheet like the men's is also worn, and some of the women wear the Munnipore 'foorit' or jacket during the cold weather."

It is noteworthy that the development of the simplest clothing found among these tribes, the plain waist-cloth with fringed ends, leads to both the kilt and the dhoti, for both these garments are fastened below in much the same way and differ only in depth.

COIFFURE.

The Tangkhul men wear the hair in a curious manner, which is to a large extent distinctive of the tribe. They cut the hair closely at the sides, leaving a broad crest, which varies in width from five to two inches down the middle of the skull. From the point of the skull the crest narrows to the nape of the neck, where the hair, which they allow to grow long, is tied in a loop. Brown [2] says that "their tradition regarding this peculiar fashion is to the effect that formerly, ages ago, the two sexes wore their hair alike and combed back, as among the Kukis; to distinguish them the above effective plan was resorted to." We meet the legend that a distinctive method of

[1] *Op. cit.*, p. 125. [2] *Op. cit.*, p. 118.

coiffure was invented to obviate the difficulty of distinguishing between the sexes among the Marrings, but no other tribe within the territory of the Manipur State has hit on the style of coiffure adopted by the Tangkhuls.

Small boys have their hair shaved off, with a round patch left on the point of the skull. In a few villages in the south, and close to the country occupied by the Marring Nāgas, the men have adopted the Marring fashion of coiling the hair up into a spiral horn in front,[1] and the eligible bachelors keep their hair long in front, and combed into a fringe, as is the fashion practised by the *leisābis*, or unmarried girls, in Manipur. Among a few of the southern villages, the young man in search of a wife advertises the fact by painting small circles of black on his upper lip and on the tip of his nose. The Tangkhul does not wear a beard, whiskers or moustache, and those who do possess these ornaments pull them out, for fear, so I was told, of the displeasure of the women, who regard them as disfigurements.

Very young girls have their heads shaved, but on reaching a marriageable age they allow the hair to grow long, and wear a fringe combed over the forehead and parted down the middle, like the unmarried girls in Manipur. In some villages a lock of hair of a triangular shape is combed out from the middle of the head and trained over the forehead. This style of coiffure seems to be adopted during the period just before marriage. When married, they wear the hair knotted at the back, as do the married Manipuri women.

Among the Mao and Marām Nāgas, the hair of the children of both sexes is cut close until puberty, and it is reckoned a disgrace for a girl to have short hair when she marries, or to have a child until her hair has grown to some length. The men cut the hair at the sides, but not as high up as the Tangkhuls, and twist the locks at the back in rolls of cotton, a fashion that is especially popular with the younger men. At Marām I learnt that only *lung-ching-bas* (men who had erected a stone) were entitled to the distinction of a parting in the middle. Many merely combed the hair out to a fringe in front and then

[1] I was told that this used to be the common custom of the Tangkhuls, but it was so much trouble that the simpler fashion was adopted.—J. S.

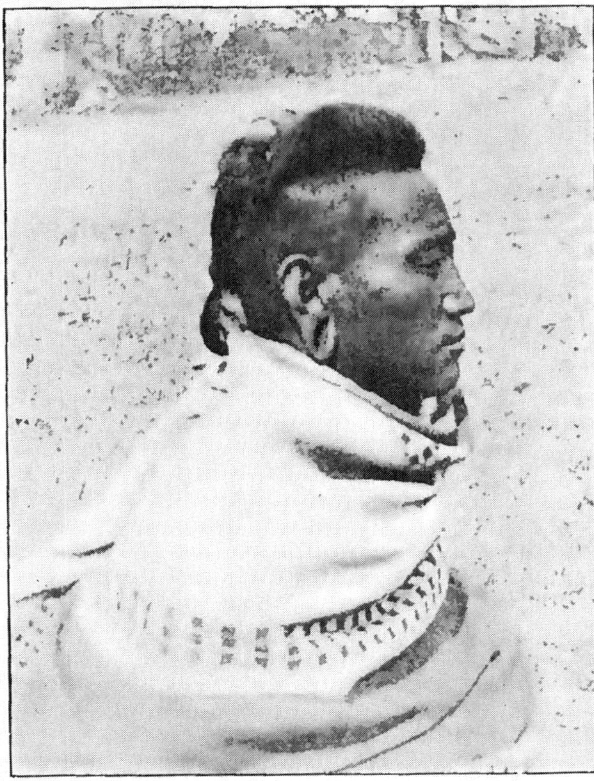

A TANGKHUL NĀGA. [*To face p.* 28

From a photograph by the Author.

combed the rest back, a fashion very common among the Mayang Khong villages south of Marām.

Both the Kabuis and the Quoirengs adopt much the same style of coiffure for both sexes, young and old, as their neighbours the Nāgas of the Mao and Marām groups. Dr. Brown gives the following description of the modes of coiffure in vogue among the Kabuis[1]:—

"The hair is worn generally short, and the favourite style among the males is sticking straight up from the head, the hair being cut to about an inch and a half from the scalp and occasionally a portion of the forehead shaved. Others wear the hair longer, and cut straight round, divided in the middle; those who adopt this fashion usually wear a fillet of bamboo round the forehead, confining the hair. Small moustaches and rudimentary beards are occasionally seen. The women wear their hair in a fashion resembling the Munnipories: the younger girls have their hair cut short all over: after this the hair is worn after the manner of the unmarried Munnipories (*i.e.* combed in a fringe over the forehead, and loose at the sides, so that it falls over the ears) the old women have the hair combed back" (and tied in a knot at the back of the neck, and supplemented often by artificial "tails," which are purchased in Manipur or are occasionally home made and eked out by bits of bark twine).

The Chirus, however, wear a curious fillet of cane round the head, and part the hair in the middle, so that it is easy to distinguish a Chiru man by this ornament.[2]

The Marrings, again, have a distinctive style of coiffure, which is thus described by Dr. Brown[3]:—"The men comb their hair from behind and from the sides, and gather it into a horn-shaped protuberance above the centre of the forehead; round the base of this horn are usually wound strings of beads of various kinds, and transfixing it crosswise is a steel bodkin-shaped instrument with a sharp point about fifteen inches long and flattened for about a third of its length at the other extremity. The story attached to this instrument is as follows:—'To the seven families of the Murrings after their

[1] *Op. cit.*, p. 101.
[2] There is good evidence that the Marring boys wear the Chiru fillet.
[3] *Op. cit.*, p. 125.

creation the deity gave pens of reed and skins of leather to write upon. The leather skins were eaten by dogs, and the pens wearing out or being lost, the art of writing was forgotten and has never been recovered ; the bodkin shaped piece of steel is retained by them as a memento of the pen.'[1] It is also stated that in order to distinguish the sexes apart, the men tied their hair in a knot in front while the women tied it behind. The hair of the women is simply parted in the centre and combed back. It is then gathered into a loose knot, which lies low down on the neck. The men shortened their cloth and made it into a waist-cloth, while the women lengthened their cloth, making of it a petticoat. It is a curious comment on this to recall the tradition of the passage through the Angāmi villages of the Manipuri force in 1833 under Gambhir Singh and Major Gordon, when the Nāgas laughed at the women, as they deemed them, who had come to fight them with sticks. The Manipuris have long hair twisted at the back, and the Nāgas till then had no knowledge of guns."

TATTOOING.[2]

Among the more distant and poorer villages on the extreme north and east of the area occupied by Tangkhuls, the women are tattooed. The pattern is very simple. Three lines about three-eighths of an inch in width start from the point of the chin round the neck, being carried in some cases right down to the navel. The upper arm is tattooed in a similar way with lines in diagonal patterns, making two crosses, which are generally kept separate. The breasts are not tattooed, and I have found that as a rule a woman who owns a necklace is not tattooed. They say that they do this because it serves to identify their women hereafter. In the beginning they learnt the art from Chom Ningthou, a monarch of a country beyond Sirohi-furar who ordered the miserable Nāgas to tattoo their women, who excited his pity by reason of their poverty-stricken appearance. This tale probably means that they learnt the art from the Shans,[3] who at various

[1] This legend is of wide distribution.—T.C.H.
[2] *Cf.* Frazer, *Totemism and Exogamy*, Vol. IV, pp. 202-207.
[3] Or Burmese.

times in the history of Manipur must have marched through the country in the occupation of the Tangkhuls.[1]

The tattooing is done by instalments, always in the cold weather. Lampblack and the juice of wild indigo are used as colouring matter, and the old woman who operates pierces the skin with a sharp bamboo splinter. The diet of the girls is restricted, and they are also subject to a tabu rule which forbids them to leave the village in which they are residing until the ceremony is over. It is often done in another village, especially when the girl's mother comes from another village. The girl then resides in the house of her mother's brother. It is obviously a pre-nuptial, and therefore to some extent an initiatory rite. Colonel McCulloch remarks,[2] that "the women of the north are much sought after by the southern men because, however fierce their feuds, a tattooed woman always goes unscathed, fear of the dire vengeance which would be exacted by her northern relations were she injured giving her this immunity." The state of things which produced this effect on the matrimonial value of the northern ladies is now at an end, and their value has fallen considerably as a result of the piping times of peace they have enjoyed under British rule.

I have not found any other cases of tattooing among the hill tribes in Manipur.

Ornaments.

Among the Tangkhuls both men and women wear ornaments. The men have their ears pierced at an early age and gradually distend the holes in the lobes until they are large enough to

[1] We may compare this with the Abor custom (Selections from the Records of the Bengal Government, No. xxiii. Papers relating to some Frontier Tribes on the N.E. border of Assam, p. 146. Major Vetch's letter, para. 20).
"Their arms are a long spear, long straight sword, dagger, and bow and arrows. Many wear a sort of helmet made of cane, plaited and ornamented with the hair of the yāk, dyed red, as well as by any trophies of the chase they consider suitable to produce a wild or warlike appearance. Many of them have the mark of the cross tattooed on their forehead, but I could get no satisfactory account of the origin of affixing this emblem. They said it was intended to stand in the place of the brass utensils and other articles buried with them at their funerals, in case they should die poor and not be able to afford them."

[2] *Op. cit.*, p. 68.

receive rolls of cotton of considerable size or bamboo ornaments. Brass cylindrical ornaments are often inserted and the young men appreciate the advantage of an empty cartridge case as a personal decoration. The ascending cartilage of the ear is frequently bored with numerous holes, into which small skeins of black or blue cotton are introduced. They wear necklaces of beads, which are often very costly, and, as a mark of distinction, a collar of red and yellow cane-work with geometrical ornamentation in cowries and three hair tails hanging down the back. Dr. Brown says[1] that "a favourite and peculiar ornament is a loose, deep collar of brass about six inches wide in front of the neck and tapering gradually to the back, where it is fastened. This collar is usually plain and projects some way in front of the chin."

They wear heavy brass armlets on the forearm and sometimes coiled wire rings. These rings serve a useful purpose as well as being ornamental, as they employ them to deliver a downward crushing blow. They also wear cane or brass rings coiled below the knee, which are said to give support when climbing hills with loads. Similar cane rings are in use in other parts of the hills.[2] In some villages smart young men may be seen who adorn these rings with small brass bells, which the children also wear as necklaces. The following description is given by Dr. Brown[3] of the *luhup* or helmet (*lu* being a common root in the languages of these tribes for head, and *hu* being connected with the root *kūp*, or *khu*, to cover),[4] an article which is not merely decorative but also serves a very useful purpose as a war helmet. "The basis of this headpiece is a conical structure of work about a foot high: over this is a layer of fur and hair black and red in colour: to the sides are stitched as wings round structures filled in with coloured seeds in rings: in front is a disc of polished brass with a button-shaped knob in the centre: slips of bamboo, feathers, etc., are also attached to the headpiece, and occasionally a long crescent-shaped piece of buffalo horn scraped thin is placed in front of the helmet. Warriors of distinction who have slain many people wear the

[1] *Op. cit.*, p. 119.
[2] *Vide* U.B.G., Vol. I., Part I., p. 385.
[3] *Op. cit.*, pp. 121, 122.
[4] The word *kūp* occurs also in Khasi in the same sense. *cf. jain kūp*, etc. —P. R. G.

KABUI GIRLS

From a photograph by the Author.

[To face p. 32

hair of their victims depending from the side ornaments of the helmet in the first instance, and, as they accumulate, made into a kind of fringe, worn round the face like the mane of a lion. Women's tresses are preferred as being longer." This description applies also to the helmet worn by the Mao Nāgas. Great use is made of the wings of beetles, the beautiful green, iridescent colours giving an extremely brilliant effect. From the fact that the northern sections of the Tangkhuls wore this helmet is derived the name *Luhupa*, which some have fancied designated a separate tribe.

The ornaments worn by the women are necklaces of the polished hexagonal cornelian beads, the number and value of which affects the price which their husbands pay for them. They have the ears pierced and wear similar but smaller ear ornaments. Young girls wear metal armlets which are coiled up on the upper arm and are made of a white metal not dissimilar to solder. In a few cases these ornaments are finished with spiral ends like the armlets of the Kabuis. Married women also wear brass armlets. Owing to the fact that the Tangkhuls are habitually employed as road coolies, they have of recent years come into contact with other tribes, from whom they have acquired some of their fashions, as their old men say that before the occupation of the State by the British Government they were not able to trade as freely as they now do.

In the Mao, Marām and Mayang-Khong groups, men and women alike wear necklaces made of rows of polished hexagonal cornelian beads which are valued highly. They are good judges of the quality of these beads, which they string themselves, adding, partly from economical necessities and in part in order to get more decorative effect, bones of deer carefully whitened and rounded and interspersed with blue beads. Many also wear a collarette consisting of four to six rows of blue beads closely strung and with white bone posts. The men also wear the half shell which is characteristic of their neighbours, the Angāmis. Women's ornaments vary rather more. At the village of Jessami I saw a woman wearing brass earrings fastened to the top of the ear and joined by thread tied across. These rings were of large diameter.[1] In general the earrings are fastened in the lower lobe of the ear and are much smaller. Bachelors anxious about their appearance wear a bright girdle of twisted cotton wool with red bands, while the knot of hair is tied up with a band of cotton wool. In the lobes of the ears I have seen ornaments of many colours, red, yellow, black, with even chillies to add a touch of colour. Thick ivory armlets are worn by the well-to-do, who alone can afford them. Here and there white wood armlets are worn in substitution for the more expensive ivory.

Of the Kabuis Colonel McCulloch states that "the women are fond of ornaments and they wear many till they are married. These consist of glass beads and brass ornaments on the arms; gold or silver ornaments do not, I think, exist among them. In their festivals, the men wear their peculiar ornaments, of which the most prized are necklaces of red pebble. A single stone of this sort is sometimes valued at five methins, but such stones are usually heirlooms and are sacredly preserved."[2] Dr. Brown's account, however, gives further particulars. "Necklaces of beads and shell are commonly worn: a reddish pebble necklace is the most highly-prized. On the upper arm an ornament of brass is commonly worn; it is made of very thick wire with a bell-shaped ball at either extremity; this is wound round the arm pretty tight about ten or twelve times until a large, deep ring is formed. Above the calf of the leg numerous rings of cane, very thin and generally coloured black, are frequently worn. The ornaments among the women are similar to those of the men, but worn in larger numbers; the earrings are always large and heavy and the necklaces numerous; bracelets of brass are also worn besides the upper arm ornaments above mentioned; the legs and ankles are bare of ornaments."[3] The necklaces are of red cornelian shells, beads and a yellow opaque stone which is rare and expensive. This last is round in shape and flat, while the cornelians are oval, sometimes hexagonal, and are polished. The ends of the spiral brass arm-ornament are

[1] I have seen these in the Eastern Tangkhul villages. The earrings are so heavy that unless supported they would tear the lobes.—J. S.

[2] *Op. cit.* pp. 51–2.

[3] *Op. cit.* p. 102.

often decorated with rude geometrical patterns which are said to add to their value greatly.

Among the Quoirengs both the men and the young girls before marriage wear the long spirally-coiled brass ornaments so common among the Kabuis. Here and there a woman may be seen with a bead necklace, but I cannot find any record of its being usual. I have seen a quaint necklace made of beetles' wings, which was pretty and effective. Such things as the wings of jays and coloured seeds are also used as ornaments, especially by the young men at the festivals.

As regards the Marrings, Dr. Brown states that "the ornaments for the men are not numerous. Before marriage, young men wear small rings in the lobes, made of brass. After marriage these are removed and a rounded piece of shell, wood covered with finely twisted horsehair, or, for the better-off, silver, about an inch and a half long of no great thickness, is worn instead. The men wear no necklaces or any other ornament round the neck; heavy bracelets of bell-metal above the wrists are occasionally worn: these are handed down from father to son for generations. Brass rings on the fingers are sometimes worn. The women wear shell ornaments in the ears, but unlike those of the men, round and fastened to the lobe of the ear by a piece of string. Long bead and shell necklaces are worn in profusion, as amongst the Kowpoees. On the upper arm is worn the twisted coil of brass, which ornament is twisted into shape before being placed on the arm. Bracelets of the same material as those of the men are occasionally worn: they are not as heavy as the men's. The women stain their teeth black."[1]

Weapons.

The weapons of offence in common use throughout the hills are the spear, the dao and the bow and arrow, with, in too many cases, firearms, some being of an excellent type. The Tangkhuls use a spear of great length, but only for thrusting; while the shorter spears used by the Mao, Marām, Kabui, Quoireng,

[1] *Op. cit.* p. 125.

Chiru and Marring tribes are thrown and used in thrusting. Of the dao we may say with Colonel Lewin:[1] "The dao is the hill knife, and used universally throughout the country. It is a blade about eighteen inches long, narrow at the haft and square and broad at the tip, pointless and sharpened on one side only. The blade is set in a handle of wood; a bamboo root is considered the best. The 'fighting' dao is differently shaped: this is a long pointless sword, set in a wooden handle or ebony; it is very heavy, and a blow of almost incredible power can be given by one of these weapons. With both the fighting and the ordinary dao one can make but two cuts: one from the right shoulder downwards to the left, one from the left, foot upwards to the right. . . . The weapon is identical with the 'parang latok' of the Malays. The dao to a hill man is a possession of great price. It is literally the bread winner; with this he cuts his joom and builds his houses; without its aid the most ordinary operations of hill life could not be performed. It is with the dao he fashions the women's weaving tools . . . and to the dao he frequently owes his life in defending himself from the attacks of wild animals." As a matter of fact there is no need for a Nāga to carry a special fighting dao, for his spear has a double edge, so that it serves as a knife if needed.

It is said that the Southern Tangkhuls used poisoned arrows. If this is true they may have been borrowed from the Marrings, who use a vegetable extract, of which Dr. Brown gives the following account.[2] "The bow is strong and the arrow-head barbed. The arrows are occasionally poisoned with some vegetable extract, the nature of which I have not been able to ascertain; they describe this poison as so potent that animals die from its effects in half an hour after being wounded by the poisoned arrow. This poison, which is also used by the Kookie tribes, is a dark brown, gummy-looking extract soluble in greater part in water. By way of experiment I had some freshly prepared poison pronounced good by the Kookies brought to me, and to judge of its effects I inserted a piece about the size of a pea into a deep incision in the thigh of a fowl. With the exception of a very temporary drowsiness, about ten minutes after the introduction of the poison, the fowl remained well and

[1] *Hill Tracts of Chittagong*, p. 12.

[2] *Op. cit.* p. 127.

unaffected. The hill-men accounted for this by saying that the poison could not have entered the system. . . . The poison used by the Bhooteahs is very much the same as that used by the Marrings and Kookies, in appearance at least."

Two types of shields are found among these tribes, the long oblong shield, sometimes curved at the top and the round buckler, the efficacy of which is really due to the skill and agility of the man behind it. The oblong shield which is usually carried by the Mao, Marām, Quoireng, and Kabui Nāgas, is about four feet long, two feet six inches wide at the top, narrowing to two feet at the bottom. It is made either of buffalo hide or of closely plaited cane, and is strong enough to turn a spear. It is held by two loops inside and decorated with plumes of toucan's feathers and pendent tassels of cock's feathers. Often it is embellished by a leopard's skin or by black cloth with a broad stripe of red in the middle. The round buckler also is made of buffalo hide, and I have seen Marrings wielding it so dexterously as to turn aside quite a shower of arrows shot at them in sport.

Among minor weapons of offence we may class the brass armlet of the Tangkhuls, which they use to deliver a crushing blow downwards. Mention has been made of the curious "tail"[1] which forms part of the warrior's dress in Mao and Marām. In the socket at the back of the tail they place their supply of panjis, bamboo spikes sharpened and hardened in the fire. These they use as darts or place in the path to the village, and the greatest care must be exercised in approaching a village when panjis have been put down, for they will cut through a boot and inflict a horrible wound.

The axe does not seem to have been adopted by the Tangkhuls, although they are in close proximity to villages which use them. A specimen in my possession is made of one piece of metal with a wooden haft let in. It has a peculiarly shaped edge, and is well balanced in the hand.

Although never used as a weapon, the ceremonial dao of the Kabuis is of interest because it differs from the ordinary dao. It is shaped with a double curve on the cutting edge, and is carried by the men when dancing or performing in gala dress.

[1] P. 23 *supra*.

I enjoyed very favourable opportunities for ascertaining the extent to which firearms were in use by the hill tribes, and found that many of them possessed Tower muskets in very good order. They obtained a crude powder from the Kukis, who probably derive their acquaintance with the art from the Meitheis. They, in turn, seem to have acquired this useful art from Chinese merchants who visited the State during the reign of Khāgenba, circa A.D. 1630.[1] Percussion caps are obtained from the plains, not without difficulty, so that a trade in paper caps, such as are used in toy pistols, was found to be carried on by Bengali traders in the Bazaar at Imphāl. I was inclined to doubt this information till I captured a gun in a distant Kabui village to which paper caps were still adhering. I made the experiment of firing a charge of home-made powder by means of a paper cap, and found that it was quite practicable. Measures were then taken to stop this illicit traffic. I have also had surrendered to me breech-loading rifles which had been ingeniously converted by a village blacksmith to muzzle loaders because cartridges could not be purchased, not even from the police.

[1] *Vide The Meitheis*, p. 21.

SECTION II.—DOMESTIC LIFE.

OCCUPATION.

These tribes are all agriculturists and to the operation of the genna system is due the exclusive attention which the cultivation receives during the greater part of the year. When the rice is safely reaped and stored, the energy of the village is turned to trade, to such small manufactures and handicrafts as are known to them, to hunting and fishing. Weaving, which is in most cases a general industry carried on by every housewife, is in one group of Tangkhul villages specialised, and, as a result, more developed there than elsewhere. The case of the pottery industry affords an example of localised industry. Daos and spears are manufactured in each village by the blacksmith and are implements which have not yet been specialised. Even in agriculture the plough is not in use and the digging stick and the dao are the main tools. They use the hoe, a small instrument used with one hand which is found all through the hills. We have in the following passage a description of the daily life of the Kabui Nāgas which is true of all these tribes now as it was when written by Colonel McCulloch nearly fifty years ago.

"In the grey of the morning the females of the family are astir and the village resounds with the blows of the long pestle in the wooden mortar beating out the rice from the husk. This finished, breakfast is cooked both for the family and the pigs, for the latter the husk mixed with other refuse serves the purpose. Breakfast over, which it usually is about sunrise, the women proceed for water, which they fill into bamboo tubes and bring on their backs in baskets. Then they go for firewood, and this brought, they set about the internal economy of the house; that is, to see to their husbands' drink being in proper quantity and quality, to their spinning or to their weaving, or any of the other household occupations except sweeping the house clean, an act in which they have no pride. In fact they rather seem to glory in a dirty house and in having the front room half covered with rice husk in which pigs are lying fast asleep or grunting about and fowls are busy seeking for food. The family, except the boys, from the time they begin to wear a cloth round their waist, sleep in the rear room of the house, and in it they cook their meals. In the front part any one who comes sits down. In it there is a fireplace and along the two sides are placed boards or bamboo platforms for sitting or lying upon. Some of these boards are as much as twenty-four feet long by four broad. They are made with their daos and little axes, a whole tree being destroyed in getting one. If not employed in the labours of the field or the chase, the men do little more than loll about the house during the day, drinking their peculiar drink, a harmless one consisting of pounded rice mixed with boiling water brought into fermentation by the addition of germinated paddy. In the mornings and evenings they will be generally found sitting in groups in front of their houses on large flat stones which cover the graves of deceased relatives.[1] They then appear to be enjoying themselves greatly, they are exceedingly loquacious and speak always in a loud tone. Pipes containing green tobacco are then smoked and at such a rate do they pull they appear to be smoking for a wager. I believe the pleasure of smoking is nothing to them compared to that of holding in the mouth a sip of the water of the bowl of the pipe which has been well impregnated with the fumes of the smoke passing through it and that it is only for the purpose of obtaining it[2] that they so laboriously pull at their pipes morning and evening."[3]

[1] This refers to the Kabui villages. Elsewhere are little platforms whereon the gossips sit and smoke.

[2] See below, p. 61.

[3] *Op. cit.* pp. 47-48.

A CHIRU NĀGA. [*To face p.* 40

From a photograph by the Author.

Houses and Villages.

The houses of these tribes are simple specimens of architectural art and Colonel McCulloch's description is generally applicable to all. "The superior elevations being the most healthy, their villages are usually to be found in them. Each house is constructed with reference to its own convenience, the regularity of the village is not cared for, but no house is so far removed from the rest as to preclude its being included in the stockade or rampart of stones which usually surrounds them as a defence, either from their enemies or wild beasts . . . . Some villages draw their supplies of water from great distances, whilst others are more fortunate in having a perennial spring or stream in their immediate vicinity. . . . . To all the villages the ascents are laborious, and to some of them from the great steepness excessively so, but throughout the hills occupied by the Songboos,[1] I am not aware of there being any roads made by them to facilitate general travelling, or for the convenience of communication between villages. Their roads are mere paths overgrown with jungle, except in the neighbourhood of their villages where it is cut down, and these paths, being selected, not for the ease of travelling by them, but for their directness, are generally over the steepest parts. . . . . The houses of the Kowpoees are well adapted to the climate. In the more flourishing villages they are large and substantially built. They are gable ended, have the ridge pole not in a horizontal position, but sloping from the front to the rear where it is in comparison with the front very low and the thatched roof on either side reaches the ground. The posts are often of great size and of such excellent quality, that for thirty or forty years the only repairs required are to the thatch, and their thatching is so good that the roof scarcely needs repair for ten or twelve years. Excellent thatching grass is found usually in the vicinity of the villages; having cut it, they divest it carefully of every weed and inferior blade, after which they tie it up in little bundles with strips of bamboo which is long between the

[1] I could not find out any Songboos, no one seemed to know them.—J. S.

joints, pliable and tough, so tightly that a blade cannot be extracted from the bundle. The method of tying is very simple and consists in passing the ligature first through the middle of the grass at the head of the bundle and then one turn round it bringing the end up and passing it in between the surrounding turn and the grass; by a slight twist a loop is formed at the end into which a short stick is thrust, with which, as a lever, the bundle itself being the fulcrum, it is tied. These little bundles are tied each separately to the bamboos of the roof running parallel to the ridge pole, and thus is formed a thatch impervious to wet and which resists effectually for years the winds of these high altitudes. Besides their grain all other articles of food and their more valuable property are kept in their granaries at a short distance from their dwelling houses. These granaries have the floors raised 4 or 5 feet above the ground, they are thatched like the dwelling houses and have their floors and walls of bamboo matting. Their positions are usually well sheltered, and their doors are secured only by wooden bolts fastened outside, but though thus easy to be opened, a theft from a granary is almost unheard of."[1] Here and there the houses of those who are better off are decorated with carvings, in some cases of animals and with paintings of rough geometrical patterns, such as circles, squares, and oblong lozenges. The scheme of decoration sometimes includes "heads," possibly of ancestors, but more probably of victims.[2] The house which is reserved for the Bachelors' Club, or Men's House, is in some villages distinguished from the rest by its great height, and the steepness of the pitch of the roof. Further south, where at one time there were settlements of the Kabuis, in the midst of jungle I have seen stone sculptures, rude, but distinct, and troughs which seem to have been used for the supply of water. The site is now occupied by the Vaiphei, a Kuki sub-tribe.

The Tangkhuls use pine planks and shingles in their houses which possess the appearance of great durability. The different style of house built by the Tangkhuls who have come up from

[1] *Op. cit.* pp. 42–47.
[2] See *Folklore*, xx. No. 2, Plate iv. Head-hunting among the Hill Tribes of Assam.

the Kubo valley shows evidence of Burmese influence. Among the Nāgas of Mao and Marām the houses of the village chiefs are distinguished by the curved and carved beams crossed in front, a style of distinction which we find in Manipur in the Kangla.[1] The description given in the *Gazetteer of Upper Burma*, Vol. I., Part I., pp. 499–510, of a Wa village would apply, with a few and unimportant modifications, to a Nāga village. It is notable that down to the detail of the curved beams on the chief's house the likeness is exact. Simple decorations in crude colours ornament the dwellings of the wealthy. The original motive of these designs is lost and they are nearly always concentric circles. Spirals and whorls are rarely, if ever, seen. Here and there the beams are handsomely carved with deers' heads.

The houses of the Kukis are totally distinct, and though smaller than the Nāga house which is not far evolved from the communal house of other early communities, are more comfortable according to European ideas than even a large morang ghar of a prosperous Nāga village.

In Marām we find an interesting regulation which requires that the houses should at least not face the west because that is the direction in which the spirits of the dead go to their resting place. I do not know whether there is any such necessity imposed on Tangkhuls who also have a definite pathway to their heaven. The prevailing wind is westerly, and it may be observed that whatever the formal sanction of the regulation, it can only have received added validity from the fact that a distinctly useful purpose is served. If a house faced west, the danger of fire would be enormously increased, and these villages, as they stand, are hazardous risks.

The houses at Uilong are of great size and have some really excellent carvings.

A Nāga village, as a general rule, is an irregularly disposed collection of houses in which the dwellings of the clans which compose the village are often huddled together. The main street serves as an outlet for the storm water which gathers all the refuse so that the narrow passage which serves as an entrance to the village is in the rains choked with filth.

[1] *Vide The Meitheis*, p. 8 and p. 124, illustration.

Great skill is often shown in the selection of a site and in some cases the village gate consists of a long plank with steps cut in it.

Among the Marrings we find houses constructed on piles in the Burmese style.

Owing to the policy adopted by the authorities of Manipur towards the Nāga villages under their sway, the village fortifications have been dismantled as far as possible.

In the vicinity of many Tangkhul villages may be found store holes dug in the earth in which the grain was placed for safety; a practice which is found in many parts of the world.[1]

FURNITURE AND HOUSEHOLD UTENSILS AND IMPLEMENTS.

Rough log planks, stools hewn from a solid log, neatly plaited cane baskets five to six feet high, in which the rice is stored, two or three dhan pounders, and some earthern pots bought by some enterprising villager from Manipur, Kohima or Cachar, a row of spears, a mat or two, of such consists the furniture of a Nāga house. Here and there, especially among the Mao and Marām people, we see handsome drinking cups of buffalo horn in imitation of the Angāmi Nāga, but as a rule the drinking vessels are made of shallow gourds. The earthenware jars in which the *zu* is kept are treasured carefully.

The implements in general use are the dao, which serves a variety of purposes, and the implements for weaving, which is a general industry, except in the Tangkhul area. The loom is of the horizontal type, the spindle consists of a pair of twisted canes working together just like cogs, a very rough bobbin and a stout crescent-shaped piece of wood. In the manufacture of earthen pots the implements used comprise a bamboo cylinder, a flat plank, and a pointed stick. The dao and the hoe are the

[1] See J. R. A., I., xxxix. p. 45-46, *Deneholes and other Chalk Excavations, their Origin and Uses. Folk Memory*, Ch. xii.

At some place in the North Lushai Hills, I forget exactly where, there are several such caches outside a village. In the same neighbourhood are found groves of deciduous oaks, which Davis attributed to previous Nāga settlements, and in one place I was shown levelled sites of houses and some defences which were attributed to Nāgas.—J. S.

implements used by the men in their field work while the women use their stick as a drill and as a support when climbing up and down. The tools of the village blacksmith are a set of hammers of graduated weight and size, bellows and stones on which they sharpen the spears and daos. The bellows are made on an ingenious principle. A pair of bamboo cylinders are placed side by side with a common exhaust pipe. The pistons are fitted fairly close and are worked by hand alternately so that the air is forced down one cylinder into the fire while an exhaust is simultaneously maintained by the other cylinder and piston.[1]

MANUFACTURES.

Six Tangkhul villages, Ukrul, Toloi, Naimu, Sandang, Toinem, Phadang, are specially engaged in the industry of cloth weaving. They obtain the raw cotton from the Manipuri women in the *Sena Kaithel* or Royal Bazaar, the main centre of the commerce of the State.[2] They, in their turn, get it from the Kukis inhabiting the hills to the west of the valley. The juice of the wild indigo is used to give a black or dark blue dye, and they purchase from the plains a bark which gives a red colour shading to terracotta. Lampblack is also used for the black dye, but the better black shades are obtained from a strong decoction of indigo. The green and yellow or orange shades are produced from the barks of jungle trees, but it is not at all easy to get the people to talk about the details of their industry, because they suspect an enquirer of ulterior motives and cannot understand his curiosity. All the implements are of a simple primitive nature. The cotton is spun into thread on a pair of naturally twisted canes which work on one another almost like cogs, and from them it is transferred to a spool. The thread is then arranged by hand on the loom, which in its essence consists of a pair of bamboo

[1] An excellent illustration of the double cylinder forge bellows is given in the *Journal of the Anthropological Institute*, Vol. xxii. Plate xiv. in connection with a most interesting article by Mr. S. E. Peal, pages 244 *et. seq.* on the *Morong*. The area over which this implement is found is mentioned on p. 250, *loc. cit.*—T. C. H. See Tyler, *Early History of Mankind*, p. 168.

[2] *Vide The Meitheis*, p. 23.

bars. The girl or woman who weaves the cloth (for the men take no part in so lucrative an industry beyond enjoying its profits) sits on a low stool a little way from the back bar and keeps the warp tight by means of a leather strap against which she leans, the ends of the strap being fastened to the back bar of the loom.[1] The shuttle containing the thread is passed over and under the warp and the woof is pushed into its place by a flat, crescent-shaped piece of wood slightly larger and wider than the warp. It is hardly necessary to say that this process is slow and laborious and Manipuri competition is beginning to be felt. Manchester goods find no market here because no attempt is made to study and understand native requirements, customs, and desires. The wise purchaser who looks for strength and durability still patronises the home article. Lozenge-shaped patterns are woven into the borders of the cloths and serve as trade-marks, possibly as "luck" marks, and therefore possessing a magical value, and as ornaments, their presence adding to the price.

The following ten patterns of cloths are manufactured:

1. Pākhon phi, worn by men, white centre with black or blue and red lines on the border.
2. Leirum phi, red and white with black marks.
3. Kairao phi, red and black or blue stripes.
4. Lai phi, worn by women, black and white stripes.
5. Longkhum kasum, women's cloth, red and white stripes.
6. Sukham phi, white ground with red or black border.
7. Pordesum phi, red with black or blue and white cross markings.
8. Langoudesum phi, women's cloth, black and red stripes.
9. Kasendesum phi, broad red and narrow black stripes, worn by women.
10. Melao phi, the waist-cloth worn by the men, blue and red stripes.

There are no variations from the "sealed patterns," except in the case of the cloths worn by the *khullakpas* or headmen of a clan or village, who are by custom permitted to decorate

[1] Cf. *Upper Burma Gazetteer*, Vol. i. Part i. p. 437.

their cloths with a handsome fringe with the loose ends of the threads tied into tassels, and a pattern of orange, red and white colours with occasionally a little green, diamond pattern on the edge. The stripes of the decorative border are pointed like the pattern on a backgammon board, and when these cloths are new and in good condition, they are very handsome.

This industry is carried on by the women alone and the six villages as far as possible prevent their girls from marrying into a village where the industry is not practised. In this way a "Clothworkers' Guild" is in process of formation, and as a proof of the hold that custom, once it has become custom, has on others outside the charmed circle, I may adduce the case of a woman from the village of Toloi who married a man of the village of Powi and wished to weave cloths in her new village but was forbidden to do so by the people of Powi who, so far from being desirous of acquiring this new and valuable accomplishment, declared that it was forbidden to them to weave cloths and declared it to be tabu, using the Tangkhul equivalent to the Manipuri *namungba*. I have always regarded this glimpse into the morality of the people as affording a valuable indication of the mechanism by means of which the differentiation of caste obtains acceptance. Every specialisation of function in this level of culture seems to derive its sanction from the idea that it is dangerous in some vague mysterious way to infringe the "patent." "Les fonctions les plus délicates se différencient les premières."[1] It was a boast of the Luhupa, the northern section of the Tangkhuls, that "their women never made cloth"[2] because their subject villages kept them supplied. India teems with examples of the tabu which a dominant tribe or caste places upon the arts and crafts of a conquered tribe. They say that they learnt the art of weaving from a Deity who noticed and pitied their naked condition and taught them to weave cloths and to be decent.

Three clans of Hundung and the village of Nungbi make earthen pots from beds of clay close to their villages. The method of manufacture is extremely simple. The clay is

[1] V. Henry, *La Magie dans L'Inde Antique*, p. 5.
[2] McCulloch, *op. cit.*, p. 67.

slightly damped and then rolled out on a board which is first powdered with fine grit to prevent the clay from adhering too closely. It is then coiled round a bamboo stem and the base of the vessel cut out. At first the shape is that of a plain cylinder. It is then moulded by hand into the curves required, and after a partial hardening in the sun is baked in a furnace outside the village. They make vessels of all sizes. These vessels are devoid of any but the simplest ornamentation, but are, nevertheless, strong and well suited to the requirements of the purchasers and command a large sale over the whole of the Tangkhul country.

Colonel McCulloch found that "all of them make earthen vessels."[1] My own experience is that the potteries at Shuganu and Chairel[2] supply the wants of the hillmen over a large area.

The salt industry provides employment for a number of villages in the North East of the Tangkhul country. The brine wells are close to the beds of rivers and are of considerable depth. Their existence is determined by watching the movements of the cattle whose fondness for salt is thus turned to good use.

Huge trees, hollowed out, are driven into the places selected and the boring cleared of the earth and stones. They evaporate the brine by artificial heat in shallow iron vessels, korais, which they obtain on payment of a small annual rent from the State. The salt thus manufactured is full of impurities but meets with a ready sale among the hill people, so that the salt wells are a meeting place for all sorts of traders, men from the Nāga Hills, from Khonoma and Jotsoma, and from the Somra villages.[3]

Mention has been made of the implements used by the village blacksmiths, and incidentally of the extent to which this craft is practised. It may be noted that the industry depends on foreign supplies of metal as ore is not obtained locally. The traders in the valley from whom the crude metal is purchased, themselves obtain it either from the Lois at

[1] *Op. cit.*, p. 74. [2] *The Meitheis*, p. 32.

[3] When the Lushais made their own salt, there was a superstition that if there was ill news in a man's household, the salt would not crystallise. Men used to come from great distances to make salt.—J. S.

Kokching or from the plains. On one occasion a Tangkhul belonging to the village of Hundung purchased a shell from a Kabui sweeper attached to the regiment in Manipur and took it to the village blacksmith. This sensible fellow at first refused to have anything to do with it as he feared there was something uncanny about it. There was a lengthy debate which terminated when the owner of the shell offered a proof of his confidence in his property by putting the shell in the fire. As it happened that the shell was a live one, the discussion was adjourned till we could take official part in it. Curiously enough, of the five people who were sitting round the fire when the shell burst, only two were injured and they both recovered from the slight wounds they received. The Tangkhul who bought the shell was fined by the village for his rash and negligent conduct in bringing dangerous substances into the village precincts. For the present this source of supply may be regarded as closed.

In common with all hill tribes, the Tangkhuls are adepts at mat and basket weaving. Some of the cane collars which are worn by those who have distinguished themselves in combat are specimens of ingenious decoration. Cowries when obtainable, and, in the absence of cowries, trouser buttons are worked in.

The Tangkhuls have earned, and very deservedly, a reputation as earth-workers, and in the cold weather they are in the habit of visiting the valley to obtain contracts from the lazy Manipuris for the excavation of works, such as trenches to drain wet fields or embankments for protection against floods.[1] They are well able to protect themselves against the rapacity of the Manipuri and measure up their work and take out rates in a style which many a Civil Engineer would approve and appreciate.

The village blacksmith is an institution throughout this area, and he forges the spears and daos which his people require. The manufacture of presentation spears is a specialised industry carried on beyond the boundary. With the exception of certain cloths which are reserved for khullākpas and lungchingbas, and which are purchased in Manipur at the Sena Kaithel, all the cloths worn by the members of the household

[1] *Vide* McCulloch, *op. cit.* p. 68.

are woven by the women during the cold weather, when alone is the practice of this accomplishment possible. The skill and ingenuity with which they make baskets, collars, gaiters, armlets, headbands of plaited cane, are very notable. Among some of the Mao villages drinking cups of buffalo horn are made up, but a silver mounted cup from Calcutta is immensely prized. The gourd platters occasionally are bartered by enterprising villagers, but the staple of trade is not so much home manufacture, for they are all on about the same level, but articles of European manufacture.

Agriculture.

We have in this area tribes who migrate periodically and practise only the jhum system of cultivation. We have tribes such as the Kabuis (and possibly the Marrings), who keep to their village sites with tenacity, but are compelled to change the area of their cultivation year by year in set rotation. They preserve the memory of other days by taking omens annually to decide the direction in which the cultivation is to be. We have large villages [1] with extensive terraced fields magnificently irrigated with water brought from considerable distances in channels so well aligned that every advantage is taken of any natural slope encountered, and awkward corners avoided or turned with admirable ingenuity. But this method of cultivation is not practicable everywhere, and fortunate are the tribes who occupy hills whose declivity is not too steep for such fields. By means of long and assiduous labour, a field may be built up and provided with water so that the large terraces represent the expenditure of a vast amount of energy and farming ability, as well as much practical engineering skill. In every village where there are terraced fields, there is a body of custom with reference to the equable distribution of the water over the fields.[2] The growth of this body of law dealing with these easements is not at all easy to trace, but its final effect is as clear as its origin is natural. The fields are embanked, where possible, with small stones which serve as boundary marks because this kind of landed

[1] *E.g.*, Mao, Marām, and Mayang Khong.
[2] Below, p. 105.

property is valuable. In many villages, especially in the Tangkhul area, may be seen abandoned fields, which, according to tradition, were cultivated when the village was larger and more prosperous than it now is. But in crowded villages, as in the Mao group, patches of jhum cultivation exist which are semi-permanent, as they are cropped one year and left fallow for two years, which is not really long enough for any heavy jungle to grow.

Nearly every tribe has some terraced fields, but among the Kabuis, Quoirengs, Marrings and Chirus, jhum cultivation[1] provides the bulk of their sustenance. The Kabuis are fortunate enough to have in the Kaopum valley an area where flat fields of the ordinary kind are possible, and there raise excellent crops. The jhum system[2] has been described both by Colonel Lewin[3] and by Colonel McCulloch as follows:—

"The mountain land around the village, within certain fixed bounds, is usually the property of the village. This they cultivate with rice in elevations suited to it, and with other crops in situations unfitted for that species of grain. The spot cultivated this year is not again cultivated for the next ten years; it having been found that the space of time is required for the formation of a cultivable soil by the decay of the vegetable matter that again springs upon it. The chief crop is rice, but the produce is very uncertain, both from the vicissitudes of weather, and the differing richness of the soil which they must of necessity cultivate in their ten years rotation. As, for instance, is the case with Nongba, when, by rotation, their cultivation falls upon the south side of the village, they reap but little and support themselves principally that year on wild yams. This root a beneficent Providence has so diffused throughout these mountains that no native of them able to dig them up can starve. The hillman, more

[1] They are, however, fast giving up jhuming for plain rice.—J.S.

[2] Under the name of Essartage, the jhum system is described by the Historian of America (Payn, *History of the New World called America*, Vol. i. p. 333) as "the primitive mode of agriculture all over the world and widely practised, even yet, where virgin forest land is abundant, for in such circumstances it is the most economical method, because it produces the largest net return."

[3] *Op. cit.* p. 10, by Forbes, *British Burma*, p. 281, *et seq.* and in the *Gazetteer of Upper Burma*, Vol. i. Part i. p. 424.

especially, lives by the sweat of his brow. The spot for cultivation being determined on, he must clear it of a jungle of ten years' growth; if the spot happens to be near to the village, he can return in the evening after a full day's work, but, if at a great distance, as it often is, he must either give up work early to enable him to get back to his village by nightfall or working late remain there. Working exposed to the full influence of the rays of the sun, thirst is soon induced, which often, from there being no water near, must be endured. A bamboo jungle of the species called "Maubee" is to cut, compared with a dense tree jungle, easy, but still it is no light labour. After having been cut down, the jungle is allowed to dry, so that it may be fired in season, for if fired out of season, as sometimes through accidental conflagrations happens, the crop to be raised will be most probably deteriorated, or the land even be rendered unfit for it. Great damage has occurred to the hill people from the carelessness of travellers on the Munnipore Road, in lighting fires and leaving them burning in the neighbourhood of dry jungle. These fires communicating with the jungle have sometimes been the cause of the premature burning of the newly felled jungle, not of one, but of many villages. A premature fire caused by a hillman is visited upon him with severe punishment, and before a village sets fire to the jungle cut down on the spot about to be cultivated, it gives some days' notice to the neighbouring villages of the day on which it means to do so. At the season of firing the jungle cut for cultivation, as all the low uncut jungle is comparatively dry, on setting fire to the former the latter also ignites, and the whole mountain becomes a sheet of fire. This to a person safe from it forms a most magnificent spectacle, but one of fear and the greatest danger to those exposed to it. If the felled jungle has been thoroughly dried, the whole is, with the exception of the larger trees, reduced to ashes. The soil for an inch or two is thoroughly burnt, and having been scratched up with their little hoes, is mixed with the ashes and becomes ready for the reception of seed, which is sown broadcast. They measure their cultivation by the number of baskets required for seed.[1]

[1] This is not done by the Lushais.—J. S.

Across the field in parallel lines, at no great distance apart, they lay the unconsumed trunks of the trees; they serve as dams to the water which comes down the face of the hill when it rains, and prevents the soil being carried away with it. In bamboo jungle the bamboo stumps serve the same purpose. The field has to be constantly watched against the depredations of birds and wild beasts, and, weeds being very rapid in growth, to be frequently weeded. The rice raised by the Kowpoees generally is of inferior quality. But the villages around the beautiful little valley of Kowpoom, and near the vale of the Laimatak River, having plain surfaces of fertile soil to cultivate, raise crops of the same superior description as that of the valley of Munnipore. Although these villages possess buffaloes, they do not use them to plough with, but only to harrow after they have dug up the soil with their hoes. The crop having been cut, is beat out on the field, and the grain carried to and deposited in the granary close by the village. In the carrying, the whole village joins, receiving as recompense a certain proportion of the loads carried and their drink. In the best seasons it is only by the most unremitting attention that the Kowpoee reaps his crop, and anything at the cultivating season occurring to interrupt his labours may be attended with the serious result of a lessened supply of food. After all their labours, when the grain is ripe and ready to be cut, they lose it sometimes by a high wind sweeping the field. This wind, they assert, does not merely shake the grain out of the ear, but carries it away bodily. In such cases the grain, they say, has been taken up by the divinity. In the same manner I have heard Munniporees, when the crops are ripe, and it thunders accompanied by the wind, say that the divinity is 'carrying up' the crop, and that the grain is carried away bodily they also positively assert. A slip of the face of a hill sometimes ruins all, and another calamity consists in the visits of immense quantities of rats. These, in their progress, destroy everything before them; they nip down the standing corn, ascend the granaries, fill the houses and leave nothing behind them fit for human subsistence. Neither fire nor water stops the progress of the innumerable host. After a time these rats, they say, become birds, to eat of which produces a pestilence. That this transformation takes place they hold to be proved by the birds having tails like rats. The visitations of rats are fortunately infrequent; during the last thirty years none have occurred, but the signs of their advent are, they say, apparent, and that it will take place next year (1859) is generally expected."[1]

When felling the jungle for the jhums, it is usual to leave one tree in the middle of the field as a refuge for the tree spirit. Indeed the scorched, scarred, twisted horror of some of these solitary stumps is enough to account for belief that some spirit has chosen them as an abode. It is interesting to note the skill with which advantage is taken of the tree logs to employ them as retaining walls to keep the moisture in the ground, thus making use of the principle of the terraced field in places where terraced fields are impossible on a large scale. One of the interesting questions which arise in the course of an investigation such as this is the relationship in point of evolutionary age of two systems of agriculture such as these. Is the terraced field system evolved from the jhum system and is it legitimate to see in the details of jhum cultivation rudiments of the principles that govern the construction of the terraced fields? This question has been raised by Davis,[2] who thought that the terraced "system of cultivation gradually spread northwards from Manipur until it reached the Angamis who adopted it for the following reasons: (1) a desire for a better kind of food . . . . (2) the impossibility of raising a sufficient crop of this better kind of food, *i.e.* rice, except by a system like that of irrigated terraces . . . . (3) a good water supply. The same method of extending and enhancing the cultivable area has been employed all over the world. There are traces of terraced fields in England[3]—and in America the system received remarkable development.[4] We have to deal with people whose habits move slowly, so slowly that no use is made of plough

[1] *Op. cit.*, pp. 45–47; *Cf.* Forbes, *op. cit.*, p. 282.
[2] *A. C. R.*, 1891, Vol. i. pp. 237–8.
[3] The existence and ethnological significance of terraced fields in Great Britain have been discussed by Mr. G. L. Gomme, *The Village Community*, see pages 76 to 101. *Cf.* W. Johnson, *Folk Memory*, Ch. xiii.
[4] Payn, *op. cit.* Vol. i. p. 339 *et. seq.*

cattle though they have the sight of it under their eyes in Manipur. The digging stick is still the implement used by the women and the hoe is the only specialised tool in general use.

If we could be certain as to the original habitat of these tribes, we could settle this and many other questions without difficulty, but as it is, we can only indulge in hypothetical speculations as to the course of progress made by these people.

In the villages, especially those which are permanent and large, are small gardens or patches of cultivation in which are grown such winter crops as chillies, cotton, and tobacco. The manure of the cattle is carefully kept and used, and I have seen wicker cages put over the young seeds. Near Mao is an avenue of holm oaks which have been polled, and I learnt that the poles are regularly used by the villagers for their houses. I could not ascertain how or from whom this art was acquired. Among the Tangkhuls there are signs that the cultivation of the potato may be taken up in the cold weather in favourable positions.

Crops.

Agricultural statistics are not available for this area because the crops raised barely suffice in ordinary years for the needs of the hillmen themselves[1] and because the only crop which is grown for purposes of export, or trade, is cotton. It has not been thought necessary or desirable to erect any additional barriers in the way of such small trade as is possible in the present circumstances. The activity of the Sena Kaithel (Golden Market or principal market in Manipur which is attended by large numbers of hillmen) is the safest token of the commercial industry of these people.

The rice grown in the hills is said to be very much coarser than the delicate varieties[2] cultivated in the valley, and there is a tale current that the rice grown by the Kukis in their jhums, which is undoubtedly superior to the ordinary hill rice, was given to them by Ching Thang Khomba, who was sheltered by them when driven out of the valley by the Burmese.[3]

[1] In most parts of the hills in an ordinary year in the Lushai Hills in almost every village you can buy dhan at eight annas a load.—J. S.

[2] In the Lushai Hills about thirteen different sorts of rice are grown.—J. S.

[3] McCulloch, *op. cit.* p. 61.

The cold weather crops consist of potatoes (among the Tangkhuls only), chillies, pumpkins, tobacco, ginger, Job's tears, millet, and cotton.

There can be no doubt that there is still a source of wealth in the forests which clothe the hills, especially in the west where the annual rainfall is at least three times as great as that of the hills on the east of the valley. The tea tree grows wild, and might still be profitable but for the extravagant haste of traders who sold immature seed in the early nineties. There is—or was—a fair amount of wild rubber. There are lac-bearing trees. No systematic investigation of the forest produce of this area has as yet been attempted—perhaps because difficulties of transport render its economic development almost impossible.

HUNTING.

The methods of hunting which are possible among the comparatively open hills east of the valley of Manipur are not practised among the luxuriant jungles of the lofty ranges west of the valley. As a rule Nāgas hunt in large numbers, all the men turning out to drive the game from ravines into more open country where it can be chased by the dogs and speared or shot. The Tangkhuls of the villages Hundung and Ukrul possess a special variety of dogs which resemble the "Chow." They are good watchdogs, and are often used for driving game. This fine creature is black with white feet, and wiry hair which thickens into a ruff at the neck. They cut the tail and clip the ears. Parties of men occupy the points of vantage commanding the ravines and the dogs drive out the game. As far as possible they confine their shikar operations to their own territory, but pursue it wherever it goes. If they kill on land belonging to another village, that village is entitled to a share of the game if any of its men be present at the kill. We may presume that if no representative of the strange village be present the honest hunters will be discreetly silent about their trespass and will go home with their trophy with all speed. The ribs are usually given to the strange village. Custom provides for the dogs (or the owner of the dogs) a share of the quarry which is known as the dogs' share.[1] At Jessami I was told that the lower part of the back was the dog's share. At Laiyi the entrails were thus reserved, while at Liyai they gave the head for this purpose. In a case of homicide which arose out of a breach of these laws of venery among the Nāgas of Mao and a neighbouring village, it was contended that the members of another village were only entitled to a share of the game if they were present at the kill and aiding. A part, sometimes the head, is reserved for the man who kills. If, as sometimes happens, a single man starts the chase and others join in, he is entitled to a special share which is less than the portion appropriated to the man who actually kills.

The Kabuis hunt in numbers like other Nāgas, and, unlike their neighbours the Kukis, also make considerable use of traps and snares. Dr. Brown[2] remarks on the absence of game in the area occupied by the Kabuis and notes that the head is reserved for those who draw first blood. Some of the traps are very ingenious. They erect a long fence and leave an opening in it through which they drive the game. At the opening is placed a weighty spear attached to a pliant and elastic creeper coiled like a spring so that the animal in its mad rush for safety spears itself. I have also seen them notch a creeper along which monkeys have been seen to play. Immediately below they place panjis. Presently a band of monkeys, the worst pests the cultivators have to contend with, comes dancing along and finds the creeper particularly elastic and interesting. They dance vigorously, with the result that one of their number breaks the creeper at the notch and falls on the panjis below on which it is impaled. The Nāgas dig pitfalls but are careful to avoid any track along which human beings are likely to travel.

Hunting is prohibited during the cultivating season and the game have thus a close season which is extremely beneficial, for they have no scruples as to killing does.

[1] A similar custom exists amongst the Khasis. See *Khasis*, p. 48.—P. R. G.

[2] *Op. cit.* p. 110.

I have no direct knowledge that they set snares for birds and small game in openings in these fences. So far as I know the game is always driven. The Lushais trust a good deal to the chance wanderings of animals to take them into the snares at the openings.—J.S.

The Khul-lākpa has a customary right to a portion of all game and to royalties on catches of fish.

FISHING.

Fishing rights become valuable in the lower reaches of the hill rivers, for the upper waters are too shallow and the current too swift for much to be done there. However, I have seen Tangkhuls not far from the source of the Lanier who regularly fished the pools. They used seine nets and swept the pools down, driving the fish to the shallows, where they were netted easily. On another occasion a party of men took weighted nets attached to long bamboos twenty to twenty-five feet in length, and waded down the pool in an echelon formation, driving the fish into the shallows, where they were either caught by hand or taken in small nets. The nets were made of twine, woven of bark fibre, which is very strong and resists the water. In many cases the nets are purchased in Manipur, and the use of the weighted nets is, I think, derived from Manipur, where these nets are in common use. Fishing baskets are used occasionally, and I saw them in an excellent place at the edge of a weir near Liyai. The Quoirengs, Kabuis, and Marrings use poison, especially in the smaller streams. The poison used is identical with that used on the arrows, and stupefies the fish so that they float on the top of the water. There are no ill effects on those who eat the fish thus captured. The Chirus use weirs [1] but not nets.

Fishing [2] is usually prohibited during the cultivating season, from the time of sowing to the harvest home, a regulation which rests on the usual vague sanction attached to so many gennas, but which operates in the useful direction of affording the fish a close time.

I have no doubt that the description given in *The Khasis* of the method of using the poison applies to its employment among the Nāgas of these hills. I believe that a road con-

[1] The Lushais build fishing weirs far up all rivers, and these suitable sites belong each to a particular village site. So frequent were the disputes that the Chin Hills Lushai Superintendents issued a joint order prohibiting the making of weirs in the streams which were the boundaries between the two districts.—J. S.

[2] So also is hunting.

[3] *The Khasis*, p. 50.

tractor did once use dynamite to destroy the fish in one of the best pools in the upper waters of the river Barāk, but so far as my memory goes, he was not encouraged to repeat this unsportsmanlike and wasteful method of replenishing his larder.

Food and Drink.

The dietary of the inhabitants is naturally restricted by the limitations on the capacity of the country to produce foodstuffs, by the ignorance of the people themselves of the possibilities of the soil, and by the remarkable prohibitions, which from long custom possess great force, against the use as articles of food of products of the country both by whole classes of persons and by individuals either generally or under special conditions. It may be convenient to defer the details of these prohibitions as well as a full discussion of their precise significance to the section on genna, although it will be necessary to refer to them when describing the internal structure of Nāga society with which they are closely connected.

The cereals which have been mentioned in the preceding sections as cultivated by the people are all used as articles of food. The staple is, of course, rice, which is cooked in earthen pots or in bamboo tubes, a fashion of great popularity among the Meitheis.[1]

Among the jungle products which are regarded as edible are the yam, which Kabuis use to supplement their rice when forced to do so, the young shoots of the bamboo which possess a crisp and delicate flavour, a ground orchid which is rather devoid of flavour but is harmless, and the wild tomato, the fruit of which is quite small but excellent.[2]

All domestic animals are eaten with the exception of the cat, which is treated with respect and is buried with some semblance of funeral rites by the old women in one or two villages. It is said among the Tangkhuls that a man who kills a cat will lose his power of speech. I must include dogs in the

[1] I think bamboos are only used on journeys, or when for some reason pots are not available.—J. S.

[2] The young shoots and pith of sago palm are probably used extensively.—J. S.

category of domestic animals, for they are purchased in numbers in the Sena Kaithel for consumption. It is often said, though no one has seen it, that the most dainty dish which can be set before anyone is rice cooked in the following manner. A young, hungry puppy is selected and given as much rice to eat as he can hold, till at last he drops into sleep. He is knocked on the head, his feet tied together on a pole, and roasted in a fire, and after but a very few minutes taken out, cut open, and the rice extracted in perfect condition for immediate consumption.

Game of all sorts is freely eaten, and by old custom the Nāga villages in the neighbourhood of the Valley have a right to all cattle that die in the area near them. The law's delays and the genial heat of the climate occasionally accelerated the dissolution of the carcase of some cow or bullock, but it did not seem to matter to the Nāgas interested, for they often preferred to wait until the meat was, to a European palate, disgustingly high, before thinking of beginning a feast. Elephants that died in the Royal Pīlkhāna were similarly disposed of, and McCulloch tells how a store of dried meat was kept for the Haochongba,[1] the festival when men of the various tribes came down to Imphāl to perform feats of strength and agility. With ample store of ardent spirits distilled at Sengmai or Andro the evening was spent in a gorgeous feast, when ere long they were as Colonel McCulloch remarks, "o'er all the ills of life victorious."[2] The flesh of snakes is eaten, but it is necessary to have a village genna when a python is killed and eaten. I found great reluctance among the Tangkhuls whom I questioned to enter into a discussion on the merits of the grass snake which is eaten by some of them. I have reason to suspect that those who do not eat it look down on those who do, much as frog eating is elsewhere a source of similar feeling. Locusts are also eaten. The Nāga, especially the Tangkhul, is fond of dried fish, which is imported into Manipur in large quantities from Cachar. They also eat fresh fish.

The common drink is zu, rice beer which is variously flavoured. The commonest variety is very acid, pleasant enough but thin. Among the Tangkhuls, and especially at

[1] Hao = Nāga, chongba = to jump. [2] *Op. cit.* p. 24.

Longoi, a variety is made which is thicker, yellowish in colour and sweeter. They use jungle herbs for flavouring, and I am told that Kukis often use the leaves of the datura plant, stramonium, which accounts for the strength of their brew. I have not made the acquaintance of the Nāga who would refuse other varieties of alcoholic liquor; and to prevent any excessive consumption of the ardent spirit distilled at Sengmai, it was ordered that no Nāga should purchase liquor there without the permission of the Political Agent.

I was once entertained by a village where roasted beans, garnished with pepper, were served as stimulants to thirst, and the maidens waited on us with huge zu jars. One poor girl was well scolded because my glass was left empty for a moment.

It is perhaps open to objection on scientific grounds to regard tobacco as either food or drink; but, since a Nāga will go for miles sustained by the sips he takes from time to time of the juice of tobacco which his wife has collected in her pipe for him, we may here notice Dr. Brown's[1] account of their habits in this respect.

"The juice is not swallowed, but a small quantity is tossed under the tongue and there retained for some time: it is afterwards spat out. It is an ordinary civility for the hillmen who practise this custom to hand each other the small bamboo tube containing the juice, just as the snuff-box was formerly so commonly tendered among Europeans. The tobacco juice is prepared in a kind of hookah filled with water, made of bamboo among the Nāgas and of clay or bamboo among the Kookies. One of the main objects of the excessive smoking that goes on from morning to night, among the women especially, is the preparation of this juice, which is of poisonous strength." I may add that I have been informed that the juice acts as a tonic,[2] and I have travelled with Kukis who ate nothing all day but kept their strength up by constant sips of this juice, which they retained in the mouth not more than three minutes at a time. Its odour is very pungent and penetrating. The

[1] *Op. cit.*, p. 98.

[2] It has a wonderfully rapid effect. I have seen a Chin chief who was entirely nonplussed by a sudden home question, recover at once on getting a sip, and lie with his usual freedom.—J. S.

pipes smoked by women have a receptacle fitted underneath in which the juice is caught very much on the same principle as a certain popular patent pipe is constructed.

The practice seems to be confined to Nāgas more or less in touch with Kukis. The Nāgas of the north smoke but do not gather (or make the women gather) the nicotine.[1]

GAMES.

Two games are common among these tribes, the first being the game known to the Meitheis as Kāng,[2] to the Khyoungtha or tribes of the Hill Tracts of Chittagong as Konyon,[3] while the other is the game of draughts together with variants or derivatives, which they call the tiger and the men, and which resembles our game of fox and geese.

The game of kāng is played with the round seed of a creeper that grows in the jungle and is like a horse-chestnut in colour and smoothness. It is round or flat with a small indentation or nick in order to make it stand up. Each player has his own kāng and they put them up and flick the other kāng by pulling back the middle finger of the right hand with the left. At Mao I saw girls playing it and raising it to the level of the right knee and then dropping it with a hop.[4]

I have observed four kinds of boards for use in the draughts or fox and geese games and give below diagrams of them. The draughts game is played in much the same way as ours, with the exception that they have no rule "crowning" pieces that succeed in reaching the back line and permitting them to move either way. The Kabuis, however, use for draughts the same board as is used by the Mao folk for the game of tiger and the men, and in addition have the board marked "three" below. They dispose the pieces along the base lines and their object is to get the pieces into lines of three, when they may take one of the opposite side if it is not one of a line. The game of the tiger

[1] See above, p. 40.
[2] McCulloch, *op. cit.* p. 26.
[3] Lewin, *op. cit.* p. 40.
[4] The Kāng has to be propelled in a different method each turn. I gathered that the Manipuri and Lushai rules are identical. The kāng is placed on the instep, held between the knees, balanced on one cheek, &c., all in a regular rotation.—J. S.

and the men as I saw it played at Mao requires twenty-two pieces, two tigers and twenty men. The men are placed in groups of five, on the points marked A, B, C, D, in the diagram No. 2,

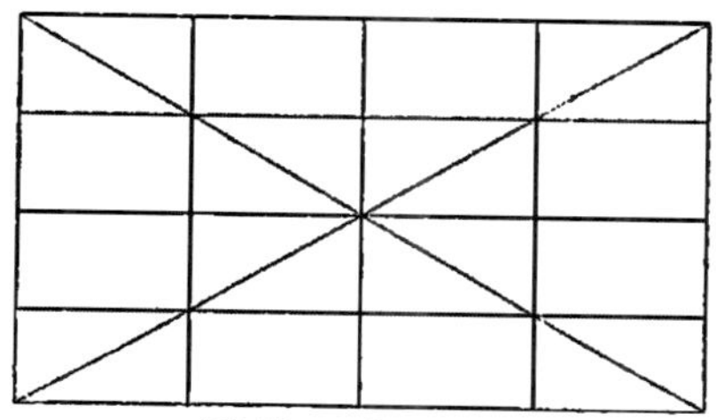

(1) Draughts only.

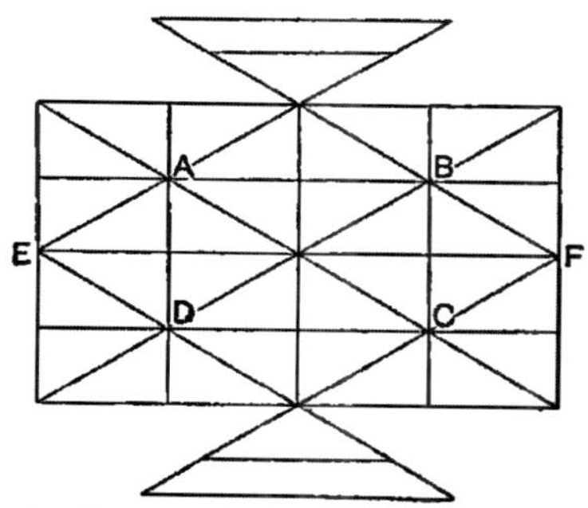

(2) Tiger and Men; also

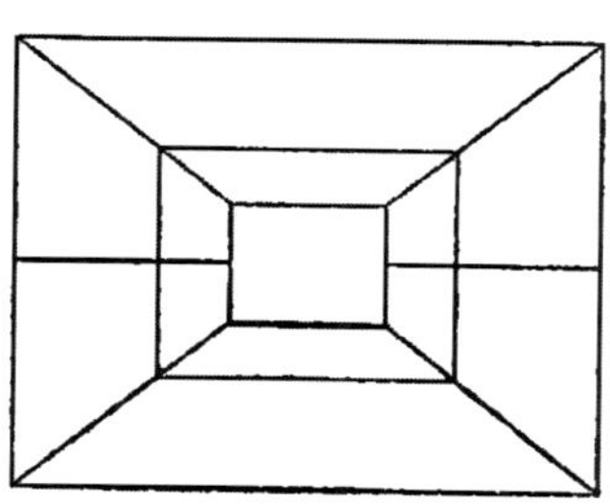

(3) Kabui Game.

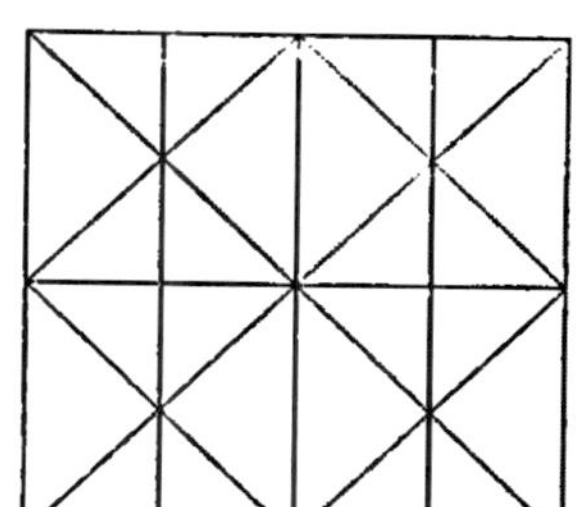

(4) Kabui: Tiger and Men.

while the two tigers are placed at E and F. A tiger kills a man each time he jumps over a pile with a clear square beyond. When the tiger is hemmed in by men with non-open squares behind them, he is killed.

Wrestling (which in the Marām group possesses an additional interest from the fact that a set bout of wrestling forms part of the "marriage ceremony"), long jump, putting the stone, spear throwing and stone lifting, an amusement also practised by the Tibetans,[1] are other forms of amusement common in every village. I have seen pegtops in use by the small boys, while in a Kuki hamlet I witnessed an exciting match between two boys with whipping tops who showed great skill in managing to drive them in and out of lines marked by stones. I may note that in the same village boys were using stilts. In a Marring village I saw children swinging between two trees on a swing hung on the branches. Among the Tangkhuls we find the tug-of-war, but as part of a ceremony of religious purpose connected with the crops. What with them is of serious import, is with the Meitheis a matter of pastime.[2] Games such as dancing are so closely connected with the religious life of the village that we realise that in the words of a French writer on this subject, "leur vie n'est pas divisée dans compartiments étanches." The dances of the Tangkhuls are thus described by Dr. Brown.[3] "The Tankhool of both sexes sing and dance together. The Loohoopa men only dance a sort of war dance, the women supplying them with liquor the while: they have drums, but only use gongs for their dances." I was informed that at Ukrul, a large, if not the largest, Tangkhul village, they have a dance for girls only, which is very similar to the Manipuri dance—called Khubei-sei-sakpa.[4] My information about dances as practised by the Mao and Marām groups is incomplete, but so far as it goes it indicates that the only dances are those of the warriors, with which the women are not associated. Of the dances of the Kabuis we have an excellent account by Dr. Brown.[5]

"Dancing is a steady source of amusement amongst them, and I here note the various dances practised by them. In nearly all cases the dancing is accompanied by a chant in unison with the music of their only instrument, the drum, which scarcely varies in spite of the number of dances they have. In their festivals

[1] *Sarut Chandra Das*, p. 180, with illustration.
[2] *Vide The Meitheis*, p. 57.
[3] *Op. cit.* p. 123.
[4] *Vide The Meitheis*, p. 54.
[5] *Op. cit.* p. 109.

KABUI NĀGAS IN DANCING COSTUME.

[To face p. 64

and dances the costume for the men consists of a kilt-shaped piece of red cloth round the loins, a Scotch wool cravat of gay colours is worn as a scarf round the waist: gaiters of white cloth with worked spots are also commonly worn. Tinsel ornaments and long feathers are worn on the head, and a favourite ornament with the men only is a broad gaudy coloured natural butterfly's wing attached to and spreading wing-like from each ear. In their dances the men carry daos with the handles ornamented with coloured bamboo strips and occasionally spears; these are twirled round in the hand in unison with the music. The dress of the girls—for only the younger of the women who are unmarried engage in them as a rule—is similar to their everyday costume, but of better quality and gayer colours. Tinsel ornaments are worn in circlets round the head. Dance first: "Hansengay." In this a circle is formed by young men and girls who move round, singing at the same time, the men heading the circle, the women bearing bamboo tubes which they rap on the ground in time with the music of the drum. The step used is one step forward, then a hop, using alternate feet. The movement is slow at first, gradually increasing. At the close of the dance, as in most of the others to be described, the dance closes by two girls dancing together in the centre of the circle; the step is the same, but they change about as in a quadrille, and great use is made of movements by the hands. This and all the dances end by the men meeting in a close circle, holding up their daos and giving vent simultaneously to a long drawn hoey, once repeated. Dance second, in this, named "Toonanga lomna," or the young women's dance, a circle is formed of young men and girls who dance but without moving round so quickly; in the centre are two couples, men and girls, facing each other. These dance, the girls opposite each other changing side and turning round as in a quadrille: the step is the same as in the last. Dance third, "Hengnaga Toona," two rows of men and girls mixed, opposite each other holding the hands clasped, which are occasionally lifted together in time with the music, step from side to side alternately, then the lines advance and retire, moving the joined hands backwards and forwards. Dance of two or four girls by couples in the centre to finish. Dance fourth, "Tinkoom Gneina Tanagga

Lamay." In this only two girls dance in the centre of a circle, using much motion with the hands; the circle is stationary. Dance fifth, "Gnan lam," young men's dance. In this only the men engage two and two abreast in a circle which moves round at first all together; the step is a single step forward, followed by a pause in the stopping position, a sort of goose step, everyone shouting ho! ho! ho! In the latter part of the dance, the circle divides into two and go round, one within the other, in opposite directions; the circle again forms as before, and they meet in the centre and indulge in hoeys in quick time, finishing up with howls. This is a very favourite dance, probably from the opportunity it affords of making a din, and they carry it on sometimes for days with scarcely an interval for repose or refreshment."[1] I have to add that the curious figure described in the last sentences of the above extract is also employed in the dance No. 1, in which both men and girls take part.

At the village of Impāmi, which belongs to the Quoireng tribe, I witnessed a series of dances which began with a dance consisting of two large parties with practically six figures. First the two parties moved in front and across one another, they then turned in opposite directions, this figure being followed by a movement intertwining the two parties which in the next figure broke into a snake-like figure. They then formed a grand circle which was then formed into two small circles from which they again formed the original two lines. It must not be supposed that there was any pause or delay in the execution of this dance, which went on without interruption, each figure and formation being harmoniously and rapidly formed. This dance was succeeded by foursomes in which the men always turned to the outside. At the beginning of the dance the men faced one another and turned at the end of the measure, then they faced the same way and again turned at the end. They kept their hands in the air twirling sticks or daos, which as with the Kabuis were of a peculiar shape. The girls kept their hands close to their sides, moving the fingers all the time. After this came the girls' foursomes with much the same figures as in the mixed foursomes, but the hands were then

[1] *Op. cit.* pp. 109-10.

placed on the hips as they moved backward. In the girls' twosomes, one hand was on the hip the other bent to the waist as in a reel. The step seemed to be the same in each dance, a step forward, balance on that foot, a step forward on the other foot half to one side, then balance, then on the first foot again. On this occasion I was told that the Kukis had four dances similar to these, but that they were inferior to the Nāgas in dances, though superior in singing.

Among the Marrings we find two dances, in the first of which the men only perform. This is a war dance and the agility with which the men advance, leap in the air, parry imaginary spear-thrusts, retreat and go through the pantomime of attack and retreat is very interesting. The second dance, in which both women and men take part, is very simple and consists of two lines alternately advancing and retreating to the accompaniment of a not very melodious chant.

The Tangkhuls are expert buglers and use a simple piece of bamboo with a vibrating reed. They give the various regimental calls with great accuracy. An instrument resembling the Jew's Harp, of which an illustration is given by Peal,[1] is also used among the Mao Nāgas. Other musical instruments are gongs made of bell-metal, which are purchased either in Burma or in Cachar. I have seen a fiddle imitating the "pena" used in Manipur, with a gourd covered with leather as a sounding box, hair strings and a bow fashioned from a bent bamboo with a string of horsehair. The drums are often of considerable size, and are made of skin stretched tightly over a hollowed frame.

In a Chiru village near Thobal, in the valley, I saw the men playing on a goshem,[2] or Kuki reeded instrument, which is described by Colonel Lewin[3] as in use among the Mrungs.

The study of the songs of the people demands more thorough investigation than I found possible, but even a slight acquaintance with this feature of native life convinced me of the importance, especially from a linguistic point of view, of further research into the language of the songs, which is known in many cases

[1] *Loc. cit.*
[2] Lushai Rotchem (R in Lushai = Y in Thādo). This instrument is distinctly Kuki as opposed to Nāga. I believe every Kuki clan uses it.—J. S.
[3] *Op. cit.* p. 87.

to be now unintelligible to those who sing them. Of the Tangkhuls, Dr. Brown,[1] remarks that:—Their singing is pleasing, being executed in well toned parts, blending together and forming a pleasing melody. Men and women in equal numbers sing thus together and sometimes men alone. The melody is always in slow time, whatever the nature of the song, joyous or otherwise. They understand the meaning of their songs as a rule, and these vary, though those of a melancholy nature prevail. The burden of one which I have heard is to this effect. "A young woman and man were attached to each other: the youth proceeded into the jungle for cane to make a basket for the girl; he is devoured by a tiger and announces his fate to his lover in a dream." There are songs which old custom determines to be appropriate for the evening of a marriage. The young friends of the newly wedded couple gather and sing these songs to them while the young men wrestle. I was told that these songs were not understood, but this may be an euphemistic concealment of the fact that the songs were not particularly decent. The wrestling determines, so they believe, the length of the union and its fertility. If the bride's champions win, she is sure to outlive her husband and to present him with many olive branches.

At Mao there is a song about the great schism which caused the breach with Maikel, but I did not get it.

Among the Kabuis as far back as the days of McCulloch[2] and Brown,[3] the difference between the language of the songs and that in daily use was conspicuous. The meaning is preserved by oral tradition and there are war songs, love songs. One, according to Dr. Brown, relates how a young man was disappointed in love and the girl married into a strange village. In a dream he beheld her as dead, and so set forth to her village, where he stealthily sought her house and found her alive and well. So he returned home comforted. Dr. Brown has preserved an interesting folk tale about the ignorance of the Marrings of matters musical.[4] "When the Deity distributed songs to the inhabitants of the world, some caught them in their hands, some secured them carefully in their clothes and

[1] *Op. cit.* pp. 122 and 123.
[2] *Op. cit.* p. 27.
[3] *Op. cit.* p. 109. *Cf.* Forbes, *op. cit.* p. 251.
[4] *Op. cit.* p. 128.

thus retained them, but the Marrings unfortunately caught their share in a wide meshed basket, through which the songs escaped, never to be recovered." This tale is also told by the Kukis, who explain their superiority in this respect by the fact that on this occasion they caught their share of songs in the leather bag (khau) which they always carry.

SECTION III.—LAWS AND CUSTOMS.

INTERNAL STRUCTURE.

THE smallest social unit is the family or extended household. In its present form it usually consists of a married couple, man and wife, and their unmarried children, living in a separate house in the area occupied by the clan of which the head of the household is a member. The parents of the paterfamilias may be living with him, or rather he may be living in their house with his wife and children. There is evidence, to which I shall refer later, that not so long ago the only permanent inmate of the separate house was the mother. She kept with her, of necessity, her young children, but as soon as they were old enough they left the house to sleep, if boys, in the Bachelors' House, if girls, in the Girls' House. Her husband slept in the Men's House and was not allowed to sleep as a permanency in the separate house occupied by his wife till past the duties of active manhood.

Nāga society is patrilineal and male ascendancy is complete with them. The essential feature of the Nāga family is that its members are descended from the eldest male resident in the house, the mother being, under the rule of exogamy, brought in from another clan, that is, an entirely different group of families. The household is a true social unit, as is proved by the fact that the head of the family has to perform certain religious duties in reference to the House Deity, or to use Meithei nomenclature, the Imung Lai, the area of whose influence is strictly bounded by the limits of the eaves of the house and the noonday shadow. There are gennas, temporary tabus, imposed on households as units in the structure of society viewed from a religious aspect.[1]

The family structure is breached by the marriage of its members. The sons set up for themselves. The daughters are removed by the law of exogamy into another clan or group of consanguineous households. The severance of the woman from her clan of origin is not complete, as the duty of revenge, should she be hurt, is with her clan of origin.[2] The custom of Mandu may be argued with Hartland[3] as indicating "the alien character of husband and father." It certainly proves that the interest of the clan of origin of any woman is not completely destroyed by her marriage and severance from them. Among the Tangkhuls the marriage of a son still further breaks up the original family, because, by an interesting custom,[4] on the marriage of a son the parents are dispossessed of the bulk of their property and required to evacuate, if not the whole, at least the best part of the house. This custom extends to the tenure of village offices out of which it probably originated, and since it takes effect on and by reason of marriage is to be differentiated from the ordinary rules of inheritance which only come into play after the death of the head of the family.

The clan or sub-group is composed of families, that is, groups of agnatic kin. It occupies a definite portion of the village, and is strictly exogamous. The clans are believed to be descended from a common ancestor by whose name, in many cases, the clan is known. In many, perhaps most, of the villages in this area these clans are also known by the Manipuri titles, Ningthajā, Kumul, Luang, but it is safe to say that these names are not found in that portion of this area where Meithei rule was not really effective before the days of the British occupation. Nevertheless, although this fact gives a clue to the origin of this dual nomenclature, it requires some discussion, for it was made the basis of an ingenious theory by McLennan[5] who urged that this phenomenon is due to the migration of these tribes to the hills before they were subdued by the Meithei. In the first place this theory does not satisfactorily

[1] See below, gennas, p. 177. [2] See McCulloch, *op. cit.* p. 68.
[3] *Primitive Paternity*, Vol. I., p. 278.
[4] McCulloch, *op. cit.* pp. 66 and 68, and Brown, *op. cit.* p. 121. See below p. 100. [5] *Primitive Marriage*, pp. 109-111.

account for the presence of the Ningthajās in the hills. If the Meitheis, really at the present time the name of the whole collection of Ningthajās, Kumuls, Luangs, Khābanānbas, Angoms, Chengleis and Moirangs, are capable of special identification with one of these clans, we are compelled to select the Ningthajā clan because to it and to no other must the Meithei Ningthou belong. Now among the Tangkhuls we find the names Ningthajā, Kumul, and Luang in every village; Khāba occurs twice; in one village only, Nungbi, we have clans bearing the names Angom and Angānba, and in addition clans which possess names, Atum and Kasu, believed to be Manipuri names but which are not now known to the Manipuris themselves. We have reason [1] for holding that there were at one time ten clans in Manipur which have been reduced to seven by the disappearance of two clans and the amalgamation of the clans Khāba and Angānba into one. Perhaps as a small essay in political palaeontology, we may conclude that the names of the two Manipuri clans which have been in their own picturesque phrase, "extinguished," were Atum and Kasu. Now in no village do we find a Nāga clan having as the Manipuri equivalent for its Nāga name either Moirang or Chenglei,[2] yet these clans still exist in the valley. The Moirang clan is distinguished from the other Manipuri clans by its remarkable homogeneity, its special localisation in the south of the valley, and therefore in contact with Kuki rather than with Nāga tribes, and its independence and by the fact that it has preserved in greater vigour than any other Manipuri clan the system of communal or clan genna which constitutes so important a feature of Nāga life. The only attempt at an explanation of this duality of nomenclature was given me by a Kabui, who said it was entirely due to the fact that the Manipuris saw that the internal structure of the tribes was very similar to their own and being too lazy to learn the Nāga names gave the clans of their Nāga subjects the names of the exogamous clans into which they themselves divided. This explanation meets most of the facts fairly

[1] See The Meitheis, p. 74.

[2] Chenglei may mean dweller in the hills. Ching=hill; lei=to be or to dwell.

enough, for in such portions of this area as in the Mao and Marām group the exercise of real power by the Meitheis was only consolidated in 1891, and it is in precisely these groups that we find no trace nowadays of dual nomenclature.[1]

The clan is, however, sociologically of importance as the marriage unit. The law of exogamy obliges marriages outside the clan, though the active participation of the clan in marriage rites is not now very marked.

The clan is recognised as a unit for genna purposes among these tribes, especially in cases of death of what we should call an ordinary and intelligible nature. Incidentally it may be pointed out that there are tribes which are genna for the death of one of their members and that they do not observe the general genna for laying to rest the spirits of those who have died within the year, as is customary among those who have clan gennas for ordinary deaths. There are indications, especially among the Tangkhuls, of religious duties being attached to the office of the head of the clans.

In the Mao group at Liyai (Nāga name Yemi) there are four clans, Doe, Kopumai, Yena, Bekom, which are grouped together in pairs which forbid inter-marriage. Doe and Kopumai may not inter-marry. Yena and Bekom are similarly prohibited. The people themselves refer this to a common relationship. This is the only instance of such segmentation in one village which has come to my notice.

The clan is also the unit of blood revenge. The feuds of clan with clan were as sanguinary and as frequent as feuds between whole villages.[2]

Food gennas applying only to clans are rare—I know of one instance—at Aimol—where the "Ningthajā" or Khul-lākpa's clan are not allowed to eat tigers' flesh. Aimol is, however, distinctly of Kuki affinities.

A Nāga village consists of at least two clans of the constitution described above. In rare cases there are as many as ten clans. Each village possesses a well-defined area of territory, not only of cultivated and terraced land, but of jhum and waste land as well. In cases where fishery rights possess a value, we find that village rights are similarly defined and restricted.

[1] See McCulloch, *op. cit.* p. 75. [2] Davis, *A.C.R.* 1891, p. 238.

Serious disputes have often had their origin in a disregard of the territoriality of one village. Hunting rights are also included. In some cases there are ascertained boundaries with either natural marks or with stones to indicate the boundary. There are instances among the Tangkhuls of small villages formed by emigrants from one centre who recognise their connection with their mother village by observing the same restraints as regards marriage with the girls of the village as if they had not moved away.

Not only is the village a distinct unit of political and economic importance, but it is organised as a religious community, acting as a whole, affected as a whole by food gennas, participating in the ritual associated with and intended to assist the cultivation of the staple of the country.

Here and there it is possible to discern faint traces of a higher organisation of villages into something almost resembling a tribe. I have mentioned "tribal colours," or tribal tartans as Sir Bampfylde Fuller describes them.[1] There are food gennas observed by a number of villages all speaking a language more or less mutually intelligible. If, as a general rule, the village forms the upper limit, so to speak, of marriage, there are no marriages among Nāga tribes, outside the tribal limit as defined by community of speech. The political supremacy of one village over small weak neighbours has for a time assisted the development of the sense of tribal unity, but never for long. As political units they have at the best shown themselves capable of only very feeble attempts at concerted and united action against a common foe. The Mao group of villages perhaps offers the best example of a unity in religious matters extending beyond the narrow limits of a single village.

There are certain facts which seem to me to be perhaps related and, if collected in one place, may serve to throw light on the history of the internal growth and development of these tribes.

In nearly every Tangkhul village we find two village officers, the khullākpa and the lūplākpa. In the village of Liyai in the Mao group we have two pairs of exogamous divisions with a prohibition against the intermarriage of the members of the paired clans. The Mao group is internally divided into two

[1] *Studies of Indian Life and Sentiment*, p. 169.

groups, the cause of their separation being, according to tradition, religious rather than social. The groups intermarry it is true, but not to any very great extent. At Marām there are two khullākpas who are both under the same extended range of prohibitions. The Kabui tribe, according to Colonel McCulloch,[1] consists of two divisions, Songboo and Pooeeron.[2] Dr. Brown groups the Quoirengs with these two, but admits the existence of a very considerable linguistic divergence between them.[3] The Marrings again possess two divisions, Saibu, the elder and Marring the younger,[4] which do not intermarry. Each of these divisions was further subdivided into seven exogamous clans the names of which were identical in each division. Two of these clans have now disappeared and we have fortunately the names recorded of the seven clans which existed in Dr. Brown's days[5]:—Khool-boo, Churung-na, Kun-se-wa, Makoonga, Tangsowa, Tungtangna, Klaya. I found evidence of a similar organisation among the Chirus.[6] These facts are too slender to warrant us in deducing from them the inference that at one time each tribe consisted of two divisions each endogamous with clans which were mutually exogamous.

The institution of a communal house strictly reserved for the use of males or of females to which access is denied to members of the opposite sex, is found in so many parts of the world that it would seem to be rather symptomatic of a definite level of culture than distinctive of any special ethnic group or groups. It is found as Dr. Webster[7] has shown in Australia, Africa, North and South America, Micronesia and Polynesia as well as in India, and particularly in Assam and among the congeners of the Nāga and Kuki tribes in Upper Burma.[8] Women are forbidden to enter it.[9] In former days even married men used to sleep in the Men's House among the

[1] *Op. cit.* p. 42.
[2] I am very doubtful about the correctness of this.—J. S.
[3] *Op. cit.* p. 100. [4] Brown, *op. cit.* p. 124. [5] *Op. cit.* p. 124.
[6] The Chirus are divided into five families and so are the Chawte. In both clans the young men of each family can only marry girls of a specified family. —J. S.
[7] *Primitive Secret Societies*, Chapter I.
[8] See The Garos, p. 39. The Mikirs, p. 11. Shakespear, *Journal of the Society of Arts*, No. 2201, vol. xliii., 1895, p. 175. *Selected Records of Bengal Government*, xxiii., pp. 155, 161, 162, 164. *Upper Burma Gazetteer*, *passim*.
[9] See Peal, J.A.I. xxii, p. 244, On the Morong as possibly a relic of Pre-marriage communism. Shakespear, *J.R.A.I.* Vol. xxxix, p. 374.

Marām Nāgas and I have been informed that a similar custom obtained among the Kabuis. Colonel McCulloch[1] ascribed this custom to "their sense of insecurity from attack," a severely practical motive quite adequate to produce the effect mentioned. Among the Kabuis of to-day it is usual, as also in the Mao group, to consider it a public-spirited thing for a man to make over his house to the community for this purpose, or to allow the young men to sleep in his own house, a practice also found according to Colonel Shakespear, among the Vuite and other Kuki clans. In some villages the only relic of the institution is the gossip platform in the centre of the village where the elders gather and discuss politics over a pipe. There is, however, the sociological aspect of the matter to be taken into consideration. In these exogamous communities the male element is the permanent element of the society. The women if married are *ex hypothesi* brought in from some other clan. They live in separate houses where they used to be visited secretly by their husbands, a custom which finds, as Colonel Shakespear has noted, an interesting parallel in the practice of Kuki clans, where the woman for some time after marriage only goes to her husband after dark. The unmarried women also have, or rather had,[2] a separate house, as had their sisters in Manipur, where it was designated the Ningonvāl. Indeed there were officials, Ningon-lakpas, whose duty it was to look after the unmarried girls in these houses. The unmarried girls in exogamous society are destined to leave their clan of origin on marriage. There are thus traces of a village organisation which kept the various elements of society rigidly apart. This has been succeeded for various reasons, chief among which is the economic pressure of modern systems of taxation, by the extension of family life which makes the separate house, till then occupied permanently only by the married woman, the abode also of her husband. This again has developed into the complete family house where the children of all ages and of both sexes live in the same house as their parents.

The institution of separate houses emphasises most markedly

[1] *Op. cit.*, p. 69. *Cf.* Dalton, *Bengal Government Records*, XXIII., p. 164.
[2] *Vide* McCulloch, *op. cit.*, p. 49.

"PUTTING THE STONE."

From a photograph by the Author.

[To face p. 70

the division of society by sex and age. In further proof of the cleavage of Nāga society by lines of sex, I point to food tabus which are imposed on women but not on men,[1] to the custom which separates the sexes at village gennas,[2] and to the rigid demarcation of the economic functions of the sexes, the women, to take an instance, smoking the pipes and the men utilising the nicotine. Yet with this clear and distinct separation of the sexes there is manifested, on the occasion notably of village agricultural festivals, a recognition of the share taken by women in the communal life, since they are of necessity associated with the rites. This demarcation of functions may be observed throughout the whole of their economic life. Indeed the earliest economic differentiation seems to have been by sex, on what seem to be natural lines now sanctioned by tabus which punish the man who even touches the woman's implements.[3]

The various grades of Nāga society are also marked by distinctions ultimately resting on age and on social and physical maturity.[4] In order that the distinctive styles of coiffure may be assumed when puberty is evident the hair is allowed to grow. Where tattooing is practised the girls are then tattooed. Food tabus are not rigidly imposed on either the very young or the old. The age of marriage, though in the case of the women nearly coincident with the advent of puberty, about fourteen, is the mark both of physical and of social maturity. In the case of men some proof of their attainment of social and physical maturity was exacted, and to this in part is to be ascribed the custom of head-hunting.[5] The women in some cases put aside on marriage the ornaments which as girls it was their privilege to wear[6] or the style of ornaments worn before marriage differs from that allowed to matrons, and so far as women are concerned the style of coiffure is invariably a mark of status.[7] The duties of the married on the melancholy occasions of funeral ceremonies are distinct from those of the unmarried; and again the duties of the married who are past

[1] See below, Food gennas, p. 182 *et seq.* [2] See below, Gennas, p. 167.
[3] See Westermarck, *History of Moral Ideas*, I., 634, and Hobhouse, *Morals and Evolution*, p. 173, note.
[4] See Van Gennep, *Rites de Passage*, p. 97; Webster, *Primitive Secret Societies*, chapter ii., *passim.* [5] See below, Head-hunting, p. 121.
[6] See above, p. 32 *et seq.*
[7] See above, p. 27 *et seq.* Also Appendix I. below.

child-bearing or child-begetting age are distinct from those assigned to the married in vigorous life. In proof of the fact that marriage marks social maturity we have the evidence of Colonel McCulloch that theft by a married man, a full tribesman as we may regard him, is severely punished, while a young unmarried man might steal with impunity grain not yet housed.[1] (It may be noted that the granary is a "tabu" place and not to be violated.)

The laxity which characterises so conspicuously[2] the relations of the sexes before marriage, and is in such sharp contrast with the rigid chastity demanded of married women, may be due to the sociological fact that marriage is a rite which transfers the boys and girls from "le monde asexué[3]" to a stage or grade of social life which is organised on the basis of sex. There is a change of status. There is from the date of marriage a liability to the full obligations of membership of the clan which there was not before; there is here no horror of incest[4] between those forbidden to marry, the prenuptial lover is often of "the girl's own clan—a man whom she may not marry."[5] This ante-nuptial laxity is a phenomenon of frequent occurrence among savage races and has been discussed by Hartland[6] who deduces from it proof of the theory that ignorance of the mechanism of the procreation of children is more general than was believed to be the case. I have heard it summarily, almost contemptuously, ascribed to contamination by contact with a culture in which female chastity is held cheap. That explanation does not fit the facts very well, and it is clear that some other explanation must be found. It is significant that there is ample evidence for this area of a belief that children are "new manifestations of a previously existent personage."[7] True there is a cycle of change, an intermediate period, at the end of which the soul returns in certain cases in rebirth.[8] Whether we may explain the food tabu which forbids to an unmarried girl the flesh of

[1] *Op. cit.* p. 49.

[2] See McCulloch, *op. cit.* p. 49. Brown, *op. cit.* Davis, *A.C.R.*, 1891, p. 250. *U.B.C.*, Vol. I., Pt. 1, p. 407.

[3] Van Gennep, *Rites de Passage*, p. 96.

[4] See Crawley, *Mystic Rose*, p. 222; Westermarck, *Human Marriage*, p. 320.

[5] Davis, *loc. cit.*

[6] *Primitive Paternity*, vol. ii., chapter vi.

[7] Hartland, *op. cit.*, vol. i., chapter iii.

[8] See *Archiv fur Religionswissenschaft*, XII., p. 455.

all male animals, as Marett hints,[1] as due to the cause which holds good among the Arunta, or must leave it with so many other tabus without explanation at all, is not for me to discuss here and now.

As a general rule each village possesses at least one officer to whom the Meithei title khullākpa, is given. For convenience of administration he is often regarded as exercising secular authority, but in reality possesses in ordinary village affairs just that amount of influence to which he is on personal grounds entitled. His authority in their eyes is religious in origin and nature. We have in many villages an official entitled the Meithei lambu, who is generally invested with that dignity because he knows rather more of the Manipuri language than his fellows. Many of them owe their promotion to a temporary sojourn in the State gaol.

In nearly every Tangkhul village we find in addition to the khullākpa a village officer bearing the Manipuri title of lūplākpa who is the head of one clan just as the khullākpa is the head of his clan. The title "khulpu," which seems to mean ancestor of the village,[2] was borne in earlier days by the person now designated the lūplākpa. At Mārām there are two khullākpas or chiefs concerning whom we have the following story.[3] "A former chief had two sons, of whom the younger, who was the greater warrior, desired to usurp the place of his elder brother. He urged his father to give him the chiefship. The old chief, afraid of his youngest son, and unable to give up the birthright of the eldest, determined on a stratagem. He told his eldest son to go and secretly bring home the head of an enemy. This having been done, the old chief summoned his sons and giving each a packet of provisions, desired them to proceed in such directions as they chose in search of enemies, for he who brought in first the head of an enemy should be king. The brothers took their leave, the youngest proceeding where he thought he would soonest procure a head, the eldest

[1] *Threshold of Religion*, p. 104.

[2] I think, Protector of the village. Pū in Lushai = Protector. The Khulpu among the Aimol and other tribes an equivalent of Thempu or Lushai Puithiam, but he officiates for the whole village, and by his skill in sacrificing protects the village from the devils.—J. S.

[3] Vide McCulloch, *op. cit.* p. 66.

bending his steps to where he had concealed the one already taken. This he brought out of its concealment, and proceeded with it in triumph through the village. Nor was the youngest long in returning with a head but having been preceded by his brother, the chiefship was declared to be the right of the eldest. This, however, did not satisfy the younger son; he persisted in being called chief and the matter was compromised by both being allowed to remain, one as the great, the other as the little chief."

Of the village officers among the Kabuis, Colonel McCulloch[1] says that "Every village has three hereditary officers, namely Kool-lakpa, Looplakpa, and Lumpoo, any officers besides these are elected. If the hereditary chief or Kool-lakpa be a man of wealth, he will be also a man of influence, but usually this is not the case, and who the head of the village is would be difficult for a stranger to perceive. Before their subjugation to Munnipore, the most successful warrior would have been the most influential man in the village; now wealth and the faculty of speaking well, which doubtless in former days had their influence, render their possessors leading men."

Among the Marrings there are two hereditary officers, khulpu and khullākpa, with, in some villages, a Meithei lambu, who is the villager possessing the best knowledge of Manipuri.

The Chirus rejoice in an *embarras de richesse* of village officers, for though their villages are quite small it is usual to find four officials, khullākpa, lūplākpa, khulpu and lambu, the first three being hereditary.

Tribal Organisation.

The determining factor which we have hitherto used in ascertaining the area of the family, the clan, and the village has been religious, and we have seen how sure a test this is in practice. But it fails us almost completely when we apply it to tribal organisation, because, with one notable exception, that of the group of villages which follow the gennabura of Mao, there is no such thing as a tribal genna.

[1] *Op. cit.* p. 48.

TANGKHUL NĀGA. [To face p. 80

From a photograph by the Author.

I have often thought that the "food gennas" might perhaps afford a criterion of tribal organisation, but they fail us, though not entirely. Thus no Tangkhul keeps or eats goats, so that any Nāga who keeps or eats goat cannot be a Tangkhul. We have much the same phenomenon at Marām and its subject villages where pork is forbidden, so that it is usually correct to infer that a Nāga who eats pork is not a Marām man.

In most respects the idea of tribal solidarity meets with no recognition among them. A Kabui, for instance, owes no duty to the tribe ; he enjoys no rights as a member of the tribe ; it affords him no protection against an enemy, for as often as not his worst enemies are those of his own village or tribe. He acknowledges no tribal head either in matters of religion or in secular affairs. He is, it is true, acquainted with the general legend that all Kabuis are descended from one of three brothers, but probably regards it as a far-off event destitute of any real importance.

Yet all through this part of the hills we find a rough test in use in the rule which forbids a man to marry a woman whose speech proves her not to be of his tribe.[1] In practice this rule operates well enough, but does not avoid the possibility of excluding individuals whom we should on other grounds most certainly include in the group or tribe. For instance, it is possible to trace link by link a chain of inter-marriages from the most southerly Tangkhul villages to those in the extreme north, though a southerner will solemnly assert that it is impossible for him to marry a woman from the northern villages because her language would be unintelligible to him. The conclusions afforded by the materials collected for the Linguistic Survey of India are in harmony with connubial practice, because they show a range of variety in this particular area from dialects in the south exhibiting considerable Kuki influence to the northern dialects which approximate to the typical Nāga language.[2] My inquiries lead me to believe that this test is not supported as is the law of exogamy by a prohibition resting on a social sanction, but

[1] Among Lushais and tribes much in contact with them there is *no* restriction. As the *Lushei* form only a small portion of the Lushais, *i.e.* the subjects of the Thangur chiefs, restrictions of such a nature would have operated against the unity which was essential to success of the movement.—J. S.

[2] *L.S.I.*, Vol. III, Part II, p. 451.

by considerations of convenience. There are one or two cases where the linguistic test is relaxed. The village of Chinjaroy or Svemi was nearly destroyed by Kukis in very distressing circumstances and is now occupied by Tangkhuls from Ukrul and by Nāgas from the neighbouring villages, such as Laiyi and Chipvome, which belong to the Mao group. They wear the ring, the distinctive mark of the Tangkhuls, and keep up some of the peculiar customs of the Tangkhuls, but marry women from the Mao group. They have adopted the Deity Aru, who really belongs to Mao, and it is said that their language now resembles that of Mao. They also follow the Mao custom of having a general genna for a death of any sort, thus differing from the Tangkhuls. The village of Oinām differs in language from its neighbours but marries with them. Its customs also exhibit a degree of divergence which is notable.

I have evidence that at Laiyi, a village of the Mao group, marriages with the people of Kharasom and Chinjaroy have taken place. It seems that in these cases they pay three cloths as the bride's price and nothing when the bride comes from one of the village clans. There may be an admixture of custom and ritual in this village, which is naturally attributable to the foreign unions thus sanctioned.

We have instances of the formation of groups of villages, firstly by specialisation of employment, the interest of common employment being the factor of the union, then by the political hegemony of one large village, which becomes by sheer force the master of a number of smaller villages, and finally by religious divergence and schism. Mention has been made of the specialisation of the cloth-weaving industry among the Tangkhuls in the six villages, Ukrul, Toloi, Naimu, Sandang, Toinem, and Phadang. Ukrul is a large village which obtained a commanding position of superiority over a number of smaller villages with which it has relations, connubial and other. The others are smaller and there is evident among them a strong tendency to prevent the girls marrying outside the weaving village, naturally in order to keep valuable knowledge to themselves. In this, as I found, they were aided by the operation of the belief which underlies the whole system of genna, that one man's meat is another man's poison. "A woman whom I knew had come from a cloth-weaving village was settled with her husband in an outlying village, where I saw her. I asked her if she had woven any cloths recently, and she told me her husband's village people forbade her weaving because it was genna to them. I was well aware that by discouraging the marriage of their girls outside the group of cloth-weaving villages they were fast making themselves a close corporation in enjoyment of a valuable monopoly. I was not prepared to find others quite so ready to accept this monopoly without question . . . . I asked the headman why they forbade the women to weave cloths, and he told me they all feared something terrible would happen to them if they allowed her to make cloths. There is also the fear of the magic of the craftsmen being directed against them, for these villages which have this special industry are regarded as possessing remarkable powers which they claim, and which others believe, to have been taught them by some divine being."[1]

I have referred to the important political position occupied by Ukrul among the other Tangkhul villages. In the Mao group there are two groups, but, according to tradition, the line of divergence is in the nature of a religious schism rather than political. The village of Marām was, we know, once of considerable size, and from the 900 houses, of which it consisted in the days of McCulloch,[2] it has now shrunk to about 120. It is mentioned in the chronicles of Manipur, and according to the belief of its own people the Manipuris often took their girls in marriage in the days when such unions were lawful. It exercised great influence over a number of villages extending as far south as Mayang Khong, and received tribute from them. Some of these villages were very possibly members of other groups, but have in course of time adopted the customs of Marām, so that, to take one typical custom, the prohibition of pork, we find it recognised and followed in a large number of villages.

In the case of the separation of the fifteen villages which obey the khullākpa of Mao from the six villages under the

[1] "Genna among Tribes in Assam." T. C. Hodson, *Journal of Anthropological Institute*, Vol. XXXVI, 1906, pp. 94 and 95. See above, p. 47.
[2] McCulloch, *op. cit.* p. 69.

headship of the khullākpa of Maikel, we have an instance of religious schism as the cause of the formation of two groups. This case is the more important as it seems to me to be the only case where we have a genna extending over a group of villages, for, as a general rule, the village is in genna matters an autonomous unit.

Authorities such as McCulloch and Brown recognise two divisions among the Tangkhuls approximating to their geographical distribution. The Luhupas are the Northern division while the Tangkhuls are the Southern. Manipuris have divided them for purposes of administration into three lams, and we may certainly trace in the weaving villages the incipient development of a third group occupying a position between the Northern and the Southern Tangkhuls. Yet in the common recognition of the prohibition of goat's flesh, and in the customs of wearing the ring and of evicting the parents when the sons marry, we have enough to differentiate them from other groups.

It is less easy to find differentia between such groups as Mao Marām, Kabuis, and the Quoirengs, but we may definitely mark the Marām group by its prohibition of pork. The Mao group, which Colonel McCulloch classed with the Marāms,[1] and Dr. Brown with a large number of villages including Marām,[2] is composed of those villages which own the religious headship of either the khullākpa of Mao (Sopvome) or of Maikel. This, however, excludes the village of Jessami, which is situated at such a distance from the main group of villages that it has a khullākpa of its own. As regards the Kabuis, while their custom of "mandu" is not exclusively practised by them, yet inasmuch as it is not found in force among any other of the tribes referred to in this volume, it may be held to be adequate as a distinguishing point of difference.

I am unable to suggest any custom or tribal prohibition of general acceptance which would help us to dispense with the external differences of dress and coiffure which in practice distinguish the Marrings and Chirus from other Nāga tribes.

It is to be regretted that the materials supplied to the Linguistic Survey of India did not include specimens of the

[1] *Op. cit.* p. 69. [2] *Op. cit.* p. 111.

Marām group, a defect which is but hardly remedied by the vocabulary given by Colonel McCulloch.[1] The conclusions at which Dr. Grierson and his collaborators have arrived may very usefully be compared with the results which my own inquiries afford. At Lambui I learnt that they could understand most of the villages round them, but failed to make out the dialects of such distant places as Tussum and Kharasom. At Ukrul they understood the speech of Tussum, Kharasom, Chingai, Chatlao, as well as of nearer villages, such as Sirohi, Handang, Kalhang, and Toloi. The Huining people refuse to marry with girls from Kharasom on the score of the unintelligibility of their tongue. A small marriage group was mentioned to me at Phunggam, where it was alleged that, as a matter of fact, they rarely went beyond the neighbouring villages of Powi, Nunghar, Nungbi, and Huining for their wives.

Among the Mao Nāgas the linguistic grouping affords no distinction between the Mao and the Maikel divisions, but they declare that they do not understand the dialects of Marām and Oinām.

We find at Maikel the belief that Marām and themselves were once related, so much so that they did not intermarry because they were then living together and are of the same stock. The Marām legend does not support this, and we find that other villages, such as Mayang Khong, which claims descent from Maikel, have close relations with Marām, whose customs they follow in many respects. The linguistic test, therefore, seems to break down at this point, and we must have recourse to other material for the points of difference which enable us to distinguish the Mao, Maikel, and Marām groups.

On linguistic grounds, according to the Marām people, we must include in the Marām group such villages as Oklong, Uilong, and Mayang Khong. The first two declare themselves to belong to the Quoireng group. It is difficult to reconcile the Marām view with the equally explicit statement of the Uilong people, unless there is less linguistic difference than at first seemed the case. A possible explanation is that the Marām villagers, great warriors, so overawed the people of the smaller villages, over whom they exercised a sort of dominion

[1] *Op. cit.* pp. iv–xlii, Appendix.

that the latter learnt enough of the Marām language to make themselves understood in it.

So again, in the case of the Quoirengs and Kabuis, the differences of language are found in actual practice to be quite adequate to differentiate them and to constitute a test which the people themselves would admit of eligibility for inter-marriage.

The languages of the Chirus and Marrings very obviously belong to so distinct a group of dialects, that even less difficulty can be raised in accepting the popular use of linguistic differences as a test of tribal distinction.

The Chirus were regarded by Dr. Brown as a branch of the Kōm tribe of Kukis,[1] a view in which he differed from Colonel McCulloch, who was inclined to treat them as a link between the Kukis and the Songboos,[2] "as he dresses his hair like and approaches in habits to a part of the Songboos."

It should not be forgotten that customs are often consciously borrowed and imitated, that most of all fashions of coiffure,[3] dress, houses, are liable to variation, and that in the dominance of Meithei authority in the past, and the Pax Britannica in the present, we may see forces which are slowly breaking down the differences of language and custom which keep these villages apart. Trade is a great solvent, and its effects are coming into view. One example of the effect which the needs of modern administration have had on native custom, is that the Tangkhuls do not feel themselves inclined to insist on the full rigour of the custom of turning out the parents when the sons marry, because they have to pay house tax on each house erected. Will this result in a revival of the common house system on a large scale? If we see, as some have seen, in the institution known as the Bachelors' Hall, a survival from the times when their ancestors lived, as some tribes still live, in one large house,[4] it would be a strange thing if the effect of the measures of an enlightened bureaucracy were a return to a state of affairs from which they had emerged.

[1] *Op. cit.* p. 135. [2] *Op. cit.* p. 65.

[3] A Marring youth wears the Chiru fillet till he reaches puberty.—J. S.

[4] Surely the Bachelors' Hall arose from a desire to avoid incest. Is this not shown by the alternative systems of sleeping in well-to-do villagers' houses, or in the house of some other married person, as among the Purum? —J. S.

MARRIAGE.

One common feature of the investigations which have been made into the manners and customs of these tribes, is that intercourse between the sexes is free so long as the girl is unmarried.[1] There are however, among the Tangkhuls especially, festivals connected with the crops, a prominent feature of which is a mock contest of rope-pulling between the girls and boys, followed by a general orgy of license, at which, according to some informants, the ordinary rules are disregarded.[2] The fact that women participate in a village festival which is part of a very important genna is interesting enough, but in the rain compelling ceremony in vogue among certain Tangkhuls, women are allowed to join the procession in numbers equal to the men if we omit the khullākpa. As the common house or morung ghar is not now common among the Tangkhuls, we must notice the coincidence that in the groups where the morung ghar is found, the women do not actively participate in gennas, except the annual festival on account of those who died within the year, while in a group where the morung ghar is practically obsolete, they join in and are essential to some important agricultural ceremonies which form an integral part of the system of communal religion.

While many marriages are arranged by the young people themselves on the basis of affection, it is nearly always usual to employ an old woman as a go-between, a custom which has been held to be connected in all probability with the tabu which prohibited all intercourse between betrothed persons.[3] Marital intercourse within the dwelling house is prohibited for the initial nights of the married life. This prohibition extends in some cases over a period of a month, but is always less in cases of remarriage. Indeed, in some of the groups the married men are included in the morung ghar, so that all

[1] McCulloch, *op. cit.* p. 49. Brown, *op. cit.* p. 99. *Cf.* Lewin, *op. cit.* pp. 47, 77, 80, 93. Also see above, p. 78. Also Peal, *op. cit.* p. 248. Forbes, *British Burma*, p. 286. *U.B.G.* p. 407.

[2] *Cf.* Davis, *A.C.R.* 1891, Vol. I. p. 244.

[3] *L'Année Sociologique*, Vol. VIII. p. 422.

intercourse with their wives who live in the separate houses is necessarily of a stealthy nature.[1]

During the continuance of married life, marital intercourse is especially forbidden in connection with gennas, when the sexes are required to cook and eat apart, and to such persons as headmen on the eve of village festivals and to persons about to erect a stone monument. Warriors again, when preparing for and returning from a raid, are forbidden marital intercourse, a prohibition which leads to the inference that as they are then specially liable to danger, all acts that increase their liability to danger must be avoided. It must also be borne in mind that the successful issue of a raid at the beginning of the cultivating season brings prosperity to the crops.[2] Thus the periods when the man is in special danger are marked by the prohibition of sexual intercourse. We find that the special moments in the life of a married woman, when, as it were, the purpose of marriage is attained, the crises of childbirth, are occasions of gennas in which the husband is involved. Are these also hours when the husband and father is in any special danger? When a woman dies in childbirth, an event that happens but seldom, we shall find that the whole village is genna thereby, that the grave is dug by a special class, sometimes by old men or women past the age of child-bearing, and therefore not liable to the special danger which has just signalised its power, sometimes by men who are of the woman's kin. There are customs again, such as that called "mandu," which, whatever their origin and purpose, indicate that a woman does not completely lose touch with her birth clan[3] by reason of marriage into another clan.

These customs may well be survivals from a time when the family was not based, as now, upon male agnatic descent. They do not consort well with strict male kinship and ascend-

[1] A parallel to this state of affairs is afforded by the history of early Japanese society, in which the woman lived at home with her parents and her children, while the husband had the right of visiting her at night. Upon these facts it has been considered legitimate to base the view that the family in Japan was uterine or matrilinear in origin.—*L'Année Sociologique*, Vol. VIII. p. 422. *Cf. The Khasis*, Major P. R. T. Gurdon, p. 76. See above, p. 76.

[2] See below, Head-hunting, p. 119.

[3] Among Lushais a woman keeps her clan, though her children belong to her husband's clan. In case of her illness the sacrifices are performed in accordance with the customs of her clan.—J. S.

ancy, but it is next to impossible to get other evidence except by inferential and indirect methods.[1]

The law of exogamy prevails throughout this area in respect of the clans composing the villages, and rests ultimately on the same kind of sanction as gives validity to the various prohibitions which are classed together as genna. It may therefore be regarded as a fundamental law, and of the essence of their social fabric. A breach of this law entails at least immediate expulsion from the village, a punishment which would have meant death in days now past, but not remote, for there were no cities of refuge to afford shelter to such mistaken persons.

I have heard in a few villages that marriages with girls of the mother's clan are not liked. And also that marriages with the children of aunts on the father's side are viewed with disfavour.

Subject to the reservation that in actual practice the distinction of tribes rests on linguistic differences,[2] not on any genna ordinance, the tribe is an endogamous group.[3] We have instances where, for special reasons, marriages have taken place between persons of different tribes, as at Svemi and Laiyi.

As a rule marriage is free between all the clans in a village or group; but at Liyai we find that the four component clans are arranged in pairs which mutually forbid marriage. Among the Marrings and Chirus I have found evidence of the existence of the division of the tribe into two groups forbidding intermarriage, and with this evidence I have collated facts which seem to indicate that a similar division may have at one time existed in other cases.[4] Extended reference has been made to the formation of an endogamous group, by the efforts made by the members of the cloth-weaving villages in the Tangkhul area to discourage their girls from marrying with men of villages which lack this valuable industry.[5]

The marriage price varies very considerably, and for reasons which are worthy of note. Among the Tangkhuls it is affected

[1] See Hartland, *Primitive Paternity, passim.*
[2] See above, p. 81.
[3] Cf. *L'Année Sociologique*, Vol. I. p. 31. La Prohibition de l'Inceste, par E. Durkheim. "On ne saurait trop répéter que si le mariage est exogame par rapport aux groupes totémiques (clans primaires ou secondaires) il est généralement endogame par rapport à la société politique (tribu)."
[4] See above, p. 74.
[5] See above, p. 83.

by the station and wealth of the parents of the girl. In earlier times we have it on the authority of Colonel McCulloch [1] that "The women of the former (the Luhupas in the far north) are much sought after by the southern man because, however fierce their feuds may be, a tattooed woman always goes unscathed, fear of the dire vengeance which would be exacted by her northern relations were she injured giving her this immunity." No more do the southern bachelors seek their brides among the tattooed women of the north, preferring the attractions of cattle and other wealth. So, again, Colonel McCulloch notes that "the great expenditure of men, especially amongst the Murams, has made women exceed greatly the men, and a wife can easily be obtained for a khes or coarse cloth." [2] I have information to the effect that at a village in the Mao group which permits marriages with Kharasom and Chinjaroy (Svemi), members of the Tangkhul group, the price varies according as the girl comes from a strange village or from one of the village clans. In the latter case there is no price—a strange departure from the general rule. It is usual in the Marām group to signalise the advent of a bride from a strange village by making a wrestling bout part of the marriage festival.

Among the Quoirengs the price is paid in cash or kind and is usually a matter of arrangement.

In the days of Colonel McCulloch the price of a wife among the Kabuis was "seven buffaloes, two daos, two spears, two strings of beads, made of conch shell, two ear ornaments, two black cloths, two eating vessels, two hoes, and what is called meilon. Less than this can be given and is, usually, except with the rich, amongst whom the having paid a high price for a daughter-in-law is a subject of boasting. The meilon is given by the family of the bride, it may be an article of much value, but without it it is not thought that the bride has been fully given." [3] I was told that the price did not now exceed one hundred baskets of rice with a dao, hoe, and cloth for the girl's parents. Buffaloes and mithan are now scarce in the hills, so that substitutes have been found.

[1] *Op. cit.* p. 68.

[2] *Op. cit.* p. 69. The Lushais have a higher proportion of women to men than any other tribe, and yet the price is higher, never less than 3 mithan and about Rs. 20.—J. S.

[3] *Op. cit.* p. 50.

The regulated payment for a wife among the Marrings was in 1859 "three gongs or two methins, in fault of which the first child born becomes a slave."[1] It would hardly be legitimate to treat this statement as affording material for equating a mithan as in value one half of a slave. From Dr. Brown we gather that the price varied according to the circumstances of the husband, and that a gong in all cases formed part of the presents given.[2] To this day the gong is necessary, but thirty rupees in cash are accepted as equivalent.

Among the Chirus where I have noted the existence of two divisions, it appears that the price varies in each division, one being dear and the other cheap. It is apparently necessary for the bridegroom to work for his father-in-law as well as to pay him something as a price.

It sometimes happens that a young couple dispense with the formalities usual in such matters, but their precipitation does not set them free from the liability to follow the rule as to gifts. Sooner or later the gifts must be made, and so long as this is left undone the young couple are forbidden food in the houses of their parents.

The price is usually paid in kind, but we have instances, as the Quoirengs and Chirus, where service is accepted in lieu of the price.[3] In such cases it is nevertheless customary to insist on the transfer of some material object, such as a gong, or cloth, or spear. Among some notes prepared for me by Babu Nithor Nath Banerji in regard to the customs of the Anāl Namfau villagers, I find that three years' service is usual.[4] If this is the case, there has been a modification of local custom since the days of Colonel McCulloch, who states that the rich give "according to their means, the poorer according to theirs, not less however, than a pig and a piece of iron one cubit long."[5] We have, also on the same authority, an interesting variant in the custom of the Marrings, by which in default of the regulated payment of three gongs, or two mithans, "the first child

[1] McCulloch, *op. cit.* p. 65. [2] *Op. cit.* p. 127.

[3] *Cf.* Lewin, *op. cit.* pp. 80, 93, and Brown, *op. cit.* p. 105. See Hobhouse, *op. cit.* Vol. I. p. 45; also *U.B.G.*, Vol. I. Pt. I. p. 522 (Hka tribes), p. 586 (La'hu tribes). See Brown, *op. cit.* p. 105.

[4] The service is *in addition* to the price; in all cases where there is service there is a payment of some sort to close the deal. The Chiru bridegroom gives a gong when finally taking his bride.—J. S. [5] *Op. cit.* p. 65.

born becomes a slave."[1] It is unfortunate that the evidence stops short at this point, but it is to be inferred that the child becomes a "slave" in the family of the mother. "Slavery," as it was in the hills, is described by Colonel McCulloch[2] and by Dr. Brown[3] as mild domestic service.

It may be that some relationship exists between the marriage price and the custom of "mandu," or the price of the bones, which Colonel McCulloch thus describes as practised by the Kabuis[4]: "On the death of a man's wife the extraordinary practice exists of taking from her husband 'mundoo,' or 'the price of her bones.' If he be alive, this will be demanded by her father, in fault of the father by her nearest of kin. 'Mundoo' is also payable on the death of their children. On each demand of 'mundoo' the demander kills a pig, the 'mundoo' or price is fixed at one buffalo. No 'mundoo' is payable for persons killed by enemies or wild beasts, or whose death has been caused by any swelling, or the cholera, or small-pox. . . . She (the wife) cannot return to her parental home as long as there are any near male relatives of her husband remaining." To this account Dr. Brown adds a correction, that "mundoo" is not payable on account of the children, and makes the addition that it is not payable in the event of the woman dying in her parents' house.[5] The question arises whether this payment is, as it were, part of the marriage price which has been deferred and does not become due till the death, and thereby the final separation, of the woman from her parents' clan, or whether it is strictly the price of her bones. Another point arises on which I lack information. Wives may be sold.[6] Who is liable for mandu? The husband or the purchaser? In either case it proves that the interest of the woman's clan in her is preserved long after her marriage and removal from them. It is unsafe to build any theory as to the origin and nature of this custom upon the remark of Colonel McCulloch that mandu is payable in respect of children, because it is not confirmed either by Dr. Brown or by my own investigations thirty years later. It is quite possible that Colonel McCulloch, a shrewd observer,

[1] *Op. cit.* p. 65.
[2] *Op. cit.* pp. 24 and 25.
[3] *Op. cit.* p. 110.
[4] *Op. cit.* pp. 50, 51.
[5] *Op. cit.* p. 105.
[6] McCulloch, *op. cit.* p. 53.

is right, for in other respects we know there has been change. We have among the Kukis, some at least of whom are acquainted with this custom, the preservation of the bones as an integral part of their mortuary rites, so that in their case, while they now restrict the practice of keeping the bones to the families of chiefs, it would be literally and exactly the price of the bones which remain in the custody of the husband.[1] This explanation encounters no obstacle in the special cases of exemption which have been mentioned, as if a woman dies in her parents' house she would be buried there, and they would have the custody of her bones. If her death is due to any of the circumstances mentioned, all of which involve the village in a general genna because they indicate the presence of mysterious danger, mandu would not be payable, because the extraordinary nature of the death would release them from the obligation which they incur when the death is of an ordinary kind. By this explanation we assume that the custom has either been adopted by the Kabuis from the Kukis, their neighbours—not an impossible assumption—or that they have abandoned that part of the custom which relates and is due to the mortuary rite of preserving the bones of the dead. We know that as Colonel McCulloch observes[2]: "To their villages, which are permanent, the Koupooees are much attached. The village and its immediate precincts form their graveyard, and when for a time, from whatever cause, they have been obliged to desert their village, I have heard them more often express their wish to return to it, as being the grave of their ancestors, than to it being their own birthplace."

It may be noted that the unusual forms of death which convey exemption from mandu are associated with special funerary rites, and in the case of a woman dying in childbirth the grave is dug by her male relations or else by her husband's relations inside the house, which is then and there abandoned. I cannot say that there is absolute uniformity in this, but there is a unanimity of desire to distinguish in every possible manner such cases of death as point to special danger.

The key to the situation is, I think, on reflection, contained in the eschatological belief which denies all chance of rebirth

[1] Compare *The Khasis*, p. 77. [2] *Op. cit.* p. 43.

to persons who die in any of these ways. The connection must be disowned; the relationship must be broken finally and for ever. Hence the parents do not claim and the husband does not offer to pay, mandu in respect of a woman who has thus "disgraced" herself.

Further, mandu is paid after the burial or preliminary obsequies and before the final obsequies, that is, during a period when the soul of the deceased is in an "intermediate" condition. Is it intended to secure a wife for the widower in the world to be? The Northern Tangkhuls, whose women tattoo, declare that this is done in order that they may be identified—*i.e.* may be wives to them—hereafter. The "title" to the wife must be acquired before her ghost is finally laid to rest.[1]

Eschatological belief on this point is not perfectly clear. In some cases there is evidence that women cannot get into Heaven, that they are excluded by a watchful Deity.[2]

Polygamy is permitted among the Tangkhuls, who have a knowledge of the practice of the Manipuris in this respect. It is not very common, as separate establishments must be maintained, and custom demands that, as in Manipur, the greater attentions should still be paid to the elder wife.[3]

In the Mao, Marām and Kabui groups polygamy is very rare and is not encouraged by public opinion. I have heard of instances among the Quoirengs where the two wives lived in the same house and got on well together. As a matter of coincidence it may be remarked that polygamy is weakest in those groups in which the bachelors' hall is most definitely preserved.

The Marrings discourage polygamy by insisting upon the payment to the parents of the first wife of gifts of substantial value.[4]

There is apparently no restriction upon the remarriage of widowers, except that they are liable to the same exogamic necessity as when they first married.

In the case of widows, custom varies very much. Among

[1] Compare the Lushai Lukawng, which is paid to the deceased "Pa," who may be any person appointed by the deceased, not even of the same clan. The Pa has to provide animals for the funeral sacrifices.—J. S.

[2] See Shakespear. *J.R.A.I.* *Loc. cit.* *The Garos*, p. 103.

[3] *Cf.* Van Gennep, *Rites de Passage*, p. 252. *The Meitheis*, p. 77.

[4] Brown, *op. cit.* p. 127.

the Tangkhuls the widow is free to remarry, after the final funeral ceremony, any person to whom she might lawfully have been married as a spinster. They do sometimes marry their deceased husband's younger brother, but such marriages are entirely of inclination, not of compulsion. Much the same rule is in force among the Mao and Marām groups, in the latter of which we find an instructive regulation to the effect that a widow may remain in her husband's house and be entitled to maintenance "dum casta et sola." If she separates, she is at liberty to please herself and to keep herself.

At Yāng we begin to come upon compulsory marriage with the deceased husband's brothers, for they there preserve the tradition that in early times this regulation was in force among them. They claim to be descended from Kukis. This custom is found among some, but not in all, Quoireng villages. The remarks made by Colonel McCulloch which I have quoted in reference to mandu above, show that this obligation is in force among the Kabuis.[1] Among the Marrings it is permissive, not compulsory. Among many of the tribes which have been subject to Kuki influence, or which are of Kuki stock, we find the rule compelling such marriages, and in all cases, whether of compulsion or not, we have the additional rule that the elder brother may not take the widow of a younger brother. The object of this rule may be, firstly, to save the younger brother, if unmarried, the cost of a wife, and, secondly, to make some use of a person who would otherwise be a burden on the property of the deceased. The position of the younger brother under the laws of inheritance will be described in a later section. The "legal" effect of marriage upon rules of inheritance is traceable in these exogamic communities. If in cases where such marriages are compulsory, the younger brother refuses to marry the widow, he has to pay a fine, meithi.[2] If the woman refuses to marry her husband's brother, her price (*mangkat*) is refunded, and she is returned to her people.

There are cases, such as that of the inhabitants of Sādu Koireng, a small village of hill people in the valley of Manipur

[1] *Op. cit.* 51. See p. 92 above.

[2] Seemingly a loan-word of Meithei origin, and meaning woman's disgrace, mei = woman, and thi = shame.—T. C. H.

a few miles from Foiching, where such marriages with the deceased husband's brother are not permitted till the expiry of the general funeral rite following after the death of the husband. As we are aware, the purpose of this rite is in part to lay to rest the ghosts of those that have died in the year; the reason for this restriction is evident.[1] We may also note that in those cases where there is a genna prohibiting newly married couples from intercourse during the early days of their married life, the restriction is usually much less in the case of remarriages than of first marriages.[2] Ceremonies, such as wrestling and songs, which form part of the marriage festival are generally left out in these instances of remarriage.

Marriage is here a permanent union between two individuals, although interrupted by the occurrence of genna festivals, when society is, as it were, resolved into its primal elements as based on sex.

Marriage, therefore, is to be differentiated from the temporary unions which custom allows the young of both sexes to form, in that it definitely and permanently reserves one woman for the one man.[3] In the effect which marriage has in raising the presumption that the children born to a married woman are the offspring of her husband since "is pater quem nuptiae monstrant," we find an interesting piece of evidence as to the nature of marriage in this area. In some groups humanity permits children born to an ostensibly unmarried girl a chance of life dependent on the acknowledgment by the man of his paternity. In other groups, as at Mao, such children are abandoned without further discussion. A feature of the birth ceremonies among the Tangkhuls is that the first food taken by the newly born infant is some rice, which the father first chews, an act which seems to constitute an acknowledgment of his paternity and duty towards it, as well as to create a semi-physical bond between father and child.[4]

The Mao people punish the girls, who used in one village to be put to death, while the Marrings punish the man.[5]

[1] *Cf. The Khasis*, p. 77. [2] *Cf.* Van Gennep, *Rites de Passage*, p. 252.

[3] See Jevons, *I.H.R.* p. 71.

[4] Cf. H. Ling Roth, "Significance of Convade," *J.A.I.* xxii, p. 204 *et seq.* Also W. H. R. Rivers, *The Father's Sister in Oceania. Folklore*, xxi. p. 57. Also Frazer, *Totemism and Exogamy*, Vol. IV. pp. 244–247.

[5] Compare Lushai Sonman.

Dr. Brown makes the noteworthy statement that "should the widow not be willing to be taken by her deceased husband's brother, and her parents agree with her, her price doubled must be returned to the brother."[1] It is interesting to observe that the price doubled has to be paid in cases of adultery when the adulterer escapes the vengeance of the husband.[2]

Divorce is of rare occurrence, and among the Tangkhuls is given only on the fault of either party. My information is very scanty, but supplemented by Dr. Brown, who states[3] that: "Divorce is allowed, but seldom resorted to, on account of the great expense." It is legitimate to assume that the expense is incurred in providing the village elders with an ample store of food and drink to aid their deliberations. At Mao and Jessami, in the Mao group, I found that women occasionally divorced themselves and that in such cases the children, if and when weaned, went to the custody of the father.

Adultery is a cause of divorce among the Kabuis, who also allow divorces on such grounds as proved incompatibility of temper, as at Tamenlong, or serious ill-treatment of the woman by the husband, as at Aqui, or on her demand. In these cases, if the man is in fault or demands the divorce, the price is not returned, while it is repaid to the husband when the woman is in fault or demands the divorce.

Dr. Brown[4] remarks that, "In the event of either married party wishing a divorce, the rule is that, should the consent be mutual, there is no difficulty; the couple simply separate. If the wish for a separation comes from the woman, and the husband is agreeable, her price is to be returned; but if the man wishes to send away his wife, which he may do with or without her consent, then he is not entitled to it."

Among the Marrings divorce is given only on proof of some fault, and "even then a heavy fine is levied in the shape of feasting and drinking."[5] The Chirus do not seem to allow divorce.

The rules relating to the return of the price are also in

[1] *Op. cit.* p. 105.
[2] *Op. cit.* p. 106.
[3] *Op. cit.* p. 121.
[4] *Op. cit.* p. 105.
[5] Dr. Brown, *op. cit.* p. 127.

force among the Quoirengs, who admit barrenness as a ground for divorce, and in other cases give the children to the father.[1]

ADOPTION.

If adoption is a form of parental relation artificially created in order to supplement natural parentship, when prevented by any reason from adequately fulfilling the duties which are its essential feature, then either we may study the functions of parentship by watching the workings of a system of adoption, or by concentrating our attention on the duties and position of parents may obtain an insight into the causes which necessitate the growth of methods of adoption. Are there among these people, then, any duties attached to parentship which require issue of children for their full value? In communities with a developed system of ancestor worship every man is a potential object of worship, and, to "realise" himself, a son, in the flesh or adoptive, is necessary; but ancestor worship of this type belongs to a social system in which the family plays a much more important part than in this area. Here such ancestor worship as exists is at present closely connected with the need for laying the wandering ghosts of the dead to rest, and for that purpose we have communal ceremonies, either a general ceremony once a year, as with those tribes which practise clan gennas for ordinary cases of death, or on each occasion of death, as is usual in the Mao group. There is not, therefore, the same need for issue to perform the rites of ancestor worship when this is the business of the whole village or clan. So long as the clan or village remains in existence, there is an heir to any individual member of that clan in the person of any survivor, and consequently we do not find any ceremonies of adoption in force.

INHERITANCE.

Laws of inheritance relate to a mode of acquiring property and of succeeding to office which is occasioned by events, such as death, which cause a discontinuity of possession. Perhaps the most important form of property in this area is village

[1] Female infanticide is said by McCulloch to have been practised by Nāgas. Dr. Brown (*op. cit.* p. 115) does not accept this, and my own investigations confirm Dr. Brown's views.—T. C. H. Cf. *A. C. R.* 1891, Vol. I. p. 120.

office, because in each village the khullākpa[1] is, as we shall see, entitled to special privileges and dues, as village help in sowing and reaping and a share of all game killed or taken in the village territory.[2] In the larger villages, and most of all in the group of villages owning the authority of the khullākpa of Mao, the position of khullākpa is one of considerable value, although there are compensatory disadvantages. A common feature of the village system is that the village area is strictly defined and occasionally delimitated by artificial boundary marks within which the villagers are free to fish, if a river be in the area, to hunt, and if necessary, even in the case of permanent villages with terraced cultivation, to develop their cultivation by jhuming. In cases where permanent villages subsist by means of jhums, the rights of ownership are recognised in the jhums which are cultivated in a strict rotation, and several ownership in land is common but is limited by the condition that land may not be alienated, at any rate outside the villages, if indeed disposal outside the clan be permitted, which I am much inclined to doubt in view of the fact that the clan is the ultimate heir of a "kinless loon." As regards other property we may observe that inheritance comes into play generally on an occasion of death, and on the view that life in the next world is but a counterpart of this world's round, the property is diminished by the common practice of placing in the grave a number of articles which are destined or believed to be destined to be of advantage to the deceased hereafter, or which have been specially associated with and appropriated to the deceased during his lifetime. To the general rule that an ordinary case of death occasions only a clan genna, that is, a genna affecting only that group of individuals who comprise the heirs of the deceased, we have an exception in the case of the Mao group, where the whole village is genna and where, by a singular coincidence, the khullākpa exercises unusual authority. In other groups we have an annual festival, the purpose of which is to lay to rest the spirits of all the dead that have died since the last performance of the rite, and at which the whole village is

[1] Or gennabura. Khullākpa means leader of the village. Gennabura means authoriser of gennas.

[2] McCulloch, *op. cit.* pp. 48, 49, 53, 65, 66, 67, 69; Brown, *op. cit.* p. 112, 120, 126; Shakespeare, *J. R. A. I.* XXXIX, p. 374.

genna. In all cases of mysterious death by sudden illness, by strange misadventure, by the hand of an enemy, by wild animals or snakes, not only is the whole village genna, but also the mortuary rites are maimed, and the loss of property in the grave is much less. The ghosts of those who die in these fashions, are denied all chance of reincarnation and are consigned to a special Limbo. Thus in those rites where the khullākpa takes no part in the funeral ritual in his "representative" capacity, the destruction of property for the benefit and welfare of the deceased is large, while on the occasions when at the village genna the khullākpa exercises his authority as the religious head of the village, there is very much less placed in the grave. When we reach, as with the Meitheis, a stage of thought where the life of the world to come is viewed in the light of what Dr. Tylor[1] designates the "retribution" theory, we find that so much of the future welfare of the deceased depends on the priest that the living rather than the dead get the funeral offerings. Nāga eschatology is influenced by retributionist ideas, though obviously based on and closely related to that view of the after world which makes it a continuation of this.[2]

It is also of interest to note that the property placed in the grave to the derogation of the interests of the heirs is property that has been closely associated with the deceased and may be regarded as having gained something of his personality by long association with him. But they limit the enjoyment of the dead to articles of small value, giving them only such implements and small provision as would as it were enable them to make a start—a spear or two, sometimes the cherished umbrella, never the gun[3] or the cornelian necklace.

Hitherto I have only dealt with death as the occasion for bringing into play these laws of inheritance, but among the Tangkhuls we have a custom which in its effects makes marriage analogous in nearly every respect to death as a solvent of the continuity of possession. The details of the custom are stated by Colonel McCulloch[4] and Dr. Brown.[5] "On the eldest

[1] *Primitive Culture*, Vol. II, pp. 75, 104, 106.
[2] See below, p. 162.
[3] Stewart's gun was buried with Hausata, who headed the party that killed him. We dug him up and recovered it a year later.—J. S.
[4] *Op. cit.* pp. 66 and 69.
[5] *Op. cit.* p. 121.

son of a family marrying, the parents are obliged to leave their house with the remainder of their family, the son who has married taking two-thirds of the parent's property, not only of the household but of his father's fields, etc. Occasionally the parents are recalled and allowed to remain for some time, but eventually they have to leave and the property is claimed and divided as above stated. When the parents are well off they provide a house beforehand. On the marriage of another son the same process is repeated and may be again and again; but according to the usual custom the parents may, after the process has been repeated several times, return to the house of the eldest son. When a couple have a large family of sons who marry in succession, the poor people are often thus reduced to serious straits. May not the origin of the wearing of the ring have something to do with this practice, and may it not have been introduced by some parent anxious by placing a check upon the amatory propensity of his offspring so to put off the evil day of his own turning out? This is, however, mere conjecture as there is no trace of any story or tradition of this kind among the Tangkhuls themselves." I may add in regard to the explanation so modestly suggested by Dr. Brown that I have been told that the ring is worn because they used to quarrel so bitterly about women. Colonel McCulloch states that "On the marriage of his son, the father becomes a person of secondary importance in the house, and is obliged to remove to the front part of it[1] and again of the Luhupas whom we include among the Tangkhuls, perhaps wrongly, that "When the eldest son has brought home his wife, it is the signal for his father and mother, and the other members of the family, to quit for a new home, where they live until the marriage of the second son when they again have to move."[2] I found that this custom extends to, and I think it probably originated in, the succession to village offices. I am not certain whether it now extends quite as far as Dr. Brown would have us believe, but it is interesting to record that in one village when making inquiries into the matter I was told that it was becoming less usual because Government made them pay a house-tax and this custom led to the multiplication of taxable houses.

[1] *Op. cit.* p. 66. [2] *Op. cit.* p. 68.

The office of khullākpa or gennabura or head man is essentially representative and magico-religious. It is therefore invested with special tabus, all of which are designed to prevent any impairment of its efficiency, and we find that it can only be held by an adult male in full health both of mind and of body. From it are excluded persons who are mentally below the average and all who are blemished by any physical deformity. As with ordinary succession so the succession to office generally accrues on the death of the occupant; but among the Tangkhuls, the custom above described is held to apply to village office, and in other groups I have learnt that succession *inter-vivos* is common when the khullākpa becomes old and worn out, so that the Tangkhul custom, if not due to the desire to secure for the office a man in the plenitude of his power, physical and mental, and to secure immediate continuity in the occupation of the office, an object of the greatest social importance, is at any rate well calculated to produce these effects. This explanation extends to the private householder, who is as regards the house-spirits[1] a priest in his house and liable to tabus which are similar in nature, effect, and presumably in intent to those protecting and insulating the khullākpa. As a variant upon the custom of primogeniture we find at Purum, the old Kuki village in the S.W., a custom by which the occupants of village offices move up in regular succession. This custom provides a succession of experienced persons and has been stated to be the custom regulating the succession to the throne of Manipur.[2]

I may observe that among the Kabuis and Quoirengs the office of khullākpa seems to have lost much of its authority in religious matters.[3] Elders perform many of the religious duties which elsewhere are the task of the khullākpa, but the office exists and is still hereditary. The Kabuis especially have been exposed to Manipuri influence, and have come into close contact with Kukis among whom the hieratic functions of the chief are almost entirely atrophied.

While primogeniture is the most widely accepted rule of

[1] See below, Popular Beliefs and Worship of Deities.

[2] *Cf.* Butler, *Travels in Assam*, pp. 81–82. *The Meitheis*, p. 82. *Maine Ancient Law*, p. 241. *Early Law and Custom*, p. 146.

[3] McCulloch, *op. cit.* p. 49.

THE MAIKEL KHUL-LĀK-PA AND HIS SON.

From a photograph by the Author.

[*To face p.* 102

succession to village office in this area, there is great variety in the usages regulating succession to land and other property. Among the Tangkhuls in cases where the father dies before the marriage of a son, the general rule in many villages is that the eldest son gets a double share of the immovable property while the other sons get a single share each. The movables are then divided in equal shares, but this is by no means universal, for I know cases in the larger villages where the eldest son has taken the whole estate, a proceeding which occasioned much bitterness. In some villages, again, the estate of the eldest is distinctly burdened with the duty of maintaining his younger brothers. Daughters *dum solae* and widows *dum solae et castae* are entitled to their maintenance out of the estate. Women do not succeed to immovable property. In default of sons, the immovable property goes to the brothers of the deceased, and the movable property is distributed among the women. I have met cases of gifts *inter vivos* and their validity was fully recognised, though I learnt that the practice had its inconveniences as occasioning family quarrels. Complete disherison is, I think, impossible in view of the strength of the public feeling that it would arouse, and the right of younger sons to maintenance is safeguarded by the same bulwark.

In the Mao group we find a wide range of variety in customs of inheritance of property with an unvarying rule of primogeniture under the usual conditions as regards succession to office. At Jessami the youngest son gets the house and the best of the movable property while the other brothers take equal shares. At Laiyi, by contrast, the eldest gets half and the others divide the half share. If there are only girls to inherit, the clan (sagei) takes a share. At Liyai the sons share the property equally and the girls get a share of the domestic contents. In the event of there being no male issue to divide the property, the girls would share, but the house is reserved for the eldest surviving paternal uncle of the deceased. At Mao, again, the eldest son gets a special share, but the house is reserved for the youngest son. The share of the second son is greater than that of the third son, and so on. Girls succeed in default of male issue and their shares are made equal, the male relatives taking the house. Here, too, gifts *inter vivos* are recognised as valid, but the quarrels to which the practice gives rise tend to make it less common. At Maikel the eldest son gets the house and the others divide the fields. If there are only daughters of the marriage, they get a share of the produce of the fields, but the house falls to the nearest male relative of the deceased.

At Marām the share of the eldest son is much the largest, and the portions of the younger sons decrease according to their juniority. If there are no sons the daughters get a small share of immovable property, but no valuable immovable property, which goes to the nearest male relatives. Daughters receive maintenance *dum solae* and widows *dum solae et castae.* If a widow misconducts herself while living in the house of her deceased husband, she is turned out and forfeits her right to maintenance, but if she lives separate and misconducts herself, nothing is done to her.

Among the Kabuis we find a custom which reminds one faintly of the Tangkhul practice of turning the parents out of the house when the son marries, but here the parents only vacate a room for them. We have also the same recognition of a man's right to make a distribution of his property while living, but if no such disposition has been made when he dies the property is divided among the sons, the share of the youngest being larger than those of the other sons. The right of women to maintenance is liable to the same conditions as among the Marām people.

My information indicates some variety of custom among the Quoirengs, for in one village I was told that the eldest son took all the property, which was charged with the maintenance of the whole family; in another, that if they were all grown up, the property was divided equally, while if too young to look after it themselves, the eldest surviving paternal uncle enjoyed the property till they were old enough to manage it, and maintained them; while at a third village I learnt that the youngest son took all. All accounts are agreed that women have only a bare right of maintenance, and that in default of sons the clan would obtain the property and, presumably, divide it. I think the variations are perhaps more apparent than real, because the eldest son would be the natural "manager" of the property if he were grown up and the younger sons still children, and that the paternal uncle is the manager failing the sons, while the custom of giving the youngest son the lion's share may be associated with the custom of making provision for the others as they grow to maturity and marry.[1]

Among the Chirus if the property of the deceased be of any value it is shared, but if it is without value the eldest takes it all. So, too, among the Marrings, the eldest son is the heir general to the property, but in both these groups gifts *inter vivos* are permitted.

Laws Regarding Land.

Land is held in several ownership, but no alienation outside the clan is permitted, and in cases where attempts have been made to dispose of the land to persons who were not only not members of the clan but not even members of the village public opinion has dealt very severely with the offender. As has been pointed out above, each village possesses a well defined area which is sometimes demarcated with regular boundary stones and within which the villagers possess paramount rights of hunting, of fishing, if a river be included, and of development of cultivation either by making new terraces or by jhuming. So far as my information goes, the right of fishing extends to the middle of the stream only, and if they catch fish in the territorial waters of another village, a small share of the "take" is given to the "riparian owners." In the case of villages which possessed terraced fields, we find a mass of customs relating to the equable distribution of water throughout the terraces. The details of these easements vary from village to village, but the underlying principle remains the same and any villager who evades the rules lays himself open to much trouble.

The highest fields get the water first and then, to prevent waste, have to let it pass on to the lower fields, and each holder

[1] See p. 12 above as to the youngest son.

of a terraced field must keep its retaining walls, made as a rule of piled stones, in proper repair, lest those below should suffer by his negligence and default.

It is, I think, legitimate to discover a connection between the fact that the "crop gennas" are village gennas, and the restriction against alienation to a member of another village by which a stranger would be given an interest in the results of rites in which he could not otherwise lawfully participate.

Other Laws.

Murder within the clan is so rare an event that I have no information concerning the attitude of these groups towards the offender in such a case. The murder of a member of another clan or village would occasion a feud which would only be ended with the slaughter of a member of the murderer's clan or village, and it is known that some of the worst village feuds have originated in this manner. Accidental homicide is punished among the Tangkhuls by fine, amounting to six cows. At Jessami in the Mao group the offender has to make a short sojourn away from his house, but not necessarily outside the village; while at Liyai he is banished from the village. At Mao his punishment is seven years' banishment from the village and a fine of five cows. At Maikel banishment for one year and a fine of five cows, while murder ensuing in the heat of passion in a quarrel is punished with seven years' banishment and a fine of ten cows. The Mayang Khong people exact only a fine of one cow in cases of accidental homicide. At Marām the punishment consists of banishment for one year and a fine of six cows. In one Quoireng village it would appear that no punishment is inflicted, while in another the homicide is said to have been killed, and in a third, the punishment was said to be the cost of providing all the gear for the funeral of the dead man and the feast to the village. It is possible that my informants may have misunderstood my questions. Among the Kabuis a heavy fine is levied from the culprit. Both the Chirus and the Marrings impose a heavy fine in such cases, part of the fine being compensation to the relatives of the dead man and the rest being consumed by the village in the course of the settlement of the matter.

In some cases the weapon or other lethal instrument is forfeited to the relatives—a proceeding reminiscent of the law of Deodand.[1]

Minor assaults are punished when circumstances permit by the use of the simple law of revenge.

There is unquestionable evidence, both in the pages of McCulloch[2] and Dr. Brown[3] as well as in my own investigations, that adultery was commonly punished so far as the male offender was concerned with death, a proceeding which I learnt[4] gave no occasion for a feud. Among the Tangkhuls we now find that a fine including the mangkhat, or bride price, as well as a fine to the village is inflicted. Five cows are in some instances required for the husband and one for the village.

At Jessami the woman surrendered all she owned to her husband, who also received a fine from the lover. At Laiyi, also a village of the Mao Group, the fine is only one cow, while at Liyai, close by, the adulterer is driven out and his property seized by the injured husband, a similar punishment being inflicted on the man at Mao, where the woman was also liable to have her nose clipped or slit with a spear.[5] At Maikel also the woman is punished as well as the man, who loses all his property. The Quoirengs drive the adulterer from the village, but the customs of the Kabuis in this regard have apparently undergone some amelioration since the days of Colonel McCulloch who stated[6] that "The adulterer if he did not fly the village, would be killed; aware of the penalty attached to his offence he dare not stay and is glad to leave his house to be destroyed by the injured husband. The family of the adulteress is obliged to refund the price in the first instance paid to them by her husband, and also to pay her debts. Why these expenses are not made to fall upon the adulterer, they cannot explain." My information collected in two large villages, as Kabui villages now go, is that only a fine is imposed, and that not by any means a large one, but that, as is the case in every village, the woman

[1] *Cf.* Westermarck, *Origin and Development of the Moral Ideas*, I. 260 *et seq.*

[2] *Op. cit.* pp. 50, 65, 69.

[3] *Op. cit.* pp. 105, 115, 121.

[4] At one Tangkhul village.

[5] And her hair cut off.—T. C. H.

[6] *Op. cit.* p. 50.

is divorced from her husband, to whom her price is returned by her family. The Chirus mete out the same lenient treatment in cases of adultery, while the Marrings inflict a heavy fine.

To turn to offences against property we find among the Tangkhuls that theft was once punished with death if the offender were caught *flagrante delicto*, a statement which is made by Dr. Brown[1] and is confirmed by the information given to me. Nowadays a fine is inflicted. At Jessami (Mao Group) twelve potes of dhan must be paid by the thief as well as the restoration of the property taken. At Liyai we have an appreciation which is hardly, though possibly, attributable to the spread of the knowledge of the refined subtleties of the Indian Penal Code, of the difference between theft from a dwelling house, which is punished with a fine of fifteen potes of dhan while ordinary theft is punishable with a fine of two potes of dhan. At Marām we find the same nice discrimination, as theft from a house is punished with a fine of ten rupees while the theft of paddy from a field involves the culprit in a fine of ten potes of dhan. Matters have improved since the days of Colonel McCulloch, who declares that "Theft is of ordinary occurrence, and is not, amongst these tribes or the Loohoopas, even considered disgraceful. If the things stolen are found they are taken back, if not, it might be dangerous to accuse a man of theft."[2]

In civil debt, interest runs after the expiry of one year, when the debt is reckoned as double. In these places, the security is not good, but compositions are nearly always accepted by the creditors. The Quoirengs very sensibly give thieves a good beating, or in some villages fine them a pig, and, like railways in this country, expose the offender to public shame. Among the Kabuis we find in McCulloch[3] a different principle of differentiating between degrees of culpability, which is interesting as testifying to the educative value of matrimony in a man's life. "Theft, if the thief should happen to be a married man, is punished severely, but a young unmarried man might with impunity steal grain not yet housed, whilst theft from a granary would subject him to the severest punishment." The fine for theft from a granary is now

[1] *Op. cit.* p. 123. [2] *Op. cit.* p. 69. [3] *Op. cit.* p. 49.

one pig. A similar fine is inflicted by the Chirus and the Marrings in cases of theft. A married man therefore must be regarded as having a different status from that of the bachelor —a fact which is illustrated in other ways above.[1]

Whether exactly possessing the nature of a fine or not, the payment made by those who by accident cause the destruction of any part of the village by fire is noteworthy. The Tangkhul custom is to demand a jar of zu and a pig, which is killed when the village genna necessary on the occurrence of such events is commenced by the khullākpa.

The mere sight of the destruction by fire of a neighbouring village is enough to cause a village genna.[2]

Decision of Disputes.

When Colonel McCulloch describes the great expense to which parties in suits for divorce are put, he refers to a village council[3] as an institution to which the decision of these matters was entrusted, and to this day the elders of the village discuss any such cases, but in open court, *coram publico*, for during these discussions there is a genna. But the decision of even the elders is openly criticised by the other villagers, many of whom will take part in the debate. As a rule the procedure is simple, for the largest villages are small enough for the life of each to be well known to all, and the facts are rarely in dispute, so that only a declaration of the customary law applicable to the facts is required of the elders, who are rigorously bound by their own precedents. In cases where facts are in issue, recourse is had, as in more serious cases between clans of one village or between two villages, to the oath, by the result of which the parties agree to abide. The difficulty is always to settle the formula of the oath and in the process as much ingenuity of amendment is displayed as in the committee-rooms of more august assemblies. We find among the people of Mao that in cases in which rights to land or its produce are in dispute the oath on the earth is usual; while in cases affecting timber the oath on the axe is employed, and for the

[1] See p. 77 *et seq.*

[2] Davis, *A.C.R.* 1891, Vol. I. p. 249.

[3] *Op. cit.* p. 50.

more important cases, as quarrels between two clans or two villages, the oath on the cat is necessary. The weight of an oath is augmented by increasing its range so as to include all the members of the village in the imprecation, while it is forbidden to near relations to swear in any case between them (Mao Group). We find also that use is made of the ordeal which assumes two forms, one by water which is employed in cases between two villages, and the other in "private" as distinguished from "public" cases. In the first each village or clan proffers its khullākpa or head-man as its champion and they proceed to some deep pool, and at a signal the champions plunge into the pool and remain below the water as long as possible, for the victory is with the village whose representative stays under water longest. It once happened that this ordeal was allowed in a village case and the villagers were so enraged at seeing their khullākpa emerge puffed and nearly dead that they rushed upon him and thrust him down again to the imminent risk of his life. The khullākpa is a sacrosanct person, the representative of the village in all religious rites, and surrounded by special alimentary, social, and conjugal gennas. In the second form they agree that the village or clan which first loses a "life" shall lose the suit, and I was once asked to define a "life" for this purpose and declared it to be any living thing for whose death a genna was usual. It is also usual to introduce a "time limit," in reference to this form of the ordeal, as without this precaution further quarrels arise.

Among the Tangkhuls there are many forms of oaths, a fact which an ingenious Manipuri once attributed to the notorious reputation of the Tangkhuls for plausibility. The weightiest oath is that which concludes with the imprecation, "If I lie, may I and my family (or clansmen or co-villagers) descend into the earth and be seen no more." At Naimu I noticed a heap of peculiarly shaped stones inside the village upon which the Tangkhuls took an oath of great weight. Others swear by the Deity named Kajing Karei, by the Deity Kamyou, while oaths on a dao or tiger's teeth are common among them. Kajing Karei is a Deity by whose will, so I was told, everything happens, but they were silent as to his moral attributes.

Kamyou is associated at Powi with a stone in a sacred grove, and at Phunggam near Powi I was informed that Kamyou was the eldest of the three sons of a nameless Deity, that he went inside the earth, where he does judgment, while his youngest brother went to heaven and the middle brother stayed on earth. To Kamyou men address prayers and sacrifice when ill.

At Jessami the penalty attaching to perjury when the oath on the spear is used is a violent death, so that it is appropriately used in cases where assaults are alleged. In the oath on the earth the imprecation is identical with that current among the Tangkhuls. The oath, ordeal, or arbitrament of the cat, which is used both in the Mao Group and by Marām, is thus effected. A representative of each of the litigant parties holds an end of a cane basket inside which a cat, alive, is placed, and at a signal a third man hacks the cat in two and both sides then cut it up with their daos, taking care to stain the weapon with blood.[1] On the occasion when I saw this ceremony I was told that the ceremony was a form of peace-making or treaty, and that therefore the slaughter of the cat bound them in a kind of covenant. A cat is the only animal which is buried, though house gennas are customary on the death of any domestic animal. A cat may not be eaten by Tangkhuls, because the man who dares this thing loses his power of speech. At Jessami they say that a perjury over the cat brings sudden death and misfortune. There is also an oath upon a creeper which is believed to die when cut, and the man taking the oath cuts the creeper saying the while, "May I die as this creeper dies if I lie."

The Quoirengs make use of the oath on the dao, and also employ an oath which is as follows: "May we disappear inside the earth, may we become as black as this (the juice of wild indigo), and may we be covered with thorny spines, even as this thorn branch is covered."

At Aqui, a Kabui village, where I gathered much valuable information about the Kabuis, I found that the most important form of oath was that taken on a meteoric stone in the possession of the khullākpa. In another Kabui village they

[1] *Cf.* Owen, *Notes on the Nagas*, p. 18.

offered to swear by Kajing Karei, which I pointed out to them was not one of their oaths. They agreed, and explained that it was a Manipuri oath, which is a mistake, for it comes from the Tangkhuls. The oath we then decided to exact was in accordance with their own formularies, for it consisted of taking some salt, some ashes, and some paddy husks, with the following imprecation: "May we find our salt become as these ashes (mixing at the same time a pinch of ashes with the salt), may all our rice turn to husk, and may we ourselves perish like the husks, the spoilt salt, things that are only fit to be thrown to the winds, if we lie." I have known Kabuis agree to abide by the omens derived either from the convulsive movements of a fowl's feet in its death agony, or from the varying shapes of an egg broken on a flat stone.

The Chirus swear by the sun and on the dao, tiger's tooth, and spear. I was unable to get the formula of the oath on the sun.

The Marrings invoke the Deity Taiaru, who seems to occupy much the same relationship to them as does Kamyou to the Tangkhuls. In each village there is a circle of stones, inside of which are a few stones upon which an oath may also be taken.[1]

In oaths, the efficacy of the curse is conditional upon the truth or falsehood of the statement thus sworn to. The condition is precedent, as the truth or falsehood is really determined by past events. In the case of the oath of good behaviour taken by two villages, the efficacy of the curse which the sacrifice of the cat is deemed to assure depends upon conditions which may or may not come to pass. "The efficacy of the oath depends on the guilt of the slaughter of the cat being shared equally until one or other commits a breach of the oath, when the whole of the guilt attaches itself to the offender."[2] We may contrast this usefully with the cases where "the shedding of blood is frequently applied as a means of transferring curses."[3]

[1] *Cf.* Butler, *op. cit.* p. 154.

[2] *The Genna amongst the Tribes of Assam*, *J.A.I.* XXXVI, p. 99. *Cf.* Butler, *op. cit.* p. 154, for a similar case.

[3] Westermarck, *Origin and Development of the Moral Ideas.* Vol. II, p. 620.

I have no information as to the method of executive authority in enforcing the dooms of the elders, but may rescue from the oblivion of years the very interesting account which Major Dalton wrote of the devices of the Abor tribes in this matter.[1] "The process of realisation is a most singular one. Suppose it is decreed that in expiation of the offence a pig is to be sacrificed, the 'Raj,' that is the community, appropriate for the purpose the first animal of the kind in good condition and private property that comes to hand. The owner is then at liberty to fix his own value upon it and recover as best he can from the culprit." The system adopted provides an executive without any trouble to the "Raj" or expense to the State." If our Nāgas have not this excellent custom, they ought to be introduced to it.

WAR.

From the unanimous evidence of our authorities for the period immediately and approximately preceding British rule in Manipur,[2] it is clear that the tribes in this area were in a state of constant hostility; but it is notable that there is no evidence of any tribal organisation or of combination except among the Luhupas or Tangkhuls,[3] who sent contingents from subject villages at the behest of the dominant village. If I may paraphrase the words of Colonel Henderson, I would say that here war was at its best a blind struggle between mobs of individuals, without guidance or coherence, never a conflict of well-organised masses with a view to intelligent co-operation, acting under the impulse of a single will, directed against a definite objective.[4] The origin of many of the village feuds is lost to memory, but "the heritage of hate" persisted in full vigour. Even now one village will venture on a challenge to another village with which it has had a quarrel, and the limits, hour and weapons of the contest are duly settled. I have a

[1] *Op. cit.* p. 163.
[2] McCulloch, *op. cit.* pp. 43, 67; Brown, *op. cit.* pp 106–107; Lewin, *op. cit.* p. 105.
[3] McCulloch, *op. cit.* p. 67.
[4] Henderson, *Science of War*, p. 1.

distinct recollection of an instance where one of the villages in the Mao group sent a formal challenge to a village in the Nāga Hills district which had violated one of the hunting rules. Before daybreak on the appointed day the party sallied forth, creeping quietly past the Manipuri Police Guard, and went to the scene, where, to their great chagrin, they met an enemy who added to his offence by making use of spears in a combat which was to have been decided by sticks alone. It was bad enough to be defeated with loss of life, but to be tricked by this unsportsmanlike stratagem was an unforgettable and unforgivable injury, as the villagers in unavailing eloquence explained to me later on.

But in an ordinary blood feud or raid the essence of success, as Lewin remarks,[1] was surprise. The man who brought back the head of a woman or child belonging to a hostile village was deemed to have done a very heroic deed, because in such times the women never ventured far from the village, not even to the fields, unless protected by armed men, and their slaughter proved that the brave man had penetrated close to the enemy's own stronghold.[2]

In support of the surmise put forward by McLennan[3] that the practice of exogamy mitigated the effects of blood-feud, we have a striking piece of evidence in McCulloch's account[4] that among the Tangkhuls or Luhupas women and children were spared when the feud was not of the fiercest type, and that the northern and tattooed women always went unscathed for fear of the dire vengeance that their relations would exact.[5]

[1] *Op. cit.* p. 106.

[2] *Cf.* Davis, *A.C.R.* 1891, Vol. I. pp. 248, 249. Johnstone, *op. cit.* p. 30.

[3] *Primitive Marriage*, pp. 262-263.

[4] Pp. 67, 68.

[5] As a piece of gossip I may observe that Colonel McCulloch and Mr. McLennan were correspondents, and I have in my possession a copy of *Primitive Marriage* which McLennan presented to Colonel McCulloch.—T. C. H.

Among Lushais *War* was really war as we understand it, *i.e.* a method of settling a dispute affecting communities. It could only be undertaken by Chiefs. This seems a more advanced stage than the ambushing of small parties of any village, except those particularly allied to the warriors, for the sake of heads, or to avenge some private wrong.

The Chins used systematically to picket areas which they coveted till cultivation on it became impossible and the inhabitants moved off elsewhere. The Chin hills are fairly open, whereas the Lushai hills are thickly covered with jungle. In the former it is possible for cultivators to take sufficient care to enable work to proceed but in the latter the odds are too much in

Sir James Johnstone[1] "once knew a case of some Sephema men at feud with Mozuma, hiring two women of the powerful village of Konoma to escort them along the road, as thus accompanied no one dare touch them."

HEAD-HUNTING.

The simplest and most obvious form of head-hunting is associated with the blood feud, where the duty of vengeance remains unsated until the tally of heads is numerically equal.[2] Hence, as a matter of practical politics, it is usual when reconciling two villages to insist on the return of heads, for by this means a recrudescence of the feud is effectively prevented. But there are other causes at work to account for head-hunting raids, which have their root deep in the religious beliefs of the people.

"My[3] knowledge of head-hunting as an incident of life on the frontier of Assam dates from a visit,—with an appropriate escort of military police,—to a village in the remotest corner of the State of Manipur. My friends, as they afterwards became, did not oppose, but did nothing to facilitate, my entry, and even thought it necessary to pay us the compliment of distributing panjis, or sharpened bamboo stakes, in the pathways leading to the village. By careful strategy and neglect of the usual methods of frontal attack, we got inside unscathed, and at once proceeded to diplomatic negotiations. Two heads had been taken, and with us was the uncle of one of the gentlemen who had come to his end in the row. The first interesting fact I learnt was that, in this village, it was customary not to keep the heads of enemies inside the village, but to place them in a tree outside. Here I may observe that, among the naked

favour of the attackers. Hence the Lushais warred by raiding villages and not by ambushing.

The killing of women engaged in cultivation was freely indulged in by Chins and Thados, though it showed no bravery. I think Lewin's informant merely made an ingenious excuse to account for a practice which he knew the Sahib disapproved of.—J. S.

[1] *My Experiences in Manipur and the Naga Hills*, p. 30.

[2] See Butler, *op. cit.* p. 156. Johnstone, *op. cit.* p. 29.

[3] The following passage is a substantial reproduction from *Folklore*, Vol XX, pp. 132-143, of a paper entitled "Head-hunting among the Hill Tribes of Assam."—T. C. Hodson.

tribes of Tamlu,[1] in the hills north of Kohima, the headquarters of the Nāga Hills District, and among the Kukis [2] south of Manipur, and again south among the Lushai tribes,[3] traces of tree burial are found, so that the practice of placing the head of an enemy in a tree may be remotely connected as a ceremonial survival with a practice, once general, which has now become obsolete.[4] It was no easy matter to persuade the Nāgas of my frontier that the heads had to be restored to the friends of those to whom they had belonged, but arguments and stubborn facts prevailed in time to prevent the necessity of recourse to other methods of persuasion.

"This incident was only a case of self-defence in a sudden quarrel, and was amply punished by six months' hard labour—not, let me observe, for murder, but for the offence,—which is not yet formally in the statute book,—of cutting off the head of a fallen foe. Another incident which happened to me in the neighbourhood, but months later, brought me into contact with yet another phase of head-hunting. I myself was busy with the census, an operation which in the Meithei language is described as head-seeking (*mī kōk thī-ba*, to seek the heads of men). I was marching ahead of my commissariat, when suddenly at my feet fell a pitiable creature, a Nāga, in as abject a state of terror as poor humanity could be. It took me some time to get a clear understanding of his distress. The headman of a large and powerful village over the border and outside my jurisdiction was engaged in building himself a new house,[5] and, to strengthen it, had seized this man and forcibly cut off a lock of his hair, which had been buried underneath the main post of the house. In olden days the head would have been put there, but by a refinement of some native theologian a lock of hair was held as good as the whole head, for the ghost of the wretch would go there and seek the missing lock and be for ever compelled to remain beneath the post. This is the *motif* of the earthquake story of the Kabui Nāgas in Manipur, who declare that once

[1] *Assam Census Report*, 1891, Vol. I, p. 246.
[2] McCulloch, *op. cit.* p. 63.
[3] Capt. T. H. Lewin, *Hill Tracts of Chittagong, etc.*, p. 112.
[4] See Grant Allen, *The Attis of Caius Valerius Catullus*, *passim.*
[5] Cf. *L'Année sociologique*, Vol. II, p. 104; Grant Allen, *op. cit.*, pp. 117 *et. seq.* Westermarck, *Moral Ideas*, I, p. 461 *et seq.*

upon a time a father-in-law and a son-in-law quarrelled and fought, and the lady, seeing her husband and father locked in mortal combat, rushed on them and pulled them apart, and in so doing tore a lock of hair from her husband's head, which she threw into the fire. So the struggle still goes on, and they fight over the lost lock till parted once again. When I visited the headman who had done this evil thing to my unhappy Nāga, I had it in me to persuade him that the ghost of a stout buffalo would prop up his house as well as, possibly much better than, the thin wailing ghost of a half-starved Manipur Nāga. I succeeded in inducing him to avail himself of the law of substitution. Glimpse number two into the ethics of head-hunting was not long after followed by a rare and delicate compliment which was paid to me by the headman of an interesting village,[1] who, as a great and special favour, showed me the famous war-stone on which no woman may look and live, and to which, after a raid, the heads of the victims were shown in the bad old days, which are perhaps gone for ever, or till the next time.

"In Tangkhul villages are heaps of stones,—places of great sanctity,—*lai-pham* as the Manipuris call them,—the abodes of a *lai*, a powerful mysterious entity,—not always nor necessarily anthropomorphised. On these heaps the heads taken in a raid were placed for five days, during which the warriors were *genna*,—subjected to a process of tabu which had, I fancy, for its object the "desacralisation" of the warriors, since before they go on a raid they are similarly tabu.[2] An oath taken on these stones is regarded as most binding.

"Among the acquaintances which I made during my census tour was an elderly rather decrepit Kuki, with an unquenchable thirst, and a memory. My interest in him awoke when I saw his feats with the flagons of beer, but it was more than maintained when he opened to me the stores of his recollections. He had taken part in more than one notorious raid, and chuckled with glee over the discomfiture of the expeditionary columns which had wearily tramped the hills, burnt some villages,—in more than one case quite innocent villages (at any rate so far as the immediate outrage was concerned),—and had marched

[1] Maikel.

[2] *Cf.* Butler, *op. cit.* p. 149.

home like the King of France and his forty thousand men. In all these raids on tea gardens one and only one motive was at work, the desire to secure heads to grace the funeral of some chief. My garrulous friend was not clear as to the reason why the heads were needed, or what useful purpose they served, except that their owners became the slaves of the chief in the future world. I found this belief among my Nāga tribes, and with it the view that one of the many compartments into which heaven is divided is reserved for those whose heads have been cut off.

"Clearly the precise significance of head-hunting as ancillary to and as part of funeral rites can only be ascertained by consideration of funeral ritual as a whole, and of the causes which determine it. It is characteristic of funerary ritual [1] in this area that through eschatological belief it is affected by considerations, (1) of the social status of the deceased, and (2) of the manner of his death. In life the Kuki chief is conspicuously the secular head of his village. His funeral is incomplete without the head of a human victim.[2] His body is placed inside the trunk of a tree,[3]—surely again a survival of note,—there subjected to a desiccatory process, and his bones kept. In all funeral rites in this area I see a double motive at work, affection and respect for the dead as well as fear, not only of mortal contagiosity, but also of malignant ghostly activity. Head-hunting may serve a double purpose. It may be piacular and propitiatory, intended both to placate the powerful ghost and to prevent danger. In another aspect I venture to compare it with the interesting rites to which the Lushais give the name *ai*, a term which, as a noun, is defined by the authors of the Lushai dictionary [4] as meaning 'the power of fascinating, charming or getting power over,' and, as a verb, as meaning 'to perform a ceremony in order to get the spirit of a wild animal killed in the chase into one's power after death.' An *ai* ceremony is performed by a living person for his own benefit after death. A domesticated animal is killed, and by the sacri-

[1] *Archiv für Religions-wissenschaft*, XII, p. 417 *et seq.*

[2] *Cf.* Butler, *Travels in Assam*, p. 93.

[3] McCulloch, *loc. cit. supra.*

[4] J. H. Lorrain and F. N. Savidge, *A Grammar and Dictionary of the Lushai Language (Dulien dialect)*, p. 34.

fice and by a rite[1] the successful hunter gets power over the spirit of the animals he has killed. Is the human victim,—a stranger always,—a slave sometimes,—a Bengali sometimes,—killed by the community as a solemn communal act in order that it may get some power over, remain in possession, as it were, of, the great man who has been reft from them? In life he was a great one of this earth. It would therefore, be to their advantage as a community to keep in touch with such an one. This is at least in part the motive for preserving the bones of the chief with jealous care.[2]

"The Quoireng Nāgas, now quite a small tribe conterminous with the Kabuis on the north-west corner of the Manipur State, told me that they used to take heads because the possession of a head brought wealth and prosperity to the village.[3] They added that it was usual to keep the gruesome trophy for five days, and then to return it to the village to which it belonged. Sometimes it was put in the grave of the family of the successful warrior. This may be connected with the tree burial custom referred to above. Then for three years all raids on the particular village were forbidden. Both they and their neighbours practise a custom which I am disposed to connect with the practice of head-hunting. They erect outside the village an image of a man, made either of straw or of the stem of a plantain tree, and throw spears at it. If a spear hits the head, the successful marksman will take a head, while, if he hits the belly of the image, the crops will be good. As Colonel McCulloch remarks, 'this festival is said to be in honour of their ancestors, but the only visible sign of this is sprinkling the graves with their particular drink. Then they take the omens for their future cultivation as a ceremonial relic of former times.' There are one or two points which deserve notice in this custom. The first is that the three years' truce seems to be connected with the fact that the tribes find that even good soil is exhausted by two years of *jhum* cultivation with fire and axe. They thus change their fields every third year.[4] The next point is that we have in the shooting rite a survival of human sacrifice, so that we may fairly consider our-

[1] *J. R. A. I.* Vol. XXXIX, p. 380 *et seq.*
[2] Lewin, *op. cit.* p. 112.
[3] *Cf.* Butler, *op. cit.* p, 157.
[4] *Assam Census Report*, Vol. I, p. 243.

selves face to face with a 'trieteric'[1] agricultural rite, which has now become annual because the cultivation is changed annually, so that the rite for determining by omens the quarter of the next year's cultivation is entirely otiose. This rite had for its purposes, firstly, the fertilisation of the new area to be brought into cultivation, and, secondly, some more remote benefit to the living and the dead, especially the recently dead. It has often seemed to me, when attempting by the light of nature to work out the comparative chronology of the village festivals in this area, that,—(1) these tribes mark off the year into a cultivating and a hunting period with some sharpness, (2) that the festivals therefore which mark the conclusion of the cultivating season may also serve to mark the opening of the hunting season, (3) that the annual festival in honour of the dead that have died within the year also takes place,—when and where held,—at the end of the cultivating season, and (4) that it is quite possible that what were originally distinct and separate festivals, (*a*) for the end of the agricultural season, or (*b*) for the beginning of the hunting season, and (*c*) for the benefit of the recently dead, may now have been merged into two, or into even one festival.[2] If hunting was ever, at any stage of their tribal history, the mainstay of life, it is intelligible that the commencement of the hunting season should be marked by a rite in honour of the mighty dead whose hunting prowess was still remembered.[3] The Kukis still consult the bones of their dead chiefs,[4] and the skulls and horns of the trophies of the chase form not the least important of the decorations of the graves of the dead.

"To return to head-hunting, it is worthy of note that, in the gentle art of oneiromancy as practised by the Nāgas of these

[1] Farnell, *Transactions of the Third International Congress for the History of Religions*, Vol. II, p. 140.

[2] Seasonal festivals such as these exhibit a dual aspect which justifies us in classifying them as *rites de passage*. (See Van Gennep, *Rites de Passage*, *passim.*) Whether a fusion of festivals, as I suggested before I was acquainted with M. Van Gennep's work, or the general nature of seasonal festivals as *rites de passage* effecting the movement of society from one sharply marked stage in their life as economic groups to another stage equally well defined explains the facts I have cited, is a question worthy of fuller consideration. These phenomena are seldom due to a single cause—rather to a complexity of causes, of which now one, new another, assumes for the moment greater importance than the rest.—T C. H.

[3] Seligmann, "The Vedda Cult of the Dead," *Transactions of the Third International Congress for the History of Religions*, Vol. I, pp. 59 *et seq.*

[4] Lewin, *loc. cit. supra.*

MAO NĀGA IN THE WARRIOR'S DRESS. [*To face p.* 121

From a photograph by the Author.

hills, the accepted interpretation of dreaming that one has taken an enemy's head is that good health will be the portion of the dreamer, or that he will enjoy good hunting. I have found that actually to do the thing and to dream of doing it have in popular belief the same meaning, and, just as to dream of being attacked by a buffalo means that one will lose all one's cases in the Courts (for the law's uncertainties are as certainly uncertain in Manipur as in any other part of the King's dominions), and as any Nāga who has a case on would compromise it at any price if in the flesh he were attacked by a buffalo, so I venture to infer that the actual capture of a head would be regarded as bringing health and good hunting.

" Earlier authorities declare that no young man could find a wife for himself until he had taken a head and thereby won the right of the warrior's kilt, or of the necklace of bears' tusks and the wristlets of cowries.[1] Nowadays these are worn as ornaments without much, if any, thought of the fact that not very long ago they were regarded as affording magical protection and as bringing strength. In 1891 Davis noted the beginnings of the degradation of this custom, and observed that ' the desire for head-hunting was more the fault of the women than of the men, who were laughed at if they turned out at the village festivals without the decorations assigned to the successful warrior.'[2] Success in head-hunting was at one time, if not essential to marriage, regarded at least as a token of having passed from adolescence to maturity. At Marām I heard a folk-tale which is narrated by McCulloch,[3] and which portrays the chief sending forth his sons, who claimed the inheritance, to take a head, and awarding the prize to the beloved but unwarlike eldest son who had a head ready in a safe place, while the younger son, the bolder man, went far to win the trophy. The tale was doubtless invented primarily to explain the dual chiefship of this village, but. . . success on a head-hunting raid would fairly serve as a mark of manhood and as qualifying for promotion from one stage in tribal life to the higher stage of married man.

A raid in order to get a head is a religious business, and not

[1] *Cf.* Butler, *op. cit.* pp. 145 and 148. Davis, *A.C.R.* pp. 248 and 249. Johnstone, *op. cit.* p. 30.
[2] *Assam Census Report*, 1891, Vol. I, p. 249
[3] *Op. cit.* p. 69. See above, p. 79.

lightly undertaken, whatever its motive. They may think killing 'fine sport,'[1] but they prepare themselves for the sport with solemn rites. Before, as well as after, a raid the young warriors are *genna*, secluded from intercourse or speech with women, compelled to live apart.

"I do not think it possible to reduce head-hunting to a single formula. I have found it connected with simple blood feud, with agrarian rites, and with funerary rites, and eschatological belief. Again it may be in some cases no more than a social duty,—obligatory upon those who seek to prove their fitness for initiation into tribal rites. It is compatible and co-existent with a strong sense of social solidarity, and it may be argued to be a survival,—stripped of much of its original significance, since it is observed among people who from the aspect of material culture are not primitive in that sense of that much-abused term, since they are skilled in the arts of agriculture, weaving, and metal-work. But a society may be, in respect of its material culture, comparatively advanced, and yet exhibit a relatively low level of mentality.

"Outside, but adjacent to, this area with which I am personally acquainted and from which I have drawn my facts, there are many tribes among whom head-hunting still flourishes. The wild Wā, for instance, have introduced strictly business methods and have a definite tariff for heads.[2] Apparently there is no market in European heads as yet. Would it be out of place or unseemly to hint that the Wā country offers an admirable field for experiments in the direction of Tariff Reform?"[3]

[1] *Assam Census Report*, 1891, Vol. I, p. 238.

[2] Risley, *Ethnography of India*, quoting Sir George Scott, pp. 214 *et seq.*; *Upper Burma Gazetteer*, Vol. I, Part I, pp. 496 *et seq.*

[3] I am told that till quite recent times the Manipur Durbar or its representative, would for sufficient consideration connive at a Thados taking a head or two on occasion of a great chief's death. The Lakhus, a Southern Chin family, considered that in case of a chief's death some one of the distant village must be killed before beating of drums or gongs was allowed, but to *bring back the head* was *thiang-lo*, *i.e.* prohibited or unlucky. Dokola, a southern Chin, was imprisoned for some years in Bengal; shortly after his return he murdered a wandering Mohammedan faquir, the reason given being to regain his prestige which had suffered from his capture and imprisonment. Here we have the same idea as taking a head in return for one taken from you. The Sirkar had scored, so Dokola was disgraced till he had scored by murdering a Sirkar's man.—J. S.

In this last case the redintegration of Dokola into his original status in Chin society was effected by taking a head, in which case it is parallel to head-hunting as a proof of social maturity.—T. C. H.

SECTION IV.—RELIGION

Popular Beliefs.

"O wad some power the giftie gie us,
To see oursels as others see us!"

It is but a matter of a little patience, some knowledge of a language understanded of the people, even perhaps of sympathy, to gather the beliefs of these people; but to hold the mirror at the right angle, to know and understand the spirit in which these beliefs are held, in short, to think "*Nāga*," are matters of great difficulty, for to a consciousness of their imperfections we add an unmistakable sense of our own superiority in which they cheerfully acquiesce.

Yet a chance remark may let in more light than all the careful inquiries and systematic notes. I was once in a village far from the beaten track, and had shown them the magic lantern, I had given them practical illustrations of the utility of a repeating pistol, I had amused them with a galvanic battery, and when all was over, I was enjoying their hospitality by the camp fire and had listened to tales of the bad old days when they were left severely alone by restraining influences. The conversation flagged until I asked a man who had hung about me all day, what of all that I had shown them that day was the most surprising to him. That started a discussion which ended in a verdict that the strangest thing that the *Sahib-log* had brought within their ken was coined money, and on further inquiry I found that its uniformity was the special feature which had so excited their interest. Nor is this to be wondered at, for at the level of their civilisation all their crafts are innocent of machinery, everything they make tends to variety, everything is individual.

Dr. Grierson remarks of the Kuki-Chin languages, whose influence has been considerable in this area, that "A father cannot be imagined except as somebody's father, and a hand cannot be thought of except as belonging to someone." It is an effect of the habit of specialisation, of which there is such ample evidence in the wealth of apparent synonyms.[1] I think it is safe to extend to the Nāgas what I have in another place found to be true of the Kukis, whose language I knew, that this feature of their material life is reflected in their language, for they have a separate name for articles and actions which we classify together. They insist on the points of difference, while we classify by identities. By the absence of grammatical devices to express abstract conceptions, which forms an important characteristic of the Tibeto-Burman languages, their thought is cribb'd, cabin'd and confined to narrow limits.

The grammatical distinctions of gender reveal a curious classification into animate objects and inanimate objects. Animate objects fall into two categories, human and animal. With all this they possess, as I think, some idea of the uniformity of what we call the processes of nature. The sun that shines upon them is one sun, not a long succession of similar but not identical suns all called by the same name. The deity who caused the earthquake in 1897 is the deity who shook the foundations of the hills in 1869. He is not a different deity masquerading under the same name.

In their material development I see some proof that they possess a fair capacity. I attribute the actual state of their mentality in part to the narrow limitations imposed on them by the comparative inflexibility of their language, and in part to the absence of exterior stimulations and to the lack of opportunity for enhancing their accumulation of culture. So closely knit are the bonds of society that here very distinctly "the religious acts and ideas are themselves an organic part of the activities of the social body."[2] The ends which their religious activity seeks to compass are severely practical, material as we should judge them, and are entirely social.

[1] See Grierson, *op. cit.*, Vol. III, Part III, p. 16.
[2] *The Development of Religion*, I. King, p. 88.

When they perform rites to banish from their gates the dread pestilence that comes one knows not how or whence, that takes old and young, strong and weak alike for its victims, they are consciously busy with an act of social import and advantage. The village as a whole takes part in the cultivation rites, and I have shown that religious duties are defined by and attached to the several social units. As a rule, the ends which their religious activity subserves are capable of immediate, or at least of not long deferred, realisation. The rites themselves require the active co-operation of social units as such, and do not depend exclusively upon any individual. Even in cases where it would seem that the gennabura or khullākpa acts alone—and such cases are rare—he acts, not as an individual, but as the representative of the whole village. The rites are social means consciously directed to the realisation of a well-recognised social end. There are rites which can only be explained as intended to propitiate some Personality capable of being influenced by gifts of good cheer and strong drink. There are rites which do not admit of this explanation, and which seem to be inspired by a "blind dread of the invisible and unknown, of which they could give no reasonable account to themselves or to others."[1] Hence, though there are dealings with agencies conceived as personal, there is always present the consciousness of power, mysterious, immanent in the world around them, and manifested by dangerous activity.

Origin and Nature of Deities.

I do not think that the religious beliefs of the Nāgas have been seriously contaminated by intercourse of a pacific nature with their semi-Hinduised overlords, the Meitheis. What is possible, is that the use of Meithei as the *lingua franca* of this part of the hills may have led me to think that the hill people attached the same value to such terms as Deity, soul, or spirit as do the Meitheis. It is right that I should make it clear here and now that I always spoke Meithei when questioning the Nāgas as to their customs and beliefs, because in every village

[1] Forbes, *British Burma*, p. 271.

there were almost always several people who spoke Meithei as well as I. In the accounts of McCulloch and Brown there exists a means ready to hand for testing the extent, if any, to which the views of the hill people have been modified.

Strange-shaped stones were often pointed out to me as "*lai-pham*," places where a Lai or Deity was wont to dwell.[1] The traveller through the hills will see on the tops of the passes little heaps of rice, leaves, flowers, pice, tobacco, votive offerings to the Lai who has his habitation there, to which all alike contribute, Nāga and Kuki, Meithei pilgrim and Bengali merchant. The fantastic caves hollowed by some force of nature in the bosom of the hills were designated "*lai-pham*." Meithei and Nāga alike declared that my galvanic battery was a "*lai-upu*," a divine box.[2] The Thādos have borrowed from the Meithei the word *laili* (or in Meithei, *lairik* = *lai* + *rik* = *likh* = to write) as if they thought a written document possessed a divine potency.

At Marām is current a legend concerning the Rain Deity, who is said to have been a man of the village specially cunning in the art of rain making. The thunder and lightning which accompany the rain storms in the hills are believed by the Kabuis to be caused by the flash and clang of the massive bracelets on the arm of an unmarried girl, Kidilumai, who dances in heaven, as she danced on earth, for joy at the welcome rain.

Some at least of that great company of powers who fill earth and heaven, and dwell in strange places, are unmistakably the ghosts of the unburied, who are ever on the watch to do some hurt to mankind in vengeance for their unhappy doom.

The only instance where I got a definite description of a deity was in a Tangkhul village, when I was told that there were two deities, Uri and Ura, who had four arms and four legs each. I suspect that these deities were Loan Gods. A Tangkhul once assured me that no one had ever seen a Lai. It was, he said, when things happened that men asserted that a Lai had done it. In his view clearly a Lai was a mere

[1] Cf. Marett *The Threshold of Religion*, p. 19: "Stones that are at all curious in shape, position, size, and colour . . . would seem to be specially designed by nature to appeal to primitive man's 'supernaturalistic' tendency."

[2] Cf. *Tom Tit Tot*, p. 151.

hypothesis, an explanation of some phenomenon or occurrence which baffled their knowledge of causation.

Creation.

A common feature of the beliefs held by these tribes is that the creation of the world is ascribed to the deity who causes earthquakes. Among the Tangkhuls and Mao Nāgas it is believed that the world was once a waste of water with neither hills, nor trees, and that the deity imprisoned below made such huge efforts to escape that hills emerged. To this some of the Mao Nāga villagers add the belief that the sky is the male principle and the earth the female, and that an earthquake is as it were their conjugal embrace, whence all fertility, all growth on the earth, has its origin. The Quoirengs say that a deity named Kampinu [1] made the hills for the Nāgas to live in, and an earthquake happens when a piece of rock is cut away to mend the deity's house below. Dr. Brown [2] tells us that "The Kowpoee believes in one Supreme Deity, whose nature is benevolent. This deity is the creator of all things. Man, they say, was created by another god, named Dumpa-poee, by the orders of the Supreme Deity, but they can give no account of the nature of the creation." The belief in a divine Demiurge who, in creating the world and sending forth the race of mankind to dwell thereon, acts not of his own volition, but by the command of a Supreme Deity, is found elsewhere in this area. As a rule, this deity is devoid of colour—he is neither well nor ill disposed towards mankind—to whom he is inaccessible and from whom he receives no gratification of prayer or sacrifice. He is, it would seem, almost a metaphysical conception, originating in the desire to find an explanation for the creation of the material world, in which, except when an earthquake rends the hills and fashions their shapes anew, there is but little sign of change. At Mao the earthquake deity, Pekujike, is also associated with their belief in a future state.[3]

[1] In Lushei, Kampi-nu = Mother of the Company = Queen Victoria.—J. S.
[2] *Op. cit.* p. 107.
[3] Grierson, *Linguistic Survey Report*, Vol. II, Part II, p. 269.

Natural Phenomena.

We have seen that a deity is known to have been manufactured from the ghost of a great rain-maker: a not unnatural result of the belief that man has power of the same order as that of deities, but, as a rule, less in degree. Yet there are forces which are so far greater than the power of man, unaccountable forces, operating, as it would appear, not with any regularity, but suddenly, unexpectedly, forces of destruction. Here, in an area peculiarly sensitive to seismic disturbance, elemental forces are from time to time manifested which are greater than any man ever controls or claims to exert. A man may and does claim to be able to make rain, the successful rain-maker is deified, but I have never come across any belief in the power of man to cause or to stop an earthquake, which they regard as primordially a creative force, and from experience know to be in these latter days a force of immense destructivity. In general, they believe that in the recesses of the earth, or beneath its hills, flung over him like a blanket over a sleeper, reposes a Chief Deity whose heart is stirred from time to time with anxiety lest the race of men (whose creator he seems to be in some cases) has perished utterly from the face of the earth. Therefore they all shout, "We are alive," whenever an earthquake happens. Among the Kabuis it is said that a deity named Bangla-ong lives inside the earth. One day he sent a grasshopper to bring him some fire from above and to look round at the world. It came back and reported that there were no men left. They have also a story which is a variant of that recorded by Soppitt.[1] The son-in-law of the Deity of Heaven one day quarrelled with his father-in-law, and was on the point of worsting him when the deity's daughter, who was looking on, tore a lock of hair from her husband's head and threw it on a fire in which it was consumed. Being thus mutilated, he remains for ever inside the earth, and earthquakes are caused by his struggles to get free to seek for the lost lock of hair.[2] The thunder and lightning, accompaniments of the bursting rain, are perhaps the work of

[1] *Op. cit.* p. 16.

[2] See above, p. 116.

man, for the myths reveal them as due to personages who are, if not men deified, deities anthropomorphised.

A word may here be said of another class of natural phenomena whose causation and sequence we understand better than we yet do that of earthquakes. In every myth of the cause of an eclipse we find that the immediate cause of the phenomenon whose regularity is not obvious to people unhappily ignorant of abstruse mathematics, is always an animal,[1] generally a dog, occasionally a tiger. In the Kabui story, there was a man named Neume who had a dog. His children became leprous, and he sent them to live by themselves in the jungle. One day they caught a grass snake and cut its tail off. It got away and hid itself under the root of a tree in the jungle, and came out again with its tail healed. They themselves were healed by the wonderful properties of this tree, and returned home with some of its bark, which they wrapped up carefully in a piece of cloth and hid in a safe place inside the house. One day the children unwrapped it and put it in the sun. When they came to look for it again, it was gone. The sun had stolen it. The dog tracked the thief and ate him up, because he would not surrender the wonderful bark by whose power the sun recovered at once. The moon sometimes is caught and eaten in the same way.

Dreams and Omens.

In their belief, dreams and omens afford an unerring presage of the future. The Tangkhuls say that a man who is attacked by a buffalo will lose any lawsuit in which he happens at that time to be involved. They also believe that if a man dreams that he is attacked by a buffalo, he will suffer similar misfortune. They attach to the dream precisely the same significance as to the actual event. Does this mean that their dreams are as substantial and possess the same measure of reality as the facts of their waking vision? If this conclusion were legitimate on these facts, the dream life would have a continuity with the waking life, and possess a specific "reality" for them.

The interpretation of unusual dreams is left to the maiba, or to some wise old man. My inquiries as to the meanings

[1] *Cf.* Van Gennep, *La Formation des Legendes*, p. 71.

attached to dreams of an ordinary nature were made in the following villages:—Chimai, Liyai, Mao, Maikel (all of the Mao group), Marām, Liyāng (a village belonging to the Quoirengs), Lengpra, and Aqui (Kabui villages).

To see a plank means universally early death. To see mats spread out means good crops at Chimai, Maikel, Marām, and Lengpra, while at Liyāng it means death, and at Mao death by a tiger. At Liyai they say it means that a man will be killed. To receive a gift of a cow in a dream is at Maikel, Chimai, Mao, Liyāng, and Aqui a token of good hunting. At Liyai it means death and at Lengpra bad luck. To see paper, naturally enough, means quarrels and bad luck. To see a cat means death by tiger in all the Mao villages and Marām, and at Liyāng and Lengpra it forbodes sickness. The people of Aqui think that it portends the approach of a tiger to the village lands. To kill a man means in all the Mao villages and Marām good health and immunity from sickness, while at Liyāng, Lengpra, and Aqui it is a portent of good hunting. To be attacked in a dream by a cow or buffalo is universally held to be a sign of bad luck and sickness. To be bitten by a snake is an omen of very evil portent, and some Kukis regard it as a proof that witchcraft is directed against them. To wash the person is indicative of very good luck and prosperity. To build a house is a token of death, for, as the Kukis say, it means that they must set about building a house in heaven,[1] but at Liyāng, Lengpra, and Aqui it prophesies good luck in hunting. In the Mao villages, Marām and Liyāng, to see peas and beans means good fortune, meat for dinner and plenty, while at Lengpra and Aqui it brings sickness. To dream that a tooth falls out and is lost, is an omen of an early death in the family. A similar meaning is given to a dream that the ear is hurt. Except at Liyāng, where it means that the dreamer will be killed by a tiger, the dream that a dhoti is worn portends great wealth and prosperity. To see fire in a dream means a hot summer, and among the Kabuis of Lengpra, that the crops will be ruined, a natural consequence of a very hot summer. Again, with the exception of Liyāng, where it bears the significance that a house will be burnt, to see water in a dream

[1] Do dreams, then, come from the after world?

means good luck. To see a crow means trouble and scarcity, except at Liyāng, where it means good health. To see a pig means bad luck. There will be a village genna, or at Mao, someone will go mad. The contrary folk of Liyāng say it means good hunting. Opinion is much divided as to the meaning of a dream in which one sees the sun rise. At Chimai, Mao, and Maikel, it means an early death, while at the other villages it bears the opposite meaning. To dream that one puts a fowl in a basket is universally held to be a token of the death of a parent. A large and healthy family is indicated by dreaming that one puts a hen in a basket. To kill a hen or chicken means that a relation or child will die soon. To dream that on a journey a bridge is crossed safely means that luck will attend all enterprises undertaken. To cut the middle finger of the right hand is held to portend an early death in the family. To see a tiger is an omen of good luck, a good harvest, or the birth of a son who will be clever, according to the belief of the Mao group; while at Marām, Liyāng, Lengpra, and Aqui it means an attack of sickness due to some evil spirit. To dream of an earthquake means death, poverty, or scarcity in all cases. To dream of winning a race or such contest means success in life. To dream that a dog bites one is very unfortunate and forbodes sickness, for, as the Aqui people told me, it is a dream of a witch. To receive drink from a man who is known to be dead is a sure portent of sickness and death. To see a dog is a presage of some sickness such as a cough or bad cold, an interpretation which may be connected with the Kuki belief that the blood of a dog cures all ailments of the throat.[1] Among the lucky dreams none is more welcomed than that of climbing a tree. To go through mud possesses the same significance. To see a monkey sitting down is unlucky and is a token of a sudden violent death. To have converse, in a dream, with a girl is unfortunate at Chimai, but elsewhere means either good hunting or at any rate good fortune. To see a rope in a dream is a presage of fortune and wealth, except at Liyāng and Lengpra, where it betokens death. To climb a hill is fortunate, while to go down hill is a warning of death. To see a buffalo is universally a sign of bad luck.

[1] *Cf.* McCulloch, *op. cit.* p. 56.

To dream of a spear when seeking a name for a boy is good, and conversely bad when the child is a girl. The appropriate dream when naming a daughter is of a stick.

In some instances the method of reasoning is evident. Animals which are used in certain sacrifices, as those for sickness, are unlucky. Success in the dream portends success in waking life.

In the Meitheis[1] a case is mentioned where so-called legislation was effected as the result of a dream, and in the story of the prohibition of pork to the people of Marām the ordinance was revealed to the ancestor of the village in a dream. Such dreams as these are—properly enough—of rare occurrence.

Throughout this area we find that at all the crises of domestic and communal life omens are taken in order to determine the issue of the future. Dr. Brown thus records the superstitions of the Kabuis:—"Before going on a journey they hold up by the wings a fowl; should the animal cross its right foot over the left, the omen is good; the opposite, bad.[2] Egg-breaking, as among the Cossiah tribes, is also practised. Pigs are slaughtered, and good or bad omens read from the position of the internal organs. A number of marks is rapidly made with the finger nail or a piece of bamboo in the ground; these are afterwards counted—an even number of scratches is unlucky. A piece of green ginger is cut in two; one half is placed on the ground with the cut side up, and the other piece thrown on it from a short distance. Should the cut surfaces meet, the omen is good. On a journey, as with the Munnipories, meeting a mole is very unlucky, and they try to secure and kill the animal. The barking of a deer in front of them is unlucky, so are the cries of various birds."[3] All these methods are practised by other tribes and groups in this area. The fowl is sometimes killed and the convulsive struggles of its death agony afford a more reliable indication of the future than the economical device described by Dr. Brown. The Tangkhuls take a bamboo or cane and split it suddenly, and then if the fracture be regular,

[1] P. 131.

[2] Yen-khong-tam-na-ba in Manipuri. Yen=fowl, khong=foot, tam-na-ba= to learn.

[3] *Op. cit.* p. 107.

FLAT STONE NEAR MARĀM. [To face p. 132

From a photograph by the Author.

without any overlapping strands, the omen is good.[1] The Kabuis take a leaf and split it. If the edges are even the venture will be fortunate. At Jessami I saw them take a twig hazel and cut chips off it. If the chips fall bark downwards, the luck is good. At Mao and Marām the issue of a hunting party is prognosticated by their success in kicking small pebbles on to the top of a monolith, and I was told that before a war party set forth, it was usual to take omens by dreams, by the fowls' feet, and by taking a bundle of sticks which they threw on the ground, and if the sticks fell head over head, the raid would be successful. It is commonly believed that if an earthquake occurs just after they have had a meal, the crops will be good. In those villages where wrestling parties escort the bride to the groom's house, the fruitfulness of the marriage and its duration are foretold by the result of the wrestling. So, too, the rope-pulling ceremony, which is performed by the Tangkhuls at the beginning and at the end of the cultivating season, affords an indication of the prosperity that is in store for the village. Colonel McCulloch observes that among the Kabuis: "It is customary (after the Enghan)[2] to choose a man to go at midnight to the outer entrance of the village to take the omens regarding their welfare in the ensuing year. If whilst at the entrance he hears anything like the dragging of wood, tigers will do mischief, if like the falling of leaves, there will be much sickness. On these occasions young men have been known to cause, as Burns describes Rab to have done 'behint the muckle thorn,' the omen-taker no small fright; but such pranks are considered sure to bring punishment on their performers, and not long ago a young man after having played the tiger, having died on his way to the valley, his death was universally attributed to his having incurred the anger of the deity on that occasion." When a genna is held, whether for the whole village or for a household only, the entrails of the animals killed are always carefully examined and the omens taken, so that omen-taking is a necessary concomitant of a genna.

Twins are believed to be lucky, but among the Kukis the

[1] Paya tat-pa in Manipuri. Paya = cane, tat-pa = to break.

[2] *Op. cit.*, pp. 52, 53.

opposite belief is found. At Liyai they said that twin boys brought prosperity to the whole village, while the luck was confined to the parents if twin girls were born. But a twin birth of a boy and girl brought misfortune, a belief which is found in many parts of the world.[1]

The Quoirengs say that an eclipse portends war raids. Mention has been made of the custom of making an image of a man, at which spears are thrown, in order to ascertain whether the crops will be good or not.[2]

Omens are taken by egg-breaking among the Kabuis, and I have seen it done on a flat stone, but they were reluctant to give me any information as to the various details of the ceremony. It is quite common to see strings of egg-shells hanging outside a Kuki house as mementoes of the occasions on which this rite has been solemnised by the inmates. Among the Khasis[3] the art of taking omens by means of eggs has been brought to the excellence of a fine art. It is practised by the Mikirs,[4] by the Pankhos and Bunjogees,[5] and by the Chinbōks.[6] It is not certain that it is part of the general stock of Tibeto-Burman customs, but it is obviously practised over a wide area.

There is a tendency to specialisation in these matters. Thus dreams are often the sole means employed in deciding a child's name, while the fowls' feet are consulted before a raid, and a cane broken when other enterprises are in hand. Sometimes omens are taken in every possible manner. Among the Kabuis a special form of omen-taking is practised when the area of cultivation is to be determined.[7]

In all the villages in the immediate vicinity of Mao each house has over its door a bunch of dried leaves to keep away the evil spirits, and among the Quoirengs I learnt that, in order to notify and warn all and sundry that the inmates of a house were "genna," they put up over the lintel a bunch of grass, and the prohibition lasted as long as the grass was unwithered. The Kabuis erect a pole with a bundle of grass at the top in front of the house of the fortunate man who has had the best

[1] Cf. *Khasis*, p. 127.
[2] P. 119.
[3] *The Khasis*, pp. 119 and 221.
[4] *The Mikirs*, p. 35.
[5] Lewin, *op. cit.* p. 98.
[6] *U. B. G.* Vol. I, Part I, p. 460.
[7] See p. 172 below.

MONOLITH NEAR MARĀM. [To face p. 126

From a photograph by the Author.

crop in the year, and the Kukis also put grass and boughs in front of any house in which rice is stored. In all these cases the evil spirits are frightened off by the grass and herbs. A similar purpose is served by the cage which is so often seen outside a Nāga house. The cage itself looks to me like a head cage such as is used by the Wās.[1] It may be noted that among the Tangkhuls we find trees erected of the same shape and the same purport as among the Wās,[2] while the curved beams which mark the house of the khullākpa may possess the same significance.

When entering or leaving a strange village, and in particular when leaving after enjoying their hospitality, it is customary to pluck a sprig of wild indigo and with it to touch the ears, forehead, stomach, and then to place it in the kilt, in order to avert any evil consequences of such temerity.

Sickness and the Treatment of Sickness.

Mysterious sicknesses, the sudden appearance of boils, blindness, loss of speech, premature greyness, are regarded as, if not inevitable consequences, certainly as probable consequences of breaches of the genna prohibitions. Since their attachment to the genna rules is morality of a kind, this belief contains the rudiments of the idea that physical suffering and sickness are due to sin—to breaches of what is "tribal law." I do not think that these penal maladies are always caused spontaneously or without some intermediate agency. While breaches of these ordinances are, as a rule, the ultimate cause of these forms of sickness, their proximate cause may be, and often is, the malignant activity of some powerful offended spirit.

Among the Tangkhuls the deity Kamyou is approached by sacrifice when men are ill. Yet they have maibas, true magicians, who kill a fowl and then pick a small stone out of the side of the patient, who then gets well. When I saw this performance, both men were nearly naked. The sick man lay on the ground in a high fever. The maiba killed the fowl and

[1] *Upper Burma Gazetteer*, Vol. I, Part I, p. 503.
[2] *Op. cit.* pp. 505 and 506.

declared that the omens were favourable. He then knelt on the man, pummelled him unmercifully for about five minutes, suddenly made a dart at him, apparently bit him, and produced from a small bleeding wound in the side a tiny stone[1] about the size of a pea, which the maiba told me was the "lai" which had caused the sickness. I could not see how or where the maiba secreted the stone, as he had only a loin cloth on at the time, nor could I make out the mutterings of the maiba as he bent over his patient. Perhaps the violent massage did it, or it may have been a case of faith-healing, but the man was decidedly better in a short while. Now with all this they have sound ideas. They refuse such heating food as chillies to sick people, and diet them on rice cakes They do not put a small pox patient on a cloth, but on leaves, whether of a special kind or just picked haphazard I do not remember. They asserted to me that water in which brass armlets had been dipped was excellent for cholera. They know the use of splints, and if a man breaks his collarbone, he has a splint under his arm and must sit up. At Jessami, too, they have maibas who produce a stone from the patient as the cause of his illness. They possess a knowledge of the astringent properties of certain jungle herbs, of which they make use both in cases of dysentery and in order to procure abortion. Among the Kabuis the maibas declare the lai who is causing the sickness, and thus decide upon an appropriate sacrifice. As Colonel McCulloch[2] remarks, "whilst the Koupooee enjoys good health, he has little anxiety, but if struck by sickness for any length of time, the chances are he is ruined. To medicine they do not look for a cure of disease, but to sacrifices offered as directed by their priests to certain deities. All their goods and chattels may be expended unavailingly, and when nothing more is left for the inexorable gods, I have seen their wives and children sold as slaves to provide the means of propitiating them. In sickness, therefore, the speedy recovery or the speedy death of the patient is desirable."

Sacrifices are used as remedial measures for sickness in the whole of this area. When an epidemic sickness appears near any village, it is averted by means of a genna. The village

[1] *Cf.* Tylor, *Early History of Mankind*, pp. 275–7.
[2] *Op. cit.* p. 53.

gates at which the sacrifices are made in the case of individual illness are closed, and sacrifices offered at the village gate by the khullākpa. At Mao and in some Quoireng villages the khullākpa lets a cock go free outside the village, presumably as a sort of scapegoat. At Jessami they have annually a prophylactic genna lasting for eight days, in order to avert sickness. A bird is killed in the jungle, and if it happens to be a large one, there will be no sickness. We find among the Kabuis beliefs associating the python [1] with sickness. They kill it and worship it when dead. After killing it they are genna for three days. All men capable of field work are collected at the village gate, and then shout "We are all here." Till this is done, they may not bring it inside. The Kukis also hold that merely to see a python is a source of misfortune.[2] The great snake seems to be regarded as a water deity, and to be associated with dangerous travail, so that sacrifices are offered to it on behalf of women in labour. Either pigs, goats, or fowls may be offered to a python, but never a dog.

The sacrifices made for the purpose of effecting a cure are dogs (subject to the reservation mentioned above), fowls, eggs, or pigs. It is perhaps more than a mere coincidence that omens are taken by means of these creatures.

As a rule (to which there may be exceptions of which I have no knowledge), the patient does not eat any portion of the sacrifices, a fact which seems to distinguish them from sacrifices performed in the course of village gennas which are consumed by the villagers. If a sacrifice is offered at childbirth, in many cases only married people may partake of it, and in some cases the father is not allowed a share in it.

I have also heard of practices which are reputed to cause sickness, but it is never a fellow-villager, seldom an immediate neighbour, usually some person in a distant village, to whom these evil dispositions are attributed.

[1] I had always accepted without question the identification of the python as the snake referred to both by McCulloch and by my Nāga informants, but Colonel Shakespear holds the view that the Lairen (Meithei) is identical with the Rulpui of Lushei belief, which is undoubtedly not a python, but a mythical form of snake.—T. C. H.

[2] Cf. McCulloch, *op. cit.* p. 32.

Ancestor Worship.

It is possible that the Mangla Thā, or general village genna, held after the close of the cultivating season, is in part a ceremony of ancestor worship, although it seems to me more probable that it is intended to lay to final rest the ghosts of all the dead that have died within the year.

I think that the erection of stones has a closer connection with the rudiments of ancestor worship than is often suspected. I noted at Mao the existence of a belief that the stones are erected for the sake of a man's father, who will help his son if need arise. Hence the preservation of the stones is associated with the luck of the family. A man erects a stone in order to found a family.[1]

Nature Worship.

In the section on genna below I have described the gennas which are necessitated by their attitude towards natural phenomena, such as earthquakes and eclipses, as well as the more regular gennas which form an essential part of the rites for bringing rain when needed, and of the rites of the worship of the sun and moon, which are regarded at Mao as good deities and by the Quoirengs as malignant deities, a difference which may rest on the fact that an excess of sun is a serious matter to the jhum crops of the latter. To this difference we owe also a difference of ritual, in that at Mao a white cock is sacrificed, while a pig is the animal killed by the Quoirengs. Among the Tangkhuls and other tribes we have the legend of the angry deity who brandishes his dao and stamps in anger on the ground, thus causing the lightning and the thunder. The Manipuris preserve this legend in their words for lightning (nong-thāng-kuppa) and thunder (nong-khong-ba), while the Kukis and Nāgas have the legend but not the words.

Worship of Deities.

Among the Tangkhuls we find that the deity Kamyou, the eldest son of the Creator of all things, is worshipped by man in

[1] See below, Stone Monuments.

trouble or sickness. He is armed with a big stick, and does judgment upon evil doers, and appeals are made to him because sickness is held to be the result of evil acts. To him an invocation is made by them when entering a strange village, and they pluck a sprig of wild indigo, with which the ears and forehead are touched, in order to secure protection. I have seen Mao villagers do this when entering other villages.

Rites and Sacrifices.

The essential rite of all worship, whether by the village through its ministrant, the khullākpa, or by maibas, or by private individuals in the domestic life, is a genna, a temporary disturbance of the normal course of life. Every occasion on which a sacrifice is offered is also an occasion of a genna. Yet one or two features of the system of rites and sacrifices may be mentioned here as of special interest and importance. In the first place, whether the rite is performed by the khullākpa on behalf of the village or by the head of the household, the "celebrant" acts in a representative capacity, never alone on his own account. Then the animal offered varies, and it is notable that only domesticated animals are killed as sacrifices. I have mentioned below the specific animals that are sacrificed on specific occasions, and an instance where a certain animal is definitely forbidden, viz. the dog, when a sacrifice is made to a great snake as the deity to whom sickness is attributable. The place of sacrifice in the case of village gennas seems to be outside the village or at the village gate, but if the ceremonial offering of heads taken in war[1] is to be regarded as a form of sacrifice, it is an exception to this rule, for they are often brought inside the village and shown to the stones in the village, which are objects of great sanctity on which oaths are taken, and which are "lai-phams." In the case of domestic sacrifices, so far as I know, the sacrifice takes place inside the house, and is consumed there. In cases where a sacrifice is made on behalf of anyone in sickness, the animal sacrificed is not given to him to eat. I am inclined to think that the prohibition which refuses a share of the fowl killed on the occasion of a birth genna, is not an exception to this rule, and that the birth genna is for the "benefit"

[1] See above, p. 115.

of the father as well as of the newly-born child, because of the bond between them. It is never safe to generalise, but the sacrifice of a buffalo or cow seems to be incidental to a rite of worship of a deity, a placable being, while dogs and pigs are killed as sacrifices to beings of another order. Fowls are offered as sacrifices to the House spirit, and to the sun and moon by people who regard these last as good. Fowls are therefore appropriate for worship other than that of malignant spirits. Lastly, we find that omens are always taken when an animal of any kind is killed. It is notable that in the case of the village genna as practised at Mao, the cock is not killed, but let go, probably as a scapegoat rather than as a sacrifice. I do not think that the slender materials I have collected here are enough to warrant any definite view as to the differing purposes of the sacrifices. It may well be true that the sacrifice to a good deity is a form of communion established between the deity and his worshippers, and that the sacrifice to malignant powers is not only a form of placation, but is rather a means of removing danger from the persons on whose behalf the sacrifice is made.

PRIESTHOOD.

Both Colonel McCulloch[1] and Dr. Brown[2] identify the village priest with the maiba, who is doctor and magician in one. My inquiries show that the khullākpa is the village priest, and that the head of the household is the priest in all purely domestic worship. In many respects it is easy to distinguish the maiba from the khullākpa. The maiba is generally not an hereditary officer, while the succession to the khullākpaship is hereditary, subject, as shown in the section on inheritance above, to the condition that the khullākpa must be sound in mind and body. I know of no food or other gennas of a personal nature affecting the maiba. Such gennas may exist, but, if so, they are, I suspect, private. I know of no ceremonies of initiation or qualifications which are undergone by, or exacted from, the would-be maibas. Yet the maiba has no monopoly even of cases of sickness, for sometimes a village genna is held often as part of the cure, but

[1] *Op. cit.* p. 53. [2] *Op. cit.* p. 107.

always as a prophylactic against the sickness. The maiba cannot order a village genna. He interprets dreams and omens, but much of this has been reduced almost to the level of an exact science, so that he is not called in except in difficult cases, where there is no settled precedent. I do not think that his art is considered disreputable or anti-social. He is an empiric scientist, and has made useful discoveries, especially of the medicinal virtues of jungle herbs and roots. He is on the way to learn that man must stoop to conquer the forces of nature. The khullākpa, however, plays the leading part on all occasions when a village genna is held. He acts whenever a rite is performed which requires the whole force of the community behind it, and this force finds its operation through him. These village gennas seem in many cases to be inspired by the belief that man, *the man*, the khullākpa, when fortified by the whole strength and will of the village, is able to control and constrain forces which are beyond his control if unaided. He relies on co-operative strength while the maiba depends on his individual ability. The tabus which surround and protect the khullākpa are based, when we can identify their sanctions, upon social sanctions, behind which as the true ultimate sanction of sanctions is the vague sense of some general calamity that is bound to happen if any of the tabus are violated. The khullākpa of Mao is forbidden to eat the flesh of a number of creatures which are the very creatures which are offered as sacrifices. The "religiosity" of the khullākpa is such that it is dangerous to bring it into contact with any substance that is employed in intercourse with "powers whose modes of action transcend the ordinary and calculable."[1] He bears the brunt of it all. His special clothes mark him out among his fellows at once as a person dangerous to them and as himself peculiarly liable to danger. A plague, it may be of boils, peradventure of blindness, will come in upon the village through him by the breach of one of his gennas. The solidarity of the social structure rests on him. The maiba owes his position to his own individual talents. In these small homogeneous communities there is but little room for any individualistic tendencies. There is thus a formal but,

[1] Marett, *op. cit.* p. 90.

in this stage of imperfectly differentiated functions, not yet a fundamental difference between the maiba and the village priest. It is part of the religious belief of these people that, as proved by the care and scrupulosity with which they forbid the khullākpa to have any dealings with substances employed in intercourse with dangerous powers, some rites must be performed by the maiba.

We have in this area old women who can detect thieves, and magicians who cause sickness, but they are always to be found in the next village or a day's journey away, or over the next range of hills. These, if such exist, are the people who practise the black art, whose rites are secret, private, and disreputable, epithets which cannot be applied to the maibas whether as rainmakers or as doctors. I once had a Kabui brought before me on a charge of magical practices. He lived in the valley, and those who complained produced in Court the implements of his magic. There was a stick about ten inches long, sealed at both ends, attached to which was a wax image of what with some stretch of the imagination may be called a man. There was also a piece of mirror, doubtless used to catch the soul of the victim. The accused denied the charge and alleged that these things had been put in his house by his enemies. I took possession of them, but I have reason to believe that my faithful Uriya bearer, a devout Hindu, destroyed them while I was out on tour.

Birth Ceremonies.

The birth of children necessitates a domestic genna of which an account will be found below in the section on gennas.[1]

Dr. Brown [2] observed that among the Tangkhuls "The child immediately after birth has chewed rice placed in its mouth and is immersed in water heated nearly to the boiling point; this treatment is supposed to render the child hardy and prevent it in after life from suffering from pains about the back and loins. The mother of the child is also made to sweat profusely by being wrapped in hot water blankets until faintness ensues; this is repeated two or three times, and on the third day the

[1] Pp. 177 *et seq.*

[2] *Op. cit.* p. 120.

woman is allowed to go about as usual." The rice is first chewed by the father.[1] The navel cord[2] is buried inside the house and a small amulet given to the child, a practice which may have been imitated from Kukis.

The Kabuis bury the navel cord under the stone hearth inside the house. In some cases an old woman of the village helps the birth but in other villages the father acts as midwife. In any case all in the house are genna, secluded from the rest of the village.

Naming Ceremonies.

The name is given either during or at the end of the birth genna. The sacrifices which are made on these occasions are expressly connected with the omens which must be taken to determine the name. In addition to the omens taken by means of the fowls' feet we have among the Tangkhuls omens based on the split cane. In the Mao group and at Marām dreams supplement the omens derived from the fowls' feet. We learn that among the Quoirengs if the child cries when a name is mentioned to it, the name is abandoned, so that there even at that early age man is master of his fate. There is some variety in Kabui practice, because I find that at Tamenlong an old woman reads omens from the child's forehead, while Colonel McCulloch states[3] that "Five days after the birth of a child it is named with various ceremonies: names are not given at random but are compounds of the father's and grandfather's names, or those of other near relations." Omens are taken in order to select the most favourable compound, for the name exerts a profound influence[4] over the life of the individual, and it seems to me probable enough that the virtues and fortune of the eponymous relations are held to be thus transmitted to the child. In the Old Kuki village, Sadu Koireng, in the southern portion of the Manipur Valley, this method of nomenclature is practised. The child receives the name of his maternal grandfather.

[1] Cf. *Kinship and Marriage in Early Arabia*, p. 154.

[2] Navel cords are generally cut with sharp bamboos. A curious survival.—J. S.

[3] *Op. cit.*, p. 51.

[4] Cf. *Tom Tit Tot*, p. 80 *et seq.*, and Jevons' *Plutarch's Romane Questions*, p. lxxx.

Among the Marrings we have a system of name-giving which merits special attention. My investigations confirm the account given by Dr. Brown.[1] "The oldest male child of a family is invariably called Moba: this name is given immediately after birth. The second male child is called Koba, the third Mayba, the fourth Ungba, the fifth Kumba. After the fifth every male child is called Kumba. For female children, the first is called Tebee, the second Tobee, the third Toongbee, and fourth, Sungkobee, the fifth and others Kumbee. Thus in any village many of the same name may be found. Other names may afterwards be given, but as the giving of a second name involves a large expenditure in the shape of a feast to the village the privilege is not often taken advantage of. Amongst seventeen men I had at one time assembled before me only four of them had second names: these names were Mohseel, Modar, Morrongba, and Moteel, and the above informed me, with what truth I cannot say, that these four names, which had no meaning were all that the whole tribe possessed. Individuals of the same name are identified by the clan or family name, also by the father's number, so to speak, by personal peculiarities as long, short, stout, &c." The secret of the village genna held in consequence of the publication and loss of the original private name, is that a man has been lost to the village and a new man is thereby received into it. This system of nomenclature with different names is in force among the Old Kukis of Anāl Namfau and Hiroi Lamgang.[2] I have found it borrowed without modification by some Tangkhuls who had settled in the valley of Manipur not far from Thobal and near the area occupied by the Marrings.

Toga Virilis.

Among the Tangkhuls the assumption of the "ring"[3] may be regarded as equivalent to claiming the toga virilis. I do not know whether or not it is attended by any ceremony of a religious nature. It has been stated on good authority that the

[1] *Op. cit.* p. 126; *cf.* also McCulloch, *op. cit.* p. 66.
[2] *Notes by Babu Nithor Nath Banerji.*
[3] *Vide* Appendix I, and Brown, *op. cit.* p. 119.

kilt may not be worn by a Nāga unless he has taken heads, but many a good man in these degenerate days would go unwived and kiltless if this rule still held good.[1]

Tangkhul girls belonging to the northern section of that group are tattooed at puberty. As a general rule the hair of girls is cut short till that age is attained, when it is allowed to grow. Ornaments which are worn till then are discarded. Differences of coiffure mark the different stages of social maturity in the case of both men and women.[2]

Marriage.

Reference has been made to the effect which marriage has upon the customs of inheritance which among the Tangkhuls are brought into play by the marriage of the sons. The religious aspect of the ceremonies of marriage is enhanced by the custom of taking omens as to the day on which the marriage should take place, for marriage is the severance of the woman from her clan and the consequent accession to the man's clan and household of a member by birth of another clan. One common feature of the ceremonies is the attendance on the bride of the young men of her clan who wrestle with the bachelors of her husband's clan, so as to determine the longevity of the parties to the match. Length of life goes to the partner whose champions win. Songs are sung, but among the Tangkhuls it is expressly forbidden to sing war-songs. At Yāng spear dances are usual while in the Marām group wrestling is only permitted when the bride comes from a different village. The employment of a go-between is common, and if it is due to the avoidance which is necessary between engaged persons, it may be connected with the genna which prohibits intercourse between the newly married couple for the first few days of their wedded life. This prohibition does not operate in the case of the re-marriage of widows, a fact which suggests that the genna is in part due to the fear so often observed of entering into strange relationships for the first time.[3] The ratification of the betrothal and marriage by the

[1] Johnstone, *op. cit.* p. 30.
[2] Pp. 22, 24, 27–35, 77.
[3] *Vide* Van Gennep, *Rites de Passage*, p. 251 *et seq.*

transfer of the customary gifts rests on a social sanction, for until the price is paid over the young couple may not take any food in the house of the bride's parents.

Death Ceremonies.

All these tribes bury their dead. I have hinted above[1] that the custom of placing the heads of enemies may be a ceremonial survival of the practice common in other parts of this area of tree-burial. So far as my information goes, Jessami is the only village where the dead are regularly buried outside the village; although young children are there buried in front of the house. The Tangkhuls possess family vaults. Of the Kabuis Colonel McCulloch remarked that "The village and its immediate precincts form their graveyard and when for a time, from whatever cause, they have been obliged to desert their village, I have heard them more often express their wish to return to it as being the grave of their ancestors than as being their own birthplace."[2]

But not all the dead are buried inside the village or in the usual burying place. In the first place the children of tender years who die before they are weaned are often not buried in the ordinary grave but close to the house. In the second place, those that die outside the village must as a general rule be buried outside the village, though there is either a ceremonial burial in the usual place or the burial of some part of the remains or belongings of the deceased. Mr. Pettigrew of the American Baptist Missionary Union, who has for many years enjoyed remarkable facilities for studying the customs of the Tangkhuls, states that "in any case where the person dies away from home and where there is a difficulty in getting back —crossing a river, for instance—the person is buried near the place of death but the skull is brought to the village. . . . On burying the skull they cover it with a black cloth, and in place of the trunk left behind a piece of wood, generally the wooden pillow of the deceased, is attached to the skull, and covered also with a piece of cloth, to represent the whole

[1] Above, p. 116.

[2] *Op. cit.* p. 43.

person."[1] In the third place, under the influence of eschatological belief, the dead who die by violence, who are killed in war, whose death might, as we should say, argue a visitation of God, such as death by snake-bite, by drowning, by a fall from a tree, by a tiger in the jungle, or women who die in childbirth, are buried apart from the generality of the village. At Uilong a man killed in war is buried outside the village on the side of the village opposite to that on which live the enemies who inflict the fatal wound. Among the Quoirengs and Kabuis a woman who dies in childbirth is buried inside the house. The Quoirengs in such cases bury all the moveable articles and utensils in the house, while the Kabuis abandon the house and its contents completely. In the Kabui settlements in the valley of Manipur it is usual to carry the body out by the small door at the side of the house, or even through a special aperture cut for the purpose and then closed, and to bury it close to the house, within, so I understand, the limits of the shadow cast by the noontide sun.

Among the Tangkhuls "the dead are buried outside their houses to the depth of the length of the corpse, plus a margin for top dressing of stones, etc. Where there are no family graves near the house, other graves can be opened if there has been no burial during the past year. But before doing so a sort of ceremony has to be gone through with the bones of the departed. Some years ago one man of the village was set apart for this particular work, but now the custom is for each family to attend to same. On opening this family grave the bones are collected, cleaned with water, and then wrapped in a large cloth, new or old, and put on one side of the grave. When a great number of bones are collected and there is not sufficient room for a fresh corpse, they are taken out of the tomb; and when the fresh corpse has been buried and covered to the depth of a few feet, the bones are thrown in to help fill up the grave. The bottom of the grave is made circular to hold the corpse and the things buried with it."[2]

Among the Kabuis "the grave is thus prepared," says Dr. Brown.[3] "A trench is first made, and at right angles to this

[1] *J.A.S.B.* (N.S.), Vol. V, No. 2, 1909, p. 37.

[2] Pettigrew, *op. cit.* p. 37.

[3] *Op. cit.* p. 106.

the ground is excavated and a recess made into which the coffin is inserted, the earth being afterwards filled in: this grave is used again and again before a new one is opened . . . . A stone either flat or upright, resembling those so common in the Cossiah Hills,[1] is placed over the grave . . . . Amongst some of the Kowpoees the side of a hill is excavated for the reception of the coffin, and the vault filled and closed with earth and stones."

In ordinary cases of death, as we should classify them, the grave is dug by the Tangkhuls, at Marām by friends, among the Quoirengs by young male friends, as is also the practice among the Kabuis,[2] while custom among the Marrings imposes this task upon the relatives of the family by marriage. In cases of extraordinary death among the Tangkhuls only the immediate relations dig the grave. Among the Quoirengs when a woman dies in childbirth, either women past the age of childbearing dig it or it is begun by old men past child-begetting age and is finished by the young men. The Kabuis assign this duty to the immediate male relations of the woman. The Chirus' custom is for the elders to dig the grave in all cases of mysterious death, and for childless old men to dig the graves of women dying in childbirth. Among the Marrings it is a general task in which every household participates.

Burial takes place, as a rule, on the day following death except in the cases where children die or where death occurs before sunrise.

In the graves are placed various articles for the use and comfort of the deceased in the world hereafter. Cloths, spears, daos, sometimes as at Marām the ornaments, the shield, the drinking cup and supplies of food and drink are buried with the men. The Tangkhuls bury two old and torn cloths with a man for his own use and a new untorn cloth as a present for the Deity of Heaven. Tobacco and a pipe are laid near at hand. In the grave of a woman are placed food and drink, her tail of false hair, her cooking pots,[3] her digging stick and the brow-band which in life she used to carry loads from the fields.

[1] This is not an apt comparison, the Khāsi monuments being cenotaphs.—P. R. G.

[2] The grave is dug by those connected with the family by marriage with its females, McCulloch, *op. cit.* p. 52.

[3] *Cf.* Brown, *op. cit.* p. 106.

Among the Tangkhuls in the grave of a man whose parents have predeceased him it is customary to place food and drink as gifts for his relations. If a man dies of tiger bite, they put a bugle in his grave to scare away the tigers on the road to heaven. They also bury a thorn, or sharpened stake, rough and ready but useful weapons. Sometimes they provide a well-sharpened spear and kill a dog to keep him company on his long road. Over the body they play the bugle before burial. At Jessami they never kill an animal for a man who has met this death. At Maikel they put nothing in the grave, not even a cloth. At Marām they bury the body without a plank but put a white cloth on it and place a thorn and spear in the grave. No animals are killed.

The Quoirengs wait for five days, and then in such cases kill a dog and a pig. In ordinary cases of death these animals are killed on the day of the burial. The Kabuis seem to leave them without weapons, although wrapping the corpse in the usual cloths.

The detailed account given by Mr. Pettigrew of the burial ceremony practised by the Tangkhuls is noteworthy:—

"On the day of burial the rich kill a buffalo, others manage a cow, or a pig. They are killed before the grave is dug, and are left whole until the grave is finished. It is then cut up, the relations take half, and the grave-diggers the other half of the intestines. The head is taken always by the nearest male relative, the right hind leg is given to the eldest daughter, the left hind leg to the next daughter. If no daughters of their own, the nieces receive them. The forelegs are given to other distant female relatives. The heart, liver, kidneys, spleen, lungs, etc., are then handed to the 'Sherra,' the village priest. He first of all divides these portions up, six portions for a male and five for a female, and takes them to the next-door neighbour's house and cooks same. He then brings them to the deceased's house and places them on top of the rice and vegetables which the relatives have brought in during the morning, and placed near the head of the corpse. His next duty is to offer up this food to the 'kameo' (evil spirit) by reciting this refrain: 'Thisān yāmsanrava, shāiphung shap phungda thulu,' and calling upon the dead to eat this offering, takes the special portions on a plate of his own, and throws it away in the compound, where the dead's spirit and the 'kameo' are supposed to have appropriated it before touching the ground. The dogs, however, have a meal afterwards. Beer is also offered, and a small portion thrown away. After this ceremony of the priest, the rest of the meat and rice is divided amongst all and eaten before the burial. It is interesting to note here, that no matter what is killed in the village, or at whatever time, feast or otherwise, it is always offered to the 'kameo' before eating. The next act is for the 'sherra' to take the length and breadth of the bier, and if found too large for the grave, he alone is supposed to cut off any portion necessary. The bier is simply a plank of wood which lies outside ready. The body is then covered over with a clean white cloth before taking it out of the house. In the meantime one of the relations takes a pine torch from a house near by, and descends into the grave, and twirling it round beseeches the ancestors of the dead to come and meet him on his way to 'Kazairam.' 'O āwo āyi! ishāvā rārāli, ungngaroklu' is the prayer made. Then after the 'sherra,' according to custom, has slightly raised the head of the bier the relations carry it out, and put it on the plank of wood, and on top of same whatever cloths are to be taken to 'Kazairam.' The top cloth is never torn, as it is meant for Kokto when they meet him. Then the hands of the corpse are washed with water. The bier is lifted by the palms of the hands and taken to the side of the grave. If lifted otherwise the relations will get ill. All the relations now gather round and make great lamentation, and tramp around the grave two or three times. After a final burst of the mourners' refrain by one of the old braves of the village, those who wish to stay and mourn stay on, and the rest leave. Then tightly fastening the body to the plank, it is placed, with all the gifts for the journey mentioned above, in the grave. The wife is allowed to enter and remain till the last moment. Then around and over the body, to prevent any earth from touching it, is built a stone wall. After filling up with earth the 'sherra' is again called to place a pole above the mound, while others place six prongs of wood around a small hole made in the mound, wherein is placed a pine torch. On lighting this they all leave the grave and enter the house. Here all fires have been put out, and all ashes cleared, and on their entering, fresh fire is brought from another house near by. Around this fire the family sit and wait for any sign in the fire-place, such as the print of a foot, to see if there are any more deaths to be expected. If there are none it is a favourable sign fortunately. As a final wind-up for the night, the relations' portion of meat is cooked and partly eaten, along with the rice and vegetables left over from the morning's feast. At the same time, small portions in six or five pieces, with a small quantity of beer, is offered to 'kameo' near the bed of the deceased by the nearest relation. Next morning and evening the pine torch on the grave is again lighted. This is continued for three days. The spirit, after it has had its interview with Kokto, and has handed over the gifts taken with it to the ancestors, is supposed to return the following day after burial. For this reason the family keeps all doors open from morning to night, and from that day until the final disposal of the spirit from the village at the great feast of 'Kathi Kashām,' the family prepare with their own meals a similar one for the spirit. It is then put into a plate used when alive by the deceased, and put on his or her own seat. This is done twice a day. After ten days or a month the parents if a child has died, the wife if a husband, or vice versa, search the village for a person as like as possible in features and size as the deceased to be their representative at the ceremonies of the great feast."[1]

We have the authority of Dr. Brown for the statement that "on the death of a warrior his nearest relation takes a spear and wounds the corpse by a blow with it on the head so that on his arrival in the next world he may be known and received with distinction."[2]

But the obsequies are not really completed till the spirits of the deceased have been laid to rest finally and for ever by a second rite[3] in which the community as a whole takes part. This rite is known to the Meitheis under the name Mangla tha or month belonging to the ghosts. It may be a form of ancestor

[1] *Op. cit.* p. 38 *et seq.* [2] *Op. cit.* p. 121.

[3] Cf. *L'Année Sociologique*, Vol. X, p 48 *et seq.* "La Représentation Collective de la Mort." Van Gennep, *Rites de Passage*, pp. 201, 273.

worship, although celebrated only on behalf and in respect of the recent dead. It seems that they exclude from its purview those who have died by violence, as their deaths involve the whole village in a genna. At Mao it is usual to have a village genna whenever anyone dies and perhaps as a consequence of this there is there no such secondary funeral ceremony. This rite, which is held after the crops are gathered in, consists among the Tangkhuls of two parts, the "Wonyāi thing" ceremony and the Kathi kashām ceremony which are thus described by Mr. Pettigrew:—[1]

"*The 'Wonyāi thing' ceremony.*—After the harvest in December has been gathered in, and all instruments in connection with same have been put on one side, in the evening the rich kill a cow, the rest pigs and dogs, and for those whose children have died, eggs are boiled. After cooking same the 'sherra' is called in as usual and offers up small portions to 'kameo.' Next morning the 'sherras' from each section of the village gather together in a compound and receive from the relations of the dead special portions of the meat killed the night before, and rice beer. On finding out the number of persons who died during the past year in each section, the plates and cups of each deceased are brought to them thoroughly cleaned and put in a row before them. In these plates, etc., are placed the meat and beer. On one side the 'sherras' tear off small portions, and arrange three small heaps of same. After all is divided out they take these portions as well as the beer and offer again to 'kameo' up and down the rows of plates. After this performance whatever is left they eat, and the plates, etc., are taken back to their respective houses. This being done all friends who come forward to help in erecting the 'wonyāi thing' are counted, and to them a liberal supply of meat and beer is distributed. They then go off and bring in the wood and rope necessary to erect this structure. It is a lightly made structure, built outside the door of each deceased's house, and is shaped like a shield with a sort of small platform in front, on which the following day are placed various articles, such as Indian corn, roots, pumpkins, etc. The shield framework is covered with sheaves of rice corn, and so arranged that the birds cannot eat

[1] *Op. cit.* p. 41 *et seq.*

same. At the side of this structure is also placed a large clump of the orchid '*Cymbidium giganteum.*' All these articles are said to be for the departed spirit to show, as a sign, the fruits of the earth received during the past year. After four or five days friends from other houses and other villages who have not had any deaths during the past year present rice and beer to the mourners, and portions of same are first placed in the deceased's plate, etc., at evening. If this is not done by the friends it is feared it will be their share to receive death in their midst the following year."

The "Kathi Kashām" Feast.

This takes place about the end of January of each year. The first thing for each family to do is to procure their buffaloes, cows, pigs, and dogs. After they have procured these from near and far, the headmen of the village give orders for the beer, weak and strong, to be prepared for fermentation, and they also, after a palaver, decide what day the feast shall commence. It is a ten-day feast, and I give below particulars of each day's work.

First day.—The rope for binding up the animals before killing is procured from the jungle, also the poles for hanging cloths up (see fifth day).

Second day.—These ropes are prepared so as to withstand any strain by the animals when being killed. This work of the first and second day is performed by the males, the women, in the meantime, gathering and stacking wood in each house.

Third day.—This is the day for killing buffaloes and cows. Their mode of killing is very cruel, and would not be tolerated for a moment in any civilised state. In the more northern villages the poor animals are tied down and subjected to much torture, the animal being cut to pieces piecemeal with knives and spears, and no attempt made to end its life before almost the last shred of flesh has been torn away and the limbs torn from their sockets. It is considered quite a sight, and crowds gather round, and even sit on the house-tops, and gaze on this horrible butcher's work. After the cutting-up process in the whole village is over, the division and distribution take place in the same way as performed on the death of the person, and of course the "sherra" is called in to offer to "kameo."

Fourth day.—Both males and females join together in getting in a plentiful supply of wood; and as there is much entertaining during this feast, and all night singing and dancing performed, there is need of plenty of fires, it being the coldest part of the year. The representative of the dead finds his first occupation on this day by collecting "khamuinā," a kind of broad plantain leaf used for the unleavened bread made the next day.

Fifth day.—Unleavened bread is made into small cakes, and pigs and dogs killed, cut up into small pieces, cooked and offered to "kameo" and then distributed with a small cake of bread wrapped in the "khamuinā" leaves amongst the mourners in each section of the village. On this day also cloths of all kinds and qualities are attached to long poles and erected outside each house of the dead. The more cloths displayed the greater one is thought of.

Sixth day.—This is occupied in preparing the rice beer which has been fermenting for some days in large casks, and any other work not finished on previous days is completed.

Seventh day.—This is the day when the real excitement commences. Friends and relations from villages around come in during the afternoon, and at sunset. Before their arrival the females only give an offering to "kameo" in the shape of a sandwich of unleavened bread, sesamum seed concoction, and slices of pork, which after being offered to "kameo" by the "sherra" is placed on the platform of the "wonyāi thing." With this is also placed four pots of beer (weak and strong). After the arrival of villagers each family of the dead calls for its representative or "thilā kapo" as he is called. He in the meantime has been decked with bright head-gear, necklaces, armlets, and leglets. On his arrival at the house he performs a dance outside, and then on entering is introduced to the seat of the dead. From this point until the end of the feast he is looked upon as the dead person in life, and just as we would treat a friend or relation who was going on a long journey, with no prospect of seeing him again, so is this "thilā kapo" looked upon by the family and treated accordingly. He is presented with all the food cooked, and as the head of the house for the time being dispenses hospitality. On this evening in particular there are high jinks performed in each house. What with eating, drinking, and dancing, I am afraid they think more of their own enjoyment than of the dead. Before the day is over the cloths hung upon poles in each compound, after having been seen and admired, or otherwise, by the villagers, are taken down and brought into the house to be given to the representative later on.

Eighth day.—This day is mostly taken up with commercial pursuits, in the buying and selling of cloths, etc., brought in by the villagers. The representatives of the dead also give the villagers a specimen of their dancing powers in the large space called "Laingapha kayāng" situated in the midst of the village. They are, of course, dressed up for the occasion. The "sherras" during this performance cut up a portion of the skins of the pigs killed on the fifth day and offer to "kameo." The remaining skin of all the animals killed is eventually cooked and eaten with the other portions. After this exhibition by the "thilā kapo" they are taken and fed by the female relations, going from house to house, receiving the cloths brought in the previous night, so that by the time he has finished visiting there is a goodly pile, and he takes the first opportunity to sell all he does not require for himself, or for herself, if the representative happens to be a female.

Ninth day.—The great day of the feast. The first thing in the morning one of the family searches for plantain leaves to cover the pine torch handles, etc. These torches are made extra large, and laid aside for use at sunset. A further dish of pig's meat and rice is next prepared and placed on large plates, with salt and fish, and brought on the compound. Next a great gathering of all friends and relations with each representative. They meet at the lowest point of the village where a death has occurred, each one carrying his or her load of meat, ginger, rice beer, and cloths already given to the representative. These are all placed on mats in a row. Empty plates and pots are placed in a row near, and are then filled up. Everybody is dressed up for the occasion, especially the representatives. When all is ready some old priest of the village gives a great shout, "He, hiaina tātang tārangsa," and at this everybody suddenly takes hold of the plates and pots, etc., and holding them up above their heads, take all to the "thilā kapos'" houses. They are supposed to have another meal here, but as it is a question of eating and drinking all day long, they, if they are not gluttonous, content themselves with a small portion. They now take the place of receiving guests, friends, and relations who wish to say farewell, as they are now on the point of leaving for good. First to receive a parting gift is the head of the deceased's house, who receives a cloth from the "thilā kapo." Then come along the widows of the village, but instead of giving anything they receive a parting gift of meat and beer from him or her. After the widows come the female relations who entertained them the day before, and they also receive a present of meat and beer—a sort of mutual give and take before the final parting. It is sunset now, and a procession is formed. At the head of the same march the torch-bearers, with the leaves gathered early in the morning wound round their heads and shoulders to keep off sparks from the flaming torches. Behind these march a crowd of elders dressed in their war garb, and lastly the "thilā kapo," the representative of the dead, follow with relations crowding around them, and with much lamenting and grief the procession proceeds slowly on its way towards "Zaiphar," a spot at the north end of the village overshadowed by a large tree. To this spot the torch-bearers wend their way. The idea is that the spirits need to be led in the gathering twilight to show them the way to their final place of abode, "Kazairam," and the warriors are also needed as a guard to keep them from all harm on their way there. The spirit is supposed to enter into, or rather turned into these lighted torches as soon as they are thrown down at "Zaiphar." By the time these torches have reached this place, the "thilā kapo" have reached the limit of the village boundary, and on the supposition that the spirit has left to proceed on its way as a torch to "Kazairam," these representatives are at once denuded of all their finery. The head-gear is broken up on the spot, and as far as these individuals are concerned, their representative work is over. All the villagers return to their homes, the torch-bearers having already returned by another route. Before entering their houses, the "wonyāi thing" structure erected outside is pulled down, and the poles over the grave are pulled out and thrown away. At the front door, just inside the house, a pine torch is lighted and placed on a stone. This is done for the purpose of not allowing the spirits of the living to go off with the spirits of the dead just got rid of.

The spirits after entering the torches are declared to wend their way during the evening towards the hills on the north, and finally disappear to find themselves crossing the river in "Kazairam." On that side of the river they are believed to commence and carry on an existence similar to that enjoyed, or, otherwise, when alive on earth. The wealthy enjoy their wealth again, and the poor eke out the precarious existence suffered on earth.

Tenth day.—This and the following few days are practically days of rest, and the only thing recognised is the supposition that the embodied spirits in "Kazairam" cut all their hair off on the tenth day, and have a sort of "wash and brush up" to remove all connection with mother earth. On this day, therefore, no one is supposed to bathe or touch water."

I was informed by Manipuris that the Tangkhuls used to throw cloths away on these occasions which Manipuris collected and sold, thus exploiting the piety of the hillmen.

In December, 1900, I witnessed a similar ceremony at the Quoireng village Lemta, and noted the events of the day as they passed before my eyes. The young bachelors, the youths from twelve to fifteen years of age, assumed their best attire and paraded outside the village. Most of them smeared their legs with white earth and made a criss-cross pattern on them. A few of them decorated themselves with a quaint picturesque head-dress which resembled the glory worn by Saints in mediæval art.[1] The lads all assembled outside the village carrying spears. As they entered at the lower gate, they commenced to sing. No sooner had the procession entered the village than the women began to wail and lament. Each woman lit two torches over the graves in front of the houses. As the procession passed them, they poured water from a bamboo chunga over one torch and threw the other away into the jungle. The empty bamboo chunga was also thrown on to the grave. The women then joined the procession and accompanied it to the other gate of the village. They stayed inside and the lads then finished

[1] See above, p. 26.

their performance outside. They formed up into two lines moving one inside the other in opposite directions, singing all the while and then gathered to the centre and all shouted together to complete this part of the ceremony. They then indulged in sports, a long jump being the first event. All jumped one after another in rapid succession and then the village champions tried their skill. After that they "put" the stone and set the younger lads to wrestle. By this time it was near sunset and they re-entered the village. Not a stroke of work was done during the day. The rice was pounded overnight. No woman or married man may leave the village from sunrise to the following sunrise. I noticed that the women when following the procession carried their best cloths on their arm, perhaps as a precaution. In preparation for the ceremony they had erected a palisade of forked white carefully peeled sticks from ten to twelve feet high. On it hung imitation bears' heads with tusks of wood. There were semblances of men's heads fashioned from gourds, and swinging high above all from a long pole was a buffalo's head and horns.

General Ideas about Death.

At death something leaves the body. That something is often regarded as a winged insect of some kind, now a butterfly, now a bee.[1] In order to allow the insect to escape "a hole is made in the roof directly above the bed of the deceased."[2] I cannot be quite sure whether what assumes the shape of the insect in question is to be identified with the soul or personal essence, or with the vital principle. A false impression may be created by the use of philosophical terms in reference to savage beliefs, which are vague, shifting shadows, not modern synthetic systems. Mr. Pettigrew remarks that "after burial the form of the spirit as a "kaha" (*i.e.* the honeybee) is lost and the spirit is supposed to enter the deceased's body again and in that condition remains under all circumstances."[3] Among other tribes in the vicinity it is believed, according to Dr

[1] Pettigrew, *op. cit.* p. 37. Brown, *op. cit.* p. 116. *Cf.* Crawley, *Idea of the Soul*, Ch. IV.

[2] Pettigrew, *loc. cit.* p. 37.

[3] *Op. cit.* p. 38.

Brown, that transformation into an insect, especially a butterfly, is the last, not the first, stage in the progress of the cycle of life. So strongly is this idea held among the Angamis that "they carefully refrain from injuring" some species of butterfly on this account.[1]

Something which on and by death is separated from the body and is treated in much the same way as when united with and immanent in the body, is believed to remain at or near the place of death or at the place where the wound which caused death was inflicted, for some time after death. This came to my notice in connection with a frontier raid where a young man of a Manipur village had received his spear wound on ground belonging to another village. He actually died in his own village, but I was so fortunate as to witness the ceremony of calling his spirit home.

A party of the young men of the village all in war paint went to the boundary of the village overlooking the village where the fatal affray had occurred. A dance was solemnly performed and then zu was poured on the ground, rice scattered about and they all shouted "Nipone, come back, come back. Have no fear. We are your friends, here is food and drink. Come from that unlucky place." On this occasion, perhaps because I was there, to keep the peace, there was no answer but I was told that some answer was usual.

The "ghost" of the deceased is regarded as an exact image of the deceased as he was at the moment of death, with scars, tattoo marks, mutilations,[2] and all—and as able to enjoy and to need food and other sustenance—which are therefore given to it for a period.[3]

[1] *Op. cit.* p. 116. [2] See above, p. 151, below p. 161.

[3] The psychology of the Karens has been described by Forbes (*British Burma*, p. 272, *et seq.*). Everything, animate and inanimate, has a "la," which in the case of human beings constantly wanders from the body, so that its persistent absence causes death. To the "thah" or will, but not to the "la," is attached moral responsibility. A third principle called "tso" may be defined as Reason. How tempting to identify these terms with the psychical components of consciousness, feeling (la), will (thah), and thought (tso). In Lushai psychology, "each person has three spirits. One of these is called khawrin, and this is the one that sometimes wanders; the other two are spoken of as thlarao, and one is supposed to be wise and one foolish, and the constant struggle between these two causes men's actions to be so unreliable." (Shakespear, *Ethnography of India*, p. 226.) The Lushai term, thla, which is translated by Lorrain and Savidge (*Lushai Grammar*, p. 197), as a spirit or one's double, is no doubt identical with the Karen word

The Future Life.

The Tangkhuls say that their dead go to a heaven by a path over the crest of Sirohifurar. This is the realm of the Deity Kok-thi-yong, Kok-thi-makha, Kok-thu, or Kokto as Mr. Pettigrew finds him to be called. The place is called Ka-zai-ram or the country (ram = lam = territory) of the zai. The Deity of Heaven is fain to keep them all out. By the gates there flits a woodpecker, the type of restless vigilance. The thin ghosts cannot themselves force a way in, and so it is incumbent on the living to provide a buffalo for the burial feast in order that its mighty ghost may open the massy gates. To kill a pig were idle expense, because, as they know full well, "to drive a pig to Dublin you must set his nose to Cork." So, near the gates of Heaven, awaiting the arrival of the ghost of a rich man, there is a crowd of ghosts whose living kin are too poor or too selfish to slaughter a buffalo. The Deity judges them all, and on the occasion of the Kathi Kashām festival Dr. Brown notes that the "spirits of the departed appear at a distance from the village in the faint moonlight wending their way slowly over the hills, and driving before them the victims they may have slain or the cattle stolen during their lives; the procession disappears over the distant hills amidst the wails of the villagers. Unless the village priests are well fed, it is said this appearance will not take place."[1] Mr. Pettigrew's account differs but slightly from that given above. He says that "The king of Kazairam, what we might call the place of departed spirits, is named Kokto. He is supposed to live in a grand mansion, with sentries guarding all sides and nobody from the upper world dare enter. On the appearance of any spirit from above before the entrance to this mansion, they find him seated inside the door, and his first duty is to notice what kind of following the spirit has. They are of two kinds, one who has been a thief will be seen with the whole livestock which he has stolen trailing behind him, and the other will be seen with a following

"la." Here, at any rate, we have distinctly a belief in a sort of double, a soul to which responsibility is attached which uses the double as its vehicle, but it must be left to further investigation to decide the extent to which the beliefs of the Hill tribes of Manipur resemble those held by their neighbours and congeners, south and east of them.—T. C. H.

[1] *Op. cit.* p. 122.

of all the animals procured by honest hunting. As Tangkhul women do not hunt, it is difficult to find out how Kokto distinguishes the weaker sex. However Kokto judges them all, and, after appropriating for himself all the best cloths brought along, he sentences the thieves to go by the road to the left where there are worms and everything dreadful, and the honest spirit turns off to the right, and follows a road which can only be described as clean. It seems, however, that these good and bad spirits meet again further on near the banks of a river. Here the spirits dispose of the gifts they have brought, some to those who have not yet departed from the village, and to those who have and who are on the other side of the river, the gifts are thrown across to them. After this performance, the difficulty comes in as to how the spirit gets back to the house of the deceased, but the only way out of it seems for the spirit to dodge Kokto and come up to the upper world another way."[1] So far as my memory serves me, there was some room for improvement in the attitude of Tangkhuls towards stray cattle.

At Jessami I was told that the good go to a Heaven above but the bad are consigned to an abode beneath the earth. What exactly constituted goodness and badness, was not explained to me. At Mao there is a belief in a Deity named Pekujikhe with whom the ghost must strive in combat. Verily they take the kingdom of Heaven by violence. For this end two spears are placed in the grave and if the ghost succeeds in wounding the Deity or scores a hit, it is well with him, but if he fail, he is enslaved for ever. Then there is also a Deity named Kechira who sorts out the dead, some according to merit[2] (though in what merit consists my informant knew not), others according to the manner of their death. In their Heaven are many mansions. In one such compartment are herded together those who have died in battle, in another are those who in life have split their ears, being thus literally ear-marked by fate, while in another are the women who have died in childbirth. There is also said to be a nice place inside the earth to which the dead go, but I do not know whether it was

[1] Pettigrew, *op. cit.* p. 38.

[2] Among the Lushais "merit" consists in conspicuous success in the Courts of Love.—*Vide* Shakespear, *op. cit.* p. 379.

a place of lasting abode or a temporary sojourn. At Marām the Heaven lies in the west and it too is divided into many compartments. The Quoirengs believe that the ghosts of the dead are despatched on and as a result of the annual festival of the dead to a Heaven in the north-east. Of the Kabuis we have from Dr. Brown the statement that "After death the souls descend to an underground world where they are met by their ancestors, who introduce them into their new habitation; the life they lead in this underground world is an exact counterpart of what they have led in this—the rich remain rich, the poor, poor."[1] Heaven is in fact regarded down to the minutest details as an exact replica of this "material" world. Among the Marrings the good dead go up above, while the bad go below to a place inside the earth. Those who have died in an extraordinary manner flit about between Heaven and earth.

It is curious to note that as a matter of coincidence the tribes which claim to have sprung from the earth place their Heaven inside the earth. Marām is said to have had its origin from immigrants from the west and their Heaven is in the west. The Quoirengs say that they came from the north-east where they place their Heaven.

Mr. Pettigrew wonders how Koktho, the Lord of the Tangkhul Heaven, distinguished the weaker sex. Is there a back door, for ladies only? How would a poor old Nāga woman fare in combat with the stout Guardian of the Mao Heaven, seeing that all she has to fight with are a digging stick and some cooking pots, part worn? As I read Colonel Shakespear's account of the Lushai beliefs, much the same difficulty occurs there, since Pupaola always shoots at women whoever they may be.[2] There seems to be some hope for them, since in an earlier account[3] I find that Colonel Shakespear allows women to be taken by their husbands to Piel-rāl—the comfortable after world.

It is evident that the dead are sorted out by two methods which are not really inconsistent. In the first place there is a selection according to the life lived in this world, where the

[1] *Op. cit.* p. 107.
[2] Shakespear, *J.R.A.I.*, p. 379.
[3] *Journal of the Society of Arts*, XLIII, 1895, p. 180.

"good" so-called go to one place and the "bad" to another. Then the dead are sorted out according to the manner of the death they die. The common belief with respect to persons who meet with a violent or an extraordinary[1] death is that were they to be buried in the ordinary place, their fate would overtake others.[2] Like follows like, and there is not a Nāga who does not believe that there is a great deal of truth in the saying that the greatest of all misfortunes is always followed by one still greater. "Death is a phenomenon which touches the communal life very deeply. Apart from all considerations of private grief, the mere occurrence of death puts the tribal nerves on the stretch. The explanation of this strange discrimination between the various kinds of death is to be found in the psychological attitude of these people towards all such social phenomena. In some of the cases of death the proximate or mechanical cause of death is clear . . . . Behind these interpretations . . . . which are specifically referable to animistic concepts, there is in all these cases and in all such 'extra natural' phenomena a vague sense of terror which gives rise to the thought that what has happened is due to somebody's default. Sin, sickness and death are not for them isolated, unconnected phenomena. Sin in their view consists primarily of breaches both by accident and by intent of the unwritten laws of society. What gives validity to these unwritten laws is the vague fear that something may happen if they are broken. Something, this terrible death of a tribesman, has happened. Why did it happen? What more logical than the answer that it happened because a sin has been committed? . . . Thus they come to the belief that the occurrence of any of these 'extra natural' cases of death is good evidence of sin either in the sense of a breach of some precept of the communal law, the punishment for which follows, automatically, quasi-mechanically, without postulating the intermediary agency of spirits, or, in

[1] As Marett says, "there is plenty of proof that the savage is extremely unwilling to recognise the fact of natural death." (*Threshold of Religion*, p. 26.) The truth is that in these cases of "extraordinary" death, as we call them, the mechanical cause is generally patent and intelligible to them. The cause of death is not so patent, not so intelligible, in cases of "ordinary" death. Hence the dead in the first category are treated as dead, recognised as severed from the community, without delay.—T. C. H.

[2] *Cf.* Soppitt, *Kachcha Nāgas*, p. 6.

some cases, of an offence against some power. If any such case occurs, some Nāga tribes[1] destroy the house and property of the deceased and drive the survivors into the jungle. This is in part due to blind terror, in part to the desire to banish from their midst all possible sources of danger, and in part to the hope of propitiating the power whose might has thus been manifested to them."[2]

Among the Tangkhuls Dr. Brown found the belief that "in the future state they live and die, men six times and women five times: after this they are turned into clouds." At Jessami and at Mao I was assured that only the "good" were reborn, and that thieves were turned into animals. Those who were killed by animals were never reborn. Of the Kabuis Dr. Brown states that "after living their lives over again they return to the upper world and are born, live, and die unconscious of their former state; the bad, however, are annihilated."[3] Among the Marrings, the reward of a virtuous life is immediate, since "after death the good are born again at once into this world."[4] I was often assured that it was evident that people were reborn since there were children in the village who were the exact image of some deceased relation. This belief may have some connection with the custom of naming children after deceased relations.

GENNA.

The term "genna" means simply forbidden or prohibited.[5] It is therefore applied in its primary sense to the mass of prohibitions, permanent and temporary, periodic and occasional, which form so important a part of the tribal law of these societies. All the rites and festivals observed by social units in this area are characterised by a prohibition of the normal relations with other social units, so that the

[1] *A.C.R.* p. 249. See also *supra* as to Kabuis, p. 147.
[2] *Archiv für Religions-wissenschaft*, xii. p. 451.
[3] *Op. cit.* p. 107.
[4] Brown, *op. cit.* p. 127.
[5] *A.C.R.* p. 249. "The word genna is used in two ways: (1) it may mean practically a holiday—*i.e.* a man will say, 'My village is doing genna to-day,' by which he means that, owing either to the occurrence of a village festival or some such unusual occurrence . . . his people are observing a holiday; (2) *genna* means anything forbidden."

term has come to be applied to all occasions and festivals at and by which the social unit concerned consolidates and concentrates itself. It is not a new discovery. Colonel McCulloch remarked of the Kabuis that "A whole village or individual members of it are often 'Neina' or under prohibition. Sometimes this state of things lasts a day, sometimes several. The 'Neina' may be against the entrance of strangers, or the exit of members or of both, or, allowing the entrance of strangers, disallow their going into houses, etc. Peculiar circumstances also induce prohibitions in food and drink, but to attempt describing them would be to pretend to more knowledge of minutiæ than I possess."[1] So too Dr. Brown observed that "There is one curious custom which has a religious significance and which is common not only to all the hill tribes, but also to the half Hindooised Loee population of the Munnipore valley: this is 'Namoongba' or a periodical closing of individual villages. This custom does not take place with any regularity, and its object is some kind of worship. One of the occasions is just before the jungle which has been cut down on their jhooms is fired: this lasts two days, and the villagers are said to fast during that period: the village remains shut up during the two days, and no one is allowed either entry or exit, and it is also affirmed that anyone attempting to force an entrance during this period would be liable to be killed. On other occasions the proceedings are of a joyous nature and may take place after a successful hunt, a warlike expedition, a successful harvest, or other striking event: on these occasions feasting and drinking is the order of the day."[2]

I hope to set forth the facts which I have collected so as to show (1) the social units affected, thus giving to social structure its due prominence,[3] (2) the occurrences which bring these customs into play, (3) the activities and relations which are so forbidden, and (4) as far as possible the nature of the sanctions which give validity to these customs. It may be that this method involves some repetition, but, as I think, no more than is needed to display the ideas which inspire these customs.

[1] *Op. cit.* p. 53. [2] *Op. cit.* pp. 99 and 100.

[3] Davis, *A.C.R. loc. cit.* "Gennas sometimes affect whole villages, sometimes only chiefs or single households."

The real value of any social phenomenon cannot be estimated accurately by isolating methods but is largely determined by its relation to other social phenomena with which it forms part of an organic whole.

TRIBAL GENNAS.

There is so little tribal unity that it is difficult to assert positively that there are tribal gennas, customs affecting individuals as members of a tribe or homogeneous group of villages. Yet in the special prohibitions which deny pork to the Marām Nāgas and forbid the Tangkhuls to keep or eat goats, there is something of the nature of a tribal genna. So far as I could learn, the penalty attaching to a breach of either of these regulations falls rather on the actual offender, though it might be fairly described as a social sanction because there is always the fear of some calamity happening in their midst as the result of disregard of any one of these ordinances.

VILLAGE GENNAS.

The village is an economic unit, so that all the ritual observed for the cultivation of the staple, rice, necessitates the expenditure of communal energy in the form of village gennas. Rain compelling ceremonies are naturally part of the cultivation ritual. Their economic life is rigidly and sharply divided into two periods, one for agriculture and the other for hunting, fishing and other such subsidiary industries, so that there is again an economic basis for the gennas which are intended to promote good hunting. In the next place the appearance of epidemic sickness occasions a genna, whose purpose is obviously prophylactic. The occurrence of mysterious "extra natural" cases of death also necessitates a village genna for the purpose of separating the living as soon as possible from the dangerous dead. Except at Mao and its allied villages it is usual to hold an annual rite for the purpose of laying finally to rest the ghosts of those who have died within the year. At Mao any and every case of death is followed by a village genna. Events such as earthquakes, eclipses, probably also the appearance of a comet (though of this I have no personal knowledge[1]), are of so serious

[1] See Owen, *Notes on the Nāgas*, p. 25.

a portent as to require the community to meet the danger which they threaten or betoken by an effort of all its energy. If a village be burnt, there is a genna against all ordinary work for a short period. In some cases village gennas are caused by what are otherwise regarded as domestic events, such as sickness, when a man can afford the luxury of a village genna, and in other cases they are caused by the deliberate intentional acts of individuals, as when a man erects a stone monument. There are village gennas connected with the first fruits and with the first death in the year of any domestic animal. These are very typical of the fear of "la première fois."[1] Some village gennas are therefore of periodic occurrence while others are held only after the occurrence of some abnormal event. The latter are as much part and parcel of the village customary law as are the former.

At all these village gennas the ordinary routine of life is profoundly modified if not broken off altogether. There are special gennas imposed on these occasions which require abstinence from certain kinds of food. The duration of these gennas varies considerably, and some undoubtedly are of much less consequence than others. The ill effects of an interruption of a village genna are sometimes irremediable, while in other cases a repetition of the genna is adequate to prevent all harmful consequences.[2] At all the village gennas the gates are shut when the genna begins so that the stranger that is within the gates may not go forth and the friend that is without must stay outside. At some stage in all the village gennas husband and wife cook and eat apart and the unmarried of both sexes are rigorously forbidden food cooked by the other. Thus the society concentrates itself. The male element is sharply separated from the female element of society, thus effecting a resolution of society into its components. Among all these tribes from the day of the first crop genna to the final harvest home all other forms of industry and activity are forbidden. All hunting, fishing, tree and grass-cutting, all weaving, pot making, salt working, games of all kinds, bugling, dancing, all trades are strictly forbidden—are "genna" lest the grain in

1 Van Gennep, *Rites de Passage*, p. 249 *et seq.*

2 *Cf.* Soppitt, *op. cit.* p. 10.

the ear be lost. Some of these prohibitions exert—indirectly—a beneficial effect. The game has a close time which it sorely needs, for these sportsmen spare not the does. But after all necessity knows no law. I met a Mao villager once in the Sena Kaithel in Imphāl at a time when by rights he ought to have been at home minding his fields. I taxed him with disregard of his genna rules but he told me that once he got past the Marām hills, fourteen miles from his village, he was free of all these restrictions upon his commercial energy. The hinterland of Mao morality was limited to the boundaries of its neighbour and the sanctions of the crop gennas ceased to operate for him when he got round the corner out of sight.

Crop Gennas.

Every stage of the rice cultivation is marked by a village genna the duration of which varies.[1] At the end of March or the beginning of April the paddy is sown and the genna among the Tangkhuls lasts for five days. A month later they hold a genna for the prosperity of the rice before it is transplanted, and at this genna they celebrate the first rope-pulling festival, when the women and girls have a tug of war against the men and boys in order to take the omens for the future of the crops. This is followed by considerable license.[2] In some cases the "thauri chingba" or rope-pulling, takes place at the earlier genna when the rice is sown. In some villages, as at Sirohi, the khullākpa inaugurates the transplanting genna by sacrificing a fowl more to take the omens than to perform a sacrifice, although the connection between the slaughter of an animal for sacrifice and for omens is very close. When the transplantation is successfully completed, again a genna is held lasting for two days as does the previous one. Similarly both the beginning and completion of the harvest are marked by gennas lasting two days and there is also a repetition of the rope-pulling ceremony with its attendant license before the first fruits are cut by the hand of the khullākpa.[3] At Phadang, one of the cloth-weaving

[1] Cf. *U.B.G.* Vol. I, Part I, p. 425, where the Kachin and Chingpaw customs, which are very similar to those of the Nāgas, are fully described.
[2] *Cf.* Frazer, *History of the Kingship*, p. 268.
[3] *Cf.* Frazer, *Golden Bough*, Vol. II, p. 460.

villages, I learnt that there was a village genna to institute the planting of the ginger, which is used in the preparation of zu. I have enumerated five crop gennas (as practised by the Tangkhuls), but I find that as a rule four only are observed, the one generally omitted being that marking the end of the transplantation.

Rain compelling ceremonies are necessitated by the dependence of the rice crop (even in the best terraced fields) upon a seasonable and equable distribution of rain, and at the Tangkhul village genna for this purpose the khullākpa kills a pig and eleven rice cakes are made. Six men and five women with the khullākpa go outside the village where the sacrifices are duly offered up to the deity whom I believe to be Phiraoi the wife of Kamyou. At Chingai I found that in addition to this form of rain-compelling ceremony they practised the following rite. The khullākpa takes a water-worn pebble and wraps it in weeds from the river bed and, killing a fowl, offers it to the deity.

In the Mao group inclusive of Jessami we find four crop gennas usually observed which are called at Jessami, (1) Mongunge, (2) Killache kiche, (3) Aghrume, (4) Takkone. They last for five days each at Jessami, while at Liyai the first takes ten days, the transplantation genna one day, the genna marking the beginning of the harvest four days and the final genna of the harvest home occupies ten days. At Mao I gathered interesting information regarding the special food prohibitions associated with these crop gennas. At the genna for sowing the rice, pigs are forbidden, salt is tabu at the transplantation genna and dogs are not to be eaten at the two last gennas. At Mao I learnt that they worshipped the Sun as a good deity and sacrificed a white cock to him. The genna for this lasts for one day only.

In most of the villages I learnt that a sacrifice of zu was offered at the village gate by the khullākpa as a rain-compelling ceremony, but at Liyai the ceremony is more complicated. The khullākpa takes a brand from the fire, puts it on the grave of a man who has died of burns, extinguishes it with water, and then prays for rain. The people of Mayang Khong though remote from Mao are said to be linguistically connected with them and when rain is needed dip their large wicker shields in the pond near the village and sprinkle the water on the fields. A hen and some eggs are sacrificed and I noted at the time that this rite was performed, not by the khullākpa, but by an elder.

If duration of time be any test of importance, in the Mao group we have a village genna of much importance for the purpose of securing an abundance of game in the hunting season which cannot commence till the crops are safely stored. This genna takes place at a date which in other village calendars is that of the Mangla Thā for which it may be a substitute or with which it may have been fused.[1]

At Marām we have six gennas for the crops and one for the game. The two additional crop gennas are held one when the rice begins to show through the ground, before transplantation, and the second in connection with the growth of the ginger root. Their form of rain ceremony is to descend to the river, the Barāk, and there to fill vessels (bamboo chungas) with water, which they empty over their fields and pray for rain.

The Quoirengs have only four crop gennas, but the exact occasions of these four seem to vary. In one village which had no terraced fields, the first genna was held when they were ready to start felling the jungle for the jhums, the second when the jungle was all ready to be fired, the third when the rice was to be sown, and the last when the rice was about to be harvested. For a rain compelling rite they drown a pig in a pond or in the nearest river and ask for rain. At Lemta they told me that they took an eel from the river and cut it into small pieces, which they threw about on the top of the irrigation cuts. The sun and moon are worshipped here, but are malevolent deities. A pig is killed and omens are taken from its entrails. Apparently this rite is performed twice a year, and is associated with a village genna.

Colonel McCulloch[2] mentions a number of gennas among the Kabuis which he describes as festivals, and as connected with the crops, "The Reengnai, in or about January, which lasts for three days. In one day during this festival the men and women fetch separately the water for their own

[1] See above, p. 120. [2] *Op. cit.* pp. 52 and 53.

use. The men having killed pigs, take a portion for themselves and give a portion to the women, and having cooked them separately they eat them separately, the men in the house of the head of the family, the women each in her own house. An effigy of a man made of a plantain is hung on a tree, and at it they throw pointed bamboos or sticks. Should the javelin strike it in the head, the thrower, it is said, will kill an enemy,[1] but if it lodges in the belly the thrower is to be blessed with plenty of food.[2] . . . On the termination of the Reengnai they go through the ceremony of taking the omens in regard to their place of cultivation, but this seems to have descended to them merely as a ceremonial relic of former times, for the circle of cultivation is never broken, let the omens be what they may. . . . These festivals over (those for ear-piercing and the omen taking for the year), the cutting of the jungle for cultivation is commenced, which, when finished, is crowned with the festival of 'Oodooee yung,' or drinking the juice of ginger. . . . One night of the month of August and one of September they dedicate to feasting." Dr. Brown[3] adds the remark that "the reason for the males and females bringing water separately during this festival (Reengnai) is to begin with this ceremony the making of new liquor and the separate eating and cooking of the sexes to be a mark of respect to their gods. After the festival of the 'Oodooee yung,' or 'Mahlong,' as it is also called, when the cutting down of the jungle on the jhooms is finished, a curious ceremony takes place. All the people bathe after the work is completed, and, in addition, their agricultural implements are also dipped in a running stream as they are supposed to be exhausted by their labours; thus refreshed, the tools are hung up in their houses until again required for use."[4] According to my information we have among the Kabuis at least five, if not six, crop gennas, the first of which occurs before the jungle is cut, and is named Faidoutingan, and lasts for one day. A

[1] The Quoirengs do this also, but with them this ceremony is performed just before the crops are cut, and must be performed outside the village gate. —T. C. H.

[2] *Vide supra*, "Headhunting," p. 119.

[3] *Op. cit.* pp. 108 and 109.

[4] *Cf.* Pettigrew, *op. cit.* p. 41.

genna named Taisoipa, lasting for two days, at which no stranger may be present, is held before sowing. Strangers are also excluded from the Phuphoi genna, which happens when the crop is about a foot out of the ground. Private individuals of more than usual piety or plenty celebrate a private genna, named Latang-mai, and pluck an ear of paddy which they bring to their house. Before cutting the paddy there is a village genna named Nakonna, lasting for one day, at which a pig is killed and distributed. The last genna of all is named Pum-thummai, which lasts for one day, and celebrates the end of the harvest. The cultivation omens are taken by two elders who wash their bodies very carefully and put on new clothes that day. They must not sleep with their wives the night before the ceremony. Overnight a bamboo (umu) is split lengthwise and laid ready. They sit opposite each other holding a portion of the bamboo in either hand. If the bamboos press together the cultivation will not be prosperous in the direction proposed. If the bamboos turn outwards, the fields will be good. But as Colonel McCulloch observed, the rotation of cultivation is fixed and known beforehand.

Kabuis employ sacrifice as a means of bringing rain, and should this fail, it is necessary for the men to come out of their houses at the dead of night and then to bestride the roofs, and, stripping themselves of all their garments, to use the most obscene language to one another.

The Chirus have six crop festivals, one of which, that before the crops are cut, is marked by a rope-pulling ceremony of the same nature as that observed among the Tangkhuls. In order to get rain, they catch a crab in a neighbouring river, put it in a pot with water, having fastened a thread to one of its claws, and then keep on lifting it out and letting it fall back into the pot.

The Marrings, according to my notes, seem to have only one crop genna, that before the rice is sown, but I may be mistaken.

I may here describe a rain puja which I saw in course of performance in a small Kōm village. A fish was cut up on the embankment of the village weir and another fish hung up at the village gate, and all the men called upon the sky to give them rain. The maibas meanwhile smeared mud on small pieces of plank, which they dragged about the village.

Sickness Gennas.

Village gennas are caused by the advent or near approach of epidemic sickness, and are prophylactic measures rather than part of a cure. At Jessami one of the regular village gennas has for its purpose the prevention of sickness throughout the year. A party of young men is sent out to catch a bird, and if they are so fortunate as to bring back to the village a fine big bird such as a toucan (or hornbill), it is an unerring omen that there will be no sickness in the coming year. This genna lasts for eight days. The Kabuis observe a genna in January in order to protect themselves specially from hurt by bamboos. It lasts for one day, and on it the young men are forbidden to drink outside their houses.

In the Mao group either a cock is killed, as at Liyai and Maikel, or let go outside the village by the khullākpa who orders the genna. The Quoirengs sacrifice a goat or a cock at the village gate, and entreat the deity not to enter. The Kabuis kill either a fowl or a dog for this purpose, but on occasions when a python is killed, either a fowl or a pig or a goat may be sacrificed, but never a dog. The python[1] is closely associated with sickness, and merely to see one is most unfortunate, while if they see it and kill it, some, if not all, the trouble may be avoided by a village genna which lasts for three days. All the able-bodied men are gathered at the village gate, and all together shout out "we are all here!" Then the genna begins as the dead python is dragged inside.

Death Gennas.

The village gennas which are observed in connection with cases of death, fall into two classes, the first being gennas of regular occurrence as the mangla thā, a genna which seems to contain the germ of some kind of ancestor worship, though celebrated only for those of the recent dead whose manner of death does not argue them to have sinned and to be excluded from the privilege of rebirth,[2] and the second being

[1] See above, p. 137. [2] See above, p. 163.

gennas which are necessitated by the deaths of individual members of the village. I may remark that with the notable exception of the Mao group where it is customary to hold a village genna on each occasion a villager dies, whatever the immediate cause of his death, it is not usual to have a village genna when the cause of death is what we should call regular and without mystery. A village genna for the death of an individual villager is held when the death is "extra natural." In both cases the idea is the same, to sever the living from the dead. At the annual festival they restore to the living those of their members who have been in jeopardy of the contagion of death. The dead from whom they then separate themselves are regarded as in a state of existence from which it is possible they may return to life.[1] All seek to have done with the evil dead as soon as possible. They are denied rebirth. They are indeed dead. The wages of their sin is death. The society sets itself free at once, by an exertion of communal energy, from the taint of sin. It reacts violently in opposition to the calamity, in order to restore the equilibrium of life. "Here, then, is a twofold seed of religion—fear that prompts the immediate sepulture of the dead whose manner of death argues them to have sinned, while human affection retains its hold on the ghost of the good."[2] Yet there may be in this rite a desire to placate the ghost, almost to worship it, as well as to protect themselves against its wrathful malice. In an impressive passage, Hartland[3] remarks that "superstitions like those concerning ghosts in the West and *bhuts* in the East exhibit souls disembodied by other than a natural death as vindictive and often extremely dangerous beings who must be pacified and exorcised or even worshipped. The cult of executed criminals in . . . is therefore not an isolated example of the vagaries of human emotion. It is merely one of the many manifestations of the shock given to the collective mentality of any society by the death of a member. That shock is always deeper and more terrible where the severance from life is by violence . . . where it is imposed by arms or more

[1] See above, p. 160 *et seq.*
[2] *Archiv für Religions-wissenschaft*, XII, p. 456.
[3] *Folklore*, XXI, p. 178.

mysterious terrors . . . . then the shock and the terror reach their height, the whole sympathy of society goes out towards the victim and he is surrounded by a halo of more than common radiance."

Other Village Gennas.

A genna takes place in a village whose warriors have returned home with heads [1] taken in a foray. The Tangkhuls present the heads to the heap of stones in the village which is of peculiar sanctity as the abode of a deity or laipham. At Maikel we have the warstone, on which no woman might look, to which the heads were shown outside the village as in it, and in the Mao group it is not permitted to bring the heads inside the village. In all these cases there is a village genna and women are not allowed to have any commerce with the warriors for three days after their return. On one occasion, a woman, the wife of the headman, who was quite ignorant of the fact that her husband was returning with the party of warriors to lay the heads before the war-stone, spoke to him. He was under the same genna disability as the warriors and I was told that when she had learnt the awful thing she had done, she sickened and died.[2]

When an earthquake or an eclipse of the sun or moon occurs, the whole village is genna as a rule for one day only. These events are attributed to supernatural activity, in the first case, of a distinct deity, the deaf god who forgets whether men are alive or not, and, in the latter case, of the faithful dog, to recover the potent medicine which the sun or moon has stolen. We have a village genna when, as among the Quoirengs, the annual worship of the sun and moon takes place. A pig is sacrificed to them and from the entrails omens are taken for the coming year.

If a village is burnt, the whole village is genna, sometimes for three days, before any steps are taken to rebuild the houses.

Among the Kabuis, as was observed by McCulloch,[3] there is an annual village genna of three days "in which the ears of the children born after the last festival of this nature are pierced. This festival loses its interest for those who have frequently

[1] See above, sections on Headhunting and settlement of disputes.
[2] *Cf.* Jevon's *Plutarch's Romane Questions*, p. lxxvii. [3] *Op. cit.* p. 53.

participated in it and is looked forward to chiefly by those to whom it is new." I also find that there is an annual genna for the day when the children's hair is cut for the first time among the Quoirengs, who also have a genna for unmarried boys and girls, the exact nature of which I do not know.[1] As a rule these occurrences among other tribes occasion merely domestic gennas.

Another genna, which as I found it, clearly indicated a communal origin, was the case of the woman at Powi who came from a cloth weaving village and was prohibited by the elders of her husband's village from practising her industry on the ground that weaving was genna to them. I asked the headman why they forbade the woman to weave cloths and he told me they all feared something terrible would happen to them if they allowed her to weave cloths.

Village gennas are caused by the action of individual members of the village, as, for instance, by those who propose to erect a memorial stone. Among the Marrings, if a man desires to whitewash the front wall of his house, he must incur the expenditure of six mithan[2] which are consumed by the villagers at a feast. So again when investigating the system of nomenclature in vogue among the Marrings I found that, as Dr. Brown says,[3] "Other names may afterwards be given, but as the giving of a second name involves a large expenditure in the shape of a feast to the village and presents, the privilege is not often taken advantage of." After some trouble I was told, not by a Marring, but by a Manipuri who was well acquainted with them, that in addition to the formal names (see section above, Naming) they each possessed a "private" name and that if any man allowed this to be mentioned in public he had to provide the wherewithal for a village genna.[4] Among the Koms a village genna takes place if a kid is born still.

The Kàbuis have a village genna occasioned by the first death of an animal in the village or if an animal is killed by a tiger. Omens are then taken by dreams, and if the omens are good, the genna is over and done with in one day, lasting, however, for two days if the omens are bad.

[1] *Vide supra*, p. 77.
[2] McCulloch, *op. cit.* p. 66.
[3] *Op. cit.* p. 126.
[4] See above, p. 144.

Clan Gennas.

The clan is important, sociologically, as the marriage unit for marriage of members of the same clan is strictly forbidden. Were this rule to be broken, some dreadful calamity beyond description would happen to the village. The erring couple would be driven forth, practically abandoned to whatever may happen to them.

As a rule, to which the leaguer of Mao is an exception, an ordinary case of death necessitates a clan genna lasting until the body is placed in the grave.

Among the Tangkhuls the khullākpa's clan is generally forbidden to eat dog. Among the Marrings and at Aimol the khullākpa's clan is forbidden to touch goat and tiger's meat respectively.

At Maikel, while a rich man when sick would have and pay for a village genna, a poor man would only have a clan genna, a much less expensive remedy.

The paucity of clan gennas is all the more remarkable since the clan is the basis of their social structure in respect of marriage.

Household Gennas.

Household gennas are occasioned by events such as the birth of children, the birth of domesticated animals in the house, the first occasion of haircutting and ear-piercing, naming of children and finally the death of domesticated animals in the house. They affect all those who are normally inmates of the house and any others who are temporarily in the house, such as women acting as midwives. Their duration varies not only from tribe to tribe but from village to village.

Among the Tangkhuls the husband may not go out of the village or do any work after the birth of a child for six days if the child be a boy or for five days when the child is a girl.[1] So also strangers are forbidden to enter his house during this period lest harm should come to the child. If a woman comes in to act as midwife, she too is genna. At Sandang one of the cloth-weaving villages the period of restriction lasts for one day only and we have the interesting information that the father may not touch any one for fear of harm coming to the newly

[1] Cf. *Plutarch's Romane Questions*, No. 102.

born infant.[1] At the village of Toloi the prohibition lasts for ten days and it is expressly stated that the mother may go out of the house the day after the child is born, but the father stays inside the whole time. Apparently the man may go to the front of the house, but not into any one else's house, and as the area of the house and its noontide shadow is held to be the domain of the house spirit, we may say that he must remain within the limits of the power of the deity who is *ex-officio* most concerned with their domestic life. The head of the household is the person who performs the rites incidental to the worship of the house spirit and the sacrifice of a fowl which is part of the genna is made by him. Now the birth genna includes the ceremony of naming the child which takes place on the last day of the birth genna and for the purposes of which the sacrifice of a fowl is necessary as the name is determined by omens. Zu is given to the women of the village.

In the Mao group both parents are genna and at Jessami this lasts five days, while at Laiyi Liyai and Maikel it lasts for fifteen days at least in the case of all except the eldest child, when it is, or was, prolonged to thirty days. At Mao the genna for the first child is ten days and for the others five days.

A cock is sacrificed for a boy and a hen for a girl, but whether the taking of omens is the main or a secondary purpose is not clear.

At Marām they say that at one time this genna lasted for one month but is now observed for ten days only, during which neither parent may touch any other person nor may the woman eat any food except fish and salt. A fowl is sacrificed on the day of birth, but I do not know who eats it. At Uilong the woman goes out at the end of the genna to bathe accompanied by a village boy who must not have attained a marriageable age, and whose presence is necessary in case any evil spirit meet the woman.

At Liyang a village which I know is not a pure Quoireng village, the birth genna lasts for one month, during which the only food permitted to the parents is fish and fowl, meat of any other kind being most strictly forbidden. The same prohibition

[1] *Cf.* Frazer, *Totemism and Exogamy*, Vol. IV, p. 254. Tylor, *Early History of Mankind*, p. 292.

of meat is found among the Quoirengs who, with the exception of the village of Taron, keep the birth genna for a month. At Lemta and Maolong I was told that the fowl which is killed on the birth of a child may not be eaten by the father, who, at Taron, is kept without any food that day. The flesh of fowls is not regarded as meat. The Kabuis appear to have a birth genna for the first child and do not allow the father to eat, drink, or smoke that day. The Koms prolong the genna to one month for the birth of a son and for the birth of a daughter regard five days as sufficient for the father, who may do no work during the genna, and may not go far from the village, while exacting a month from the mother. The Chirus are genna for one month, though later information points to ten days as the period, and offer two jars of zu and two fowls to the house spirit. Some villages regard five days as long enough. If the navel cord and after-birth are buried by a person other than the father, that person shares the genna. Either a fowl or a pig or a fish are sacrificed to the house spirit.

The Marrings also require a month's genna for the birth of a child, and sacrifice a fowl to the house spirit immediately the child is born. At the end of the genna there is a feast, that is, one or more fowls are killed, which are eaten by the men of the father's clan, each of whom, on entering the house, pours a drop or two of zu inside the threshold of the house, as an offering to the house spirit.

Naming ceremonies either form part of or conclude the birth genna, and are an essential feature of this domestic genna. We may note that among the Quoirengs the fowl that is sacrificed is eaten by the youngsters and women, but not by the father.

Among the Tangkhuls there does not seem to be any fixed time for ear-piercing, but it occasions a genna. The animal sacrificed varies according to the wealth of the parents. A rich man may kill a buffalo and a poor man a fowl. At Kalhang a hen is the usual offering. In most villages this genna lasts for one day, but at Kharasom it needs six days when a son is the victim and five for a girl.

There is more variety among the Mao Nagas, for at Jessami the rite takes place three months after the birth of the child

N 2

and lasts for one day only, while at Liyai it takes place on the last day of the birth genna, and at Laiyi on the fifth day after the child is born, that is on the same day as the naming. At Liyai the parents may not eat salt on the day of the genna. At Mao and Maikel the ceremony is performed two months after birth, on the last day of the moon, for all other days are genna or forbidden. Both oil and pulse are forbidden to the parents, for serious illness would come to the child if they partook of these dainties. They are also forbidden marital intercourse on the night preceding this genna.

At Maikel the hair of the child is cut one month after birth, and a cock is killed for a boy and a hen for a girl.

At Marām the hair is cut on the ninth day after birth and on the following day the ears are pierced, and on these days salt only may be eaten with the rice consumed by the parents.

Among the Quoirengs the ear-piercing is performed in the cold weather and seems to take place during the Mangla thā, though in one village I was told that it was done five days after birth. The hair-cutting here requires a village genna.

The Koms cut the hair of the children on the day of the name genna, while the Chirus postpone both it and ear-piercing for two months. The Marrings again delay the ear-piercing for perhaps as long as three years, but cut the hair on the last day of the birth genna.

We have a set of gennas occurring as between married persons, by which all marital intercourse within the house is prohibited for the first two or three days of their married life. This prohibition does not apply to cases where a widow remarries.

The birth and death of domestic animals within the house occasion gennas, which last, as a rule, for a single day. At Mayang Khong there is an elaborate scale for birth gennas. When a cow calves, the genna lasts for five days; when a sow litters, three days' genna is necessary; while when a bitch has pups, or a cat has kittens, two days are ample. A hen hatching out a brood of chickens brings on a genna of one day. The only animal that is buried is the cat, which, at Mao, is buried in a cloth by old women. The Quoirengs seem to observe no gennas in respect of domestic animals except for goats.

Gennas on Individuals.

All these tribes impose a number of food gennas upon the khullākpas and attach special importance to them. Thus at Mao, where the khullākpa has relations with the six villages composing the group as well as with other villages which are tributary to him, he may not eat in a strange house or village. The sanction directly attached to these gennas is distinctly of a social nature, for they believe that if he ate fowl his villagers would suffer from blindness; if he ate pork, some would be insane; while bad luck would attend their hunting parties if he ate dog. The penalty that would follow the consumption by him of buffalo would be the loss of their intelligence. The animals forbidden to him and to his wife—who bears a double burden, that of her sex and that entailed by her relations with so important a person—are all domesticated animals, and used in ritual for purposes of sacrifice. He must not use abusive language to anyone, whatever the provocation, nor must he lay an imprecation on anyone.[1] Good food and bad language are forbidden to him.

"There are many prohibitions in regard to the food, animal and vegetable, the chief should eat, and the Murams say the chief's post must be a very uncomfortable one."[2] I found that dog, fowl, pān and tomatoes were forbidden to him and to his wife.

We may observe here that in disputes between near relations oaths are strictly forbidden. Khullākpas are entitled, perhaps required, to wear special cloths, the use of which is forbidden to all others except those who erect a stone monument. Before setting forth to select a stone, the household of the "lung-chingba" are not allowed any food except zu and ginger. Marital intercourse is strictly prohibited the night immediately preceding the day on which they choose the stone. The man then cuts a wedge from the stone and dreams on it, still abstaining from all food and marital intercourse. Once he has settled on the stone, all rice and meat are genna to him up to the day when the villagers drag the stone into the village. From that day forward he may not eat fowl and for a year intercourse with his wife is prohibited.

[1] Cf. *Plutarch's Romane Questions*, No. 44. [2] McCulloch, *op. cit.* p. 70.

So too it is genna to kill an animal he may meet while a stone is being brought in or while he is choosing it. On the day the stone is brought inside the village, the villagers may not use their drinking cups, but have to drink from leaves. The lungchingbas are entitled to wear the same cloths as the khullākpa, and the fortune of the family is bound up with the stone. A man who owns a drinking horn, a rare and treasured possession, must lay it aside as genna for six months after the death of his father.

Food Gennas.

Here, as elsewhere among the hills,[1] milk is never drunk, and the reason alleged is that to drink milk would be to put one's self on the level with an animal. I have also found that they refuse to sell milk to those who drink it.

No Tangkhul is permitted to eat the flesh of the goat. Some villages say that there was once a kid born with a pure white head and the appearance of this prodigy was the occasion of a warning to the tribe that if they ever ate of the flesh of the goat they would die a mysterious death. Others assert that they would go prematurely gray, and die mad if they partook of it. Others again say that a horrible death from boils carries off those who touch it, while quite the mildest story is that men who keep goats suffer from terrible headaches. Underlying all these stories there is the idea that there is something human about the animal, something uncanny. Perhaps this idea originates in the "capricious" antics of the beast which are associated with oracular methods elsewhere. As regards dog, only a few individuals, and in rare cases separate sections of the villages, are forbidden to eat the flesh of dog. In no village is the khullākpa allowed to touch it, while the prohibition extends in some villages to the whole of the khullākpa's clan. In some villages, such as those in which the cloth-weaving industry is specially carried on, unmarried girls are not permitted to eat dog or to eat the flesh of any male animal. A pregnant woman is not allowed to eat bear's flesh or the flesh of any animal that has died a natural death. The husband and father is not allowed to partake of the flesh

[1] Gurdon, *The Khasis*, p. 51.

of the fowl that he kills as a sacrifice when a child is born to him. Chillies are forbidden to people when ill.[1]

At Mao oil and pulse are forbidden to the parents of a newborn child when making ready for the ear-piercing genna. No special animal is forbidden to the whole group, but special kinds of food are forbidden during the progress of the village gennas for promoting the prosperity of the crops or for securing good hunting. On the occasion of the first crop genna, pigs are forbidden. When the rice is transplanted, dogs and salt are fordidden, while at the genna which follows the harvest home, dog is genna. If the whole group is genna for epidemic sickness, dog is not permitted to them. The gennaburas or khullākpas of the Mao and Māram groups and their wives are under many disabilities in regard to their food.[2] So, too, are persons who have erected a stone. Warriors, both before and after a raid, are not permitted food cooked by women. Pregnant women are forbidden bear's flesh and the wives of khullākpas, as at Jessami, which has a separate khullākpa owing to its distance from Mao, at Mao and at Maikel are under the same disabilities as their husbands.

In the Marām group we have the general prohibition of pork, which is associated with the story of the foundation of the village.[3] As a curious instance of the special survival of this prohibition in a village, Mayang Khong, which is some distance away from Marām, we find that only women are there liable to this disability. Bear's flesh, here also, is forbidden to pregnant women who may not eat the flesh of any animal that has died a natural death.

Among the Kabuis we find similar prohibitions. Thus women may not eat goat. Unmarried girls may not eat dog, and pregnant women should not partake of the flesh of any animal that has died with young. Old people may, but young persons may not, eat the flesh of a cat. I cannot find any general prohibition except as regards the women.

The Quoirengs have no general prohibition, but pregnant women are forbidden to eat bear's flesh or the flesh of any animal

[1] A diet of rice cakes is prescribed by custom. Some people declare that the flesh of crows is excellent for sick children, and I have often been asked to shoot them for this purpose.—T. C. H.

[2] See p. 181 above.

[3] See p. 13 above.

that has been killed by a tiger or has died a natural death. Young unmarried girls are not allowed to eat the flesh of male goats, and in one village which is not far from the influence of Marām, women are not allowed to eat pork. Those whose parents, or one of them, have died from snake-bite are not allowed to touch the flesh of a snake. Those who have killed a dog or goat as a sacrifice are not allowed to partake of it, and as regards the fowl that is killed on the birth of a child, while the mother may, the father may not, eat it.

No Marring eats dogs or cats, while the members of the clan to which the khullākpa belongs may not eat goat. No women may eat the flesh of any animal that has been killed as a sacrifice for illness, and pregnant women are not allowed to eat bear.

In a Kōm (? Old Kuki) village, situated in a remote corner of the plain at the south-west end of the valley, I learnt that women when pregnant are there forbidden to eat wild pig, deer, mithan, sapeng (serow, or mountain goat), while Kukis forbid them to eat eggs or the flesh of animals that are found dead in the jungle or that die a natural death. During the continuance of the birth genna a Kōm woman may not eat either fish or pork and may not drink cold water.

Among the Chirus there are no general prohibitions. No woman may eat dog, which is also forbidden both to the khullākpa and to the lūplākpa, when killed as a sacrifice.

Owen says of the Nāga tribes in the North that "they have such an aversion to the flesh of any female, as, in the absence of those of the male kind, to refuse this description of food altogether. They, however, eat of fish, snakes, etc., without endeavouring to make the same distinction."[1]

The first fruits are "genna" until rendered available for general use, by the action of the khullākpa. There are thus gennas affecting the various social units, the tribe, the village the clan, and the household. There are gennas based on the classification of society by age and sex and social duties. There are gennas of regular occurrence, gennas which are permanent, gennas of occasional occurrence and gennas which are necessitated by individual volition. There are gennas relating to every kind of food-stuff. Some are based "on the belief that

[1] *Op cit.* p. 10.

the qualities of the thing eaten pass into the eater."[1] To this class belong the sex food gennas. What would happen if an unmarried woman ate the flesh of a male animal? There are gennas which seem to be precautionary, others which seem to be prophylactic, others again which are propitiatory. Every event which in any way disturbs the normal routine of life, be the disturbance ever so little, necessitates a complementary or corresponding disturbance to set things straight once more. It is clear that, whether consciously or not, there is great stress laid on the concentration of society into its component elements upon the dual basis of sex and economic subsistence. The normal relations of bed and board are interrupted. Commensal and conjugal intercourse are resumed when the danger is overpast. The sanctions range from mere popular disapproval to death, and "they are cited more *exempli gratia* than as the known and experimentally verified results of such transgression. They represent the minimum, not the maximum, of the possibilities of the case. There is always the disturbing thought that not always, nor of necessity, does the sinner bear the punishment of his sin, and the genna system is strengthened, social solidarity is maintained, by the idea of vicarious punishment which makes it the business of each man to see that his neighbour keeps the law." It is clear that there is a bond between father and child,[2] such that what the father does and eats at certain periods of the child's life, crises in its life, as it were, is thought to affect the child injuriously. I think that there is some such bond between the religious head of the village and his fellow villagers. He is *the* man of the village, its representative on all occasions, which stir the community as a living organic whole into action. He cannot refuse to act; he may not depart from the line of action sanctioned by long custom. Every male who has attained full tribesmanship, as evidenced by marriage, acts in a similar representative capacity on behalf of the social unit of which he is the head, because he possesses in some degree a sanctity which enables him to do these necessary things, to have these dealings with "extranatural" powers with safety.

[1] Tylor, *Early History of Mankind*, p. 131.

[2] *Cf.* H. Ling Roth, *J.A.I.* Vol. XXII, p. 204 *et seq.* Significance of the Couvade. Frazer, *Totemism and Exogamy*, Vol. IV, p. 254.

The life of these small communities may not unfairly be described as "nasty, dull, and brutish." They make the most of every notable event, dwelling on the memories of the past and enhancing the value of the future by anticipation. The break in the routine of their lives, when it does come, produces an atmosphere of nervous exaltation. The slow progress and the extreme scrupulosity of their attention to the minute details of the periodical gennas are accompanied by, perhaps directly produce, a nervous tension often amounting to a state of frenzied excitement. The sudden swift occurrence of some terrible calamity in their midst sets them into a fever of fear and emotion, to be relieved on the principle *similia similibus curantur*, only by a solemn communal rite.

Stones and Stone Monuments.

The worship of stones in this area possesses an importance which will justify detailed treatment. Stone monuments consist of (1) monoliths, which are not as large as those in the Khasia Hills,[1] and which are found either singly or arranged symmetrically in rows, avenues, circles or ovals; (2) cairns or heaps of stones; (3) single smaller stones; and (4) the flat stones near Marām, supported on smaller stones.

Monoliths abound in this area, but the symmetrical arrangements of monoliths are found, so far as I know, in only two portions, viz. at Marām and the village Uilong and in the Marring area.[2] Outside the once large and prosperous village of Marām there is an avenue of stones, nearly all of which are still standing, and inside the village one can see the remains of, or parts of, a circle of stones. One particular monolith in the avenue is associated with hunting luck, and before a hunting party goes forth, they go down to the stone and endeavour to kick a pebble on top of it. If they succeed in this, their venture will be successful. At Uilong there is a very remarkable collection of stones, which is not mentioned in any of the earlier writers on Manipur, as McCulloch, Brown, Pemberton or Johnstone, though it is certain that more than once they were

[1] Cf. *The Khasis*, Major Gurdon, pp. 144-154.

[2] At Konga Khul there are a few which reminded me of Marām. At a site further south, the name of which I have forgotten, I came on some monoliths in a regular avenue.—J. S.

STONE CIRCLE—UILONG. [To face p. 186

From a photograph by Lt.-Col. Leslie Shakespear, Commandant Nāga Hills Military Police.

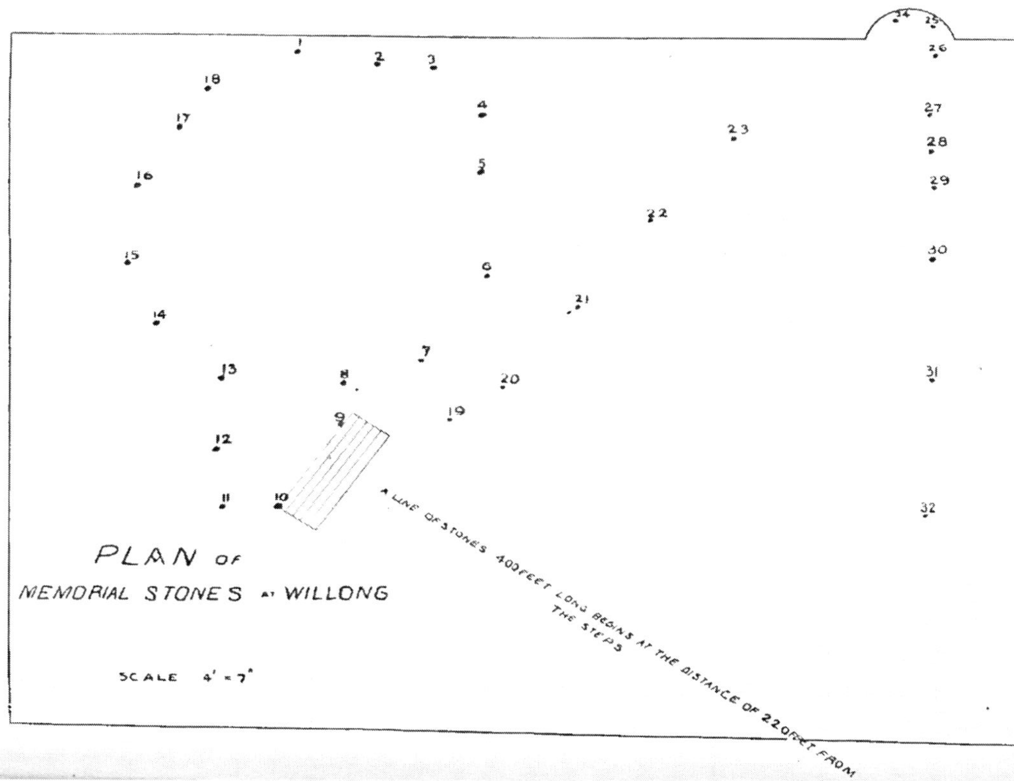
PLAN OF
MEMORIAL STONES AT WILLONG
SCALE 4' = 7"
A LINE OF STONES 400 FEET LONG BEGINS AT THE DISTANCE OF 220 FEET FROM THE STEPS
1
2
3
4
5
6
7
8
9
10
11
12
13
14
15
16
17
18
19
20
21
22
23
24
25
26
27
28
29
30
31
32

close to the village, which lies in a remote corner of the State. I visited this village in December, 1900, and to my regret had no instruments with me for determining the size and orientation of the stones. At my request Colonel H. St. P. Maxwell, C.S.I., deputed Babu Nithor Nath Banerji to measure the stones and prepare a plan which is now reproduced.[1] By the side of the winding path up to the village I noticed small stones, perhaps a foot or eighteen inches high, with a larger one at regular intervals, then I came to a flight of stone steps, close to which was a circle of stones. On investigations being made, I found that there were two contiguous series, one having a circular shape and the other, the smaller, being nearly oval. The unmarried men dance and wrestle inside the large circle on

MEASUREMENT OF THE STONES AND THEIR ORIENTATION.

	H.	B.	Th.	Orientation.
No. 1	9′0″	7′ 8″	1′ 10″	E.
No. 2	9′ 8″	4′ 6″	1′ 6″	N.E.
No. 3	12′ 10″	2′ 6″	2′ 7″	S.E.
No. 4	5′ 7″	2′ 5″	3″	S.E.
No. 5	9′ 5″	2′ 7″	8″	S.E.
No. 6	8′ 9″	4′ 0″	1′ 5″	S.E.
No. 7	13′ 4″	8′ 5″	1′ 3″	S.W.
No. 8	10′ 5″	8′ 4″	2′ 4″	S.W.
No. 9	11′ 8″	9′ 9″	2′ 2″	S.W.
No. 10	9′ 11″	7′ 8″	2″	W.
No. 11	9′ 0″	1′ 10″	1′ 2″	S.W.
No. 12	8′ 7″	3′ 8″	1′ 7″	N.W.
No. 13	8′ 9″	3′ 0″	1′ 10″	N.
No. 14	10′ 6″	3′ 9″	1′ 9″	N.W.
No. 15	9′ 0″	3′ 9″	1′ 7″	N.
No. 16	10′ 9″	4″	2′ 5″	N.
No. 17	13′ 0″	5′ 5″	1′ 11″	N.E.
No. 18	11′ 7″	2′ 8″	2′ 3″	N.E.

Dated Manipur, the 9th December, 1904 } NITHOR NATH BANERJEE.

DISTANCES OF STONES FROM EACH OTHER.

From No. 1—2 (3′ 8″).	From No. 10—11 (3′ 7″).
From No. 2—3 (2′ 6″).	From No. 11—12 (1′ 9″).
From No. 3—4 (3′ 8″).	From No. 12—13 (2′ 8″).
From No. 4—5 (2′ 7″).	From No. 13—14 (3′ 7″).
From No. 5—6 (5′ 0″).	From No. 14—15 (1′ 10″).
From No. 6—7 (3′ 3″).	From No. 15—16 (5′ 2″).
From No. 7—8 (4′ 6″).	From No. 16—17 (4′ 6″).
From No. 8—9 (2′ 3″).	From No. 17—18 (2′ 8″).
From No. 9—10 (5′ 9″).	From No. 18—1 (3′ 7″).

Dated Manipur, the 9th December, 1904 } NITHOR NATH BANERJEE.

[1] See plan and tables giving measurements.

the village genna for the annual festival of the dead. From the edge of the oval there starts a line of monoliths. There are now thirty-two stones standing, four in the small oval, fourteen in the circle, and fourteen in the long rows.[1] These stones are said to have been erected three or four centuries ago, when the village is believed to have been much larger than it now is. The erection must have been very costly and would be impossible at the present time. From the traditions of the people themselves and from the actual practices[2] as found elsewhere at the present time, we may obtain some idea of the expenditure of human energy and material resources required for the purpose.

The preliminaries have been described above.[2] On the fateful day the maiba pours zu on the stone, "utters many mantras," and lets loose a fowl, in order that there may be no difficulty in getting the stone into its appointed place. The villagers drag the stone up by sledges like those used by the Manipuris, attaching to them ropes made of the creeper. For a year the lungchingba lives apart from his family. Thereafter his descendants annually go to the stone, drink together, and clear the jungle growth away. They say that if a stone falls or cracks, it portends the ruin of the family of the lungchingba, a belief which will go far to explain the annoyance of the Nāgas at Marām when some Public Works overseers broke up a stone in order to get road metal. At Mao I was informed that the father of a man who erected a stone would help his son, so that there it has the aspect of ancestor worship. In what way the help would be rendered by the deceased parent to his son, was not made clear to me.

Among the Marrings we find stone circles, mostly dilapidated, inside the village.

Cairns and heaps of stones are found among the Tangkhuls and Quoirengs, who build them in a beehive or conical shape. Some of these beehive cairns are to be seen in the Kaithenmānbi plain close to the cart-road.

So far as I know, the flat stones, supported on three or four

[1] Cf. *Progs. Liverpool Geographical Society*, 1904, pp. 31 and 32. *Journal of Society of Arts*, Vol LIII, No. 2733, p. 559.

[2] See above, p. 181.

smaller vertical stones, are to be seen only near Marām, and I learnt that one of these flat stone monuments had been erected within comparatively recent times.

Connected with some of the stones are various legends. At Hundung is a stone commemorating the subjugation of that turbulent Tangkhul village by Ching Thang Komba, and annually worship is paid to it. Near Ukrul is a stone from which they got fire when on their migration. At that stone they divided, some going to Sirohi, while the majority preferred to go to Ukrul. At Maikel is a stone on which I was told there were pictures of men and animals. I took measures to have this stone placed in a proper position, for it had fallen down, but its inscriptions, if it ever had any, had long disappeared. The curious weathering of the stone produced effects which the Nāgas took for inscriptions. It is said that it stands on the very spot where their ancestor emerged from his sojourn in the earth. These stones are all regarded as laipham, places where a lai dwells. So, too, the heaps of stones in the Tangkhul villages and the rings of stones in the Marring villages are holy, so holy that no one dare swear falsely on them. Similar sanctity attaches to a meteor stone in a Kabui village. Good luck in war is associated with the Tangkhul cairns and with single stones such as those kept by the khullākpas at Mao and Maikel. That at Maikel is a mass of conglomerate and is always hidden inside the khullākpa's house, where, as a favour, I was allowed to see it. Heads taken on a raid were shown to these stones, and I specially observed that at Mao the khullākpa poured zu on a stone outside the village when performing a rite.[1]

Small stones are associated with sickness and it is legitimate to infer that they too are laiphams, *i.e.* not the actual spirit which causes the sickness, but the place in which he dwells.

I may add that among some of the minor Kuki tribes an interesting form of sepulchral monument[2] is erected in honour of a rich woman after her death. Small stones are erected in rows inside a fence of slightly larger stones and the heads of

[1] There is a quaintly shaped stone in a Nāga village west of the valley which receives pigs from various villages and is very holy. It is about 5 feet long.—J. S.

[2] The lady must have performed the Bah Ai ceremony.—J. S.

the creatures killed at her obsequies (a fowl, a goat, a pig, a cow) are placed on them.

Dr. Brown[1] mentions the erection by the Kabuis of upright or flat stones as marking the grave, and the only case I have known of the erection of a stone monument took place after the death of the man's father, so that the motive of honouring the dead and of exhibiting piety operates among them to the present day.[2]

Mr. Pettigrew gives a lively account of the ritual employed by the Tangkhuls when erecting a memorial stone, which I reproduce verbatim.[3]

"*The 'Onrā' (memorial stone) ceremony.*—Amongst the wealthy, the male member of the family makes a stipulation in his verbal will, that a monument should be erected in memory of him, and the wife and family suffer in consequence, as a great deal of money is spent over it. During the rainy season, before the rice begins to bear fruit, all the friends of the deceased gather together at a prominent spot outside the village which serves as a landmark and which the relations have before decided upon. The night before a cow is killed and cooked by the males only; half of the intestines is taken by the relations and the other half by the friends. It is then cooked and divided amongst them, and should there be a goodly number, say 100 or 150, their share is infinitesimal; still it has to go round. This division takes place in the morning, and after all is ready each person divides his small portion again into three pieces, and offers them to 'kameo.' The three pieces represent (1) the earth, (2) the heavens, (3) his self. With this meat weak rice beer is drunk, and after the feeding is over the strong rice beer is distributed. Then six friends are set apart to carry the wooden images shaped to represent buffalo and dogs' heads, and in the case of a brave who has taken heads, an image of himself is made. These are all to be placed on top of the memorial. Following these six friends solemnly walks the

[1] *Op. cit.* p. 106.

[2] Among Lusheis, stones are only put up as memorials of the dead. I have known two occasions on which persons having no one to put up the stone for them have put them up during their own lifetime. Stones are only put up to very important persons—chiefs or their children. Can the fear of not being honoured have led to the custom of putting up stones?—J. S.

[3] *Op. cit.* pp. 40 and 41.

'sherra' with suitable portions of cooked meat, and offers up to 'kameo' on the proposed spot. His refrain or prayer on this occasion is as follows: 'Thinghun lungkārna katatit nana yengmira,' at first offering. At second: 'Ina mashāi mashakranglaga, nathum shāirilu.' At third: 'Iwui vāng kho! khararnosan ungphāzak zāulu.' In the meantime the friends are gathering stones, and then, the 'kameo' offering being over, the earthwork is started and the stones built up all around to the height of 2 feet or more. The artists of the village then paint the different images placed on the memorial, generally with charcoal and lime. The last article to be placed on this memorial is a large stone slab, which is considered the most important stone of all, for on it the spirit is said to come and sit during his occasional peregrination around, to view his rice fields. Any removal of this stone by others means a heavy fine. The shape of this memorial is oblong, with one of the shorter sides more approaching an angle. They are about 20 feet long by 8 feet wide. Pine trees and other trees likely to afford shade to the passer-by are planted on them at the same time. The stones on the sides are used a great deal by the villagers as resting places for themselves and for loads of wood, etc., carried up from the jungle or rice field. The next day and for two days following the family take down a basket of meat and chillies and place it on a raised platform upon which the spirit is supposed to come and partake. They stay for half an hour or so, and go through the same performance at sunset."[1]

[1] *Op. cit.* p. 40.

SECTION V.—FOLK TALES

The collection of folk tales recorded in the Report of the Linguistic Survey of India possesses a charm and interest for the ethnologist apart from its value from a linguistic point of view. I have little hesitation, therefore, in making full and copious use of it, the more so because so many of the legends and myths which were narrated to me by Nāgas have already been mentioned in other connections.[1]

TĀNGKHUL.[2]

Khanongvana kahāng ji, Āramona ngană
Medicine-men-by said it-is, Forefathers-by heard
kuimaronda hāngda :—'Ithum mikumo hi kathi
transmitting say :— 'We mankind this die
maningmana,' ji, 'āphasā ngalaili phumhāi-chingda manglā
do-not,' say, 'his-body in-earth burying-always spirit
Koktoli lai-a,' ji. Kapā china nganālaga,
Death-king-with remains,' say. Madman that hearing-said,
'ino ngara! ithumli āna shothatlada. I thihāiaka i Koktoli
'my friends! us he does-kill. I when-dead I Death-king
shothatka.' Kumka shānglaga thihowa. Koktoli vāuwa.
will-kill.' One-year afterwards he-died. Death-king-to ascended.
Koktoli kapāa china kazai aina āpharuwa.
Death-king-at madman that spear with at-him-threw.
Koktoli mazatunana. Koktina,
Death-king (acc.), *did-not-touch (him).* *Death-king (said),*
'mikumo hi makaphāna; āli unguranu ; āli marālākaranu ;
'mankind this is-bad ; him let-return ; him let-never-come-here ;

[1] See sections on Origin, p. 8. Coiffure, p. 27. Manufactures, p. 47. Games, p. 68. Organisation, p. 79. Religious Beliefs, *passim*.
[2] *L.S.I.*, Vol. III, Pt. II, p. 471.

āli khi aina thirani-kala?' Ā sāraka masina panthuranu.
him what for died?' He after-doing by-wind blow-away.
Ā ungrāsāi. Āli chisanugida laisāi. 'Nathum
He returned-(to earth). His grave-at (men) were. 'You
khi sānikala?' 'Na thihoda chisanuki kajina.' 'I
what are-doing?' 'You dying grave will-make' (said). 'I
mathimana; ringli. Ina Koktoli vāi; Koktoli
am-not-dead; am-alive. I Death-king-to went; Death-king-at
ina kazai aina pharuwa; mazạtumana. Koktona ili,
I spear with threw; did-not-touch (him). Death-king me-to,
"ungulu," ji, "mikumo hi makaphāna marālākaranu,"
"return," said, "mankind this is-bad let-him-not-come-here,"
ji I mathilākmana, ili masina panthura.'
said. I have-not-died, me the-wind blew-away.'

Free Translation of the Foregoing.

Medicine men tell us by tradition from their forefathers that we men do not die, and that, when our bodies are buried in the earth, our spirits remain with the Death-king. My friends, a madman once heard this and said, 'He kills us, so when I am dead I will kill the Death-king.' A year afterwards he died, and he ascended to the Death-king. The madman threw a spear at the Death-king, but it did not touch him. Then said the Death-king, 'This is a bad man. Send him back, and never let him come here. Why did he die?' Then the Death-king blew him back to earth in a puff of wind. Men were standing round his grave. He said to them, 'what are you doing?' 'You are dead,' said they, 'and we are making your grave.' 'I am not dead. I am alive. I went to the Death-king, and threw a spear at him, but it did not touch him. "Return," said he. "This is a bad man. Do not let him come here." I have not died. The wind blew me back here.'

SOPVOMĀ OR MĀO NĀGĀ.[1]

Im mēmē thēli-a c̄hū̄ kāhē̄ ubbānā poē. Ēhū̄
We Māo-people when-dead spears two hands-by hold. Spears

[1] *L.S.I.* Vol. III, Pt. II, p. 461.

Orāmē Pēkujikhē fēlē. Fēliliā mai chanā
the-God Pēkujikhē is-for-piercing. If-able-to-pierce man that
Orāmē iniū lē chowāsoā būli sē. Fēli kokromainā
God's country in happily to-live can. To-pierce who-cannot-man
Orāmē Pēkujikhē ukrūso būdē, chilāmai soā khaidē, tinā
God Pēkujikhē serving remains, slave like is-kept, ever
fapimo. Orāmai hana pi jisūē, kota maicha. Hana
is-not-released. God's that head is-very-big, beard grows. His
kēnā, 'ochū mai nolo mai hai adasonso mathiwē,' annoē.
wife, 'aged man young man as-well-as why are-killed,' asked.
'Maina kososi miya to mima to. Mai thēfrā yiā
'Men chillies old eat unripe-also eat. Man following I-also
ochū mai nolo mai hai fūē,' sata Orāmē hananā pē-ē.
old man young man also catch,' saying God that said.

FREE TRANSLATION OF THE FOREGOING.

When any one of us Māo people dies, two spears are put into his hand. These are for piercing the God Pēkujikhē. If the dead man can pierce him, he is allowed to live happily in the God's country. If he cannot pierce him, he has to become a servant to Pēkujikhē. He is kept like a slave, and is never released.

This God's head is very big, and he has a beard. His wife once asked him why he killed young people as well as old. He replied, 'men cut chillies both unripe and ripe, and after their example I catch both young men and old men.'

KHOIRĀO NAGĀ.[1]

Kata-mi āpūi āpā cham gānghai. Sari kagāibā
Aged-men forefathers fathers words said. Enemy killing
mini sarinā sari-fi fungē; sari kagāi-kamak tang
man enemy-by enemy-dress is-carried; enemy killing-not man
fūngnāi. Sari kagāi tang sichū pāini talā
should-not-carry. Enemy killing man when-dead him-by in

[1] *L.S.I.* Vol. III, Pt. II, p. 430.

ringamang thatpā pūā wōngni pāi khāo
his-life-time who-was-killed owner (enemy) coming his basket
fūnglā gāngē 'fūng-lā-ki,' tani sarōnē, nangō haini
carry said, 'will-not-carry,' saying quarrelled, 'you I
ngamē' 'ngamakē,' tani bākathaūchē. Chithaū sibū
defeated' 'defeated-not,' saying refused. There-upon deceased
chini 'nangni bāitōmani nang jāū chi kamēt yāūlā,' tani
that 'you refuse-if your face that rubbing see,' saying
sari chini yāūchū hāng jam naini, 'jingē,'
enemy that on-seeing dao marks being-found, 'it-is-true,'
tani, 'hai-lōbāni ngamangdaiyē, fūnglē,' tan
saying, 'my-friend (you(-defeated-)me), will-carry,' saying
fūngūngē. Sari kagāi-tang sichū hāng ngāi
carried. Enemy killing-man on-being-dead dao spears
kahūchi, 'kasi bampūi kafēnga laūlō, tani chiyāngbohūē
are-given, 'death way-in will-fight again,' saying is-reason-for
ngāi jahūie, laū wālē kafū andri jahūiē.
spear is-given, land to-cultivate spade axe are-given.

Free Translation of the Foregoing.

Our forefathers have told us that when a man dies in fight, he is clad in his war-dress. If he does not die in fight, he is not so clad.

When he who killed him dies, the man who was killed comes to him and tells him to carry his basket. 'I will not carry it,' says the conqueror, 'for I defeated you in our life-time.' They fight about this. 'You did not defeat me,' denies the other. Says the conqueror, 'If you deny, rub your face and see.' Then the other rubs his face, and finds marks of a *dao* on it. 'It is true,' he says, 'my friend, you defeated me. I will carry the basket,' so he does so.

When a man who has killed an enemy dies, he is given spears and a *dao*, because he will have to fight again in the path of death. They also give him a spade and an axe to cultivate land in the nether-world.

KABUI.[1]

Taipangmai thāithai, gāinā sūraūdū-māi-mo,
Human-being when-dead, good who-did-the-one-who-that,
kai-haū laū-haū-makmai, thāithinaū Rāgāng kāi kūwē.
theft lie-who-did-not-commit, when-dead God house reach.
Gāimakmai sūmaitho thondiyāng thāin-ganthe. Ngānā
Bad-action who-did-man hell-to dies-and-is-hurled. Child
thāithai kapūi naū-naū-mai Rāgāng kāi
when-dead its-mother's bosom-which-drinks God house
kāinā-kho kapūi thāimaksān naū-ta hoinā
by-the-side-of its-mother is-not-dead-until bosom-for being-thirsty
kap bamē, kapūi dang-kho, 'Lāgānglē, āpūi
crying remains, its-mother on-being-there, 'O God, my-mother
thāiti-cho ? naū-naū-pūmathē, āpūi-tā titho,
(is)-being-dead (?) bosom-(milk)-will-drink, my-mother give,'
ngānā kuroi kap bamthē. Rāgāngloi sāpūilatsā, 'napūitā
child that crying remained. God said, 'your-mother-to
tāipāngmai kho kāihaūtinā tāo tān-kang lāū-bamthē.'
world in stealing now fetters wearing-remained.'
Nāi-khat nāi-nhāi bamlanā kalāū taroinā
Day-one days-two after-remaining her-child that
kap-lang-tithinā Rāgāngloi jiyēnā kapūitā
on-crying-very-much God (loving i.e., pitying) its-mother-for
tān-kang dapdoknā kanātā ti-naū-thē.
fetters taking-off her-child gave-the-bosom.

FREE TRANSLATION OF THE FOREGOING.

We, human beings, can after death reach the holy feet of God in Heaven, if we do not commit any sin and pass our lives honestly in this world; but those who commit theft and do many other sinful actions such as telling lies, cheating others, etc., are all sent to hell.

When a child drinking milk of its mother is dead it remains crying near God, because it is hungry and wants to drink its mother's milk; and when its mother is dead it says to God, 'O God, is my mother dead? Let me see her and satisfy my

[1] *L.S.I.* Vol. III, Pt. II, p. 423.

thirst by drinking her milk.' And God answers, 'O child, your mother cannot come here now, because she is in hell bound with fetters for committing theft in her lifetime in the world.' Nevertheless the child continues crying bitterly and makes repeated prayers for the release of its mother. At last God, being compassionate, releases the mother from confinement in hell and brings her to her hungry child. The child now drinks her milk to its heart's content.

MARING.[1]

A song sung at the death of aged or respectable men, and also the lamentation of friends and relatives of the deceased.

Kūlkūngā ūmlē piyo. Kandrāngrai?
What-was-created is-dead give. What-is-the-cause?
Thihandrāngrē? Pasāngo, samlē nungsam, hē,
Is-it-caused-by-devil? Creator, death has-occurred, O,
ponroikhā. Rūngtimā roikhlā.
clothe-the-deceased (body). O-friend gone-to-nether-land.
Kaiplūi, nang lainang nai machat thangāi taūbai
My-friend, you when-living your conduct good being
kā nūngkwāi. Āsinang, kaiplūi, nang hiworābai kā
we were-happy. Now, my-friend, you on-being-dead we
nūngāimakā. Plūiyo, Tharāi-nangn chānpiyānang, hanūi
are-not-happy. O-friend, God-by being-kind, once-more
mūrilānang kā nūngāiraūho. Nang khāinānāraū
if-allowed-to-see we would-be-happy. You-(from) separation-on
kā lāwā. Kā āpangnakāni. Kaiplūi, nang
we are-grieved. We are-like-one-senseless. My-friend, you
hiyā, nang nūngai hall khlāklē, fi khē khlāklē,
are-dead, you for cow is-given, cloths also are-given,
chāk khē khlāklē, wā khē khlāklē, tūl khē khlāklē. Ā
rice also is-given, fowl also is-given, wine also is-given. These
ānām chābai nūngkwāinē nang laūlailo.
all eating happily (may)-you live.

[1] *L.S.I.* Vol. III, Pt. II, p. 479.

The Tangkhuls of Sirohi narrated the following tales to me :—

Once upon a time a dog was about to eat the moon but the cock overheard him talking about his intentions. So the cock flew up to heaven and warned the moon. So as a reward for this the cock was given a fine crest and told to wake mankind daily with his crowings.

There is a stone near Ukrul from which their ancestors got fire by striking it with a dao. They came to the laphu (plantain) direction, but the ancestors of Ukrul came by the heimang direction, and so people preferred Ukrul to Sirohi, which accounts for the fact that Ukrul is larger than Sirohi.[1]

[1] This tale has a curious parallel in the tale reproduced in the *Linguistic Survey Report*, Vol. III, Part III, p. 71, *q.v.*, which was collected from a Kuki.—T. C. H.

APPENDIX I

The ring is worn on the penis, the foreskin being pulled through tightly. The ring is made of bone or bamboo, occasionally of cane ribbon, and is an eighth of an inch to a quarter of an inch wide. It is assumed at puberty and it at first occasions great pain, but, as Dr. Brown [1] points out, from the pressure the organ gradually alters its shape. The ring is removed at night, when their wives wear it on their finger, and for micturition. They themselves say that at one time they used to fight over women so much that the ring was adopted as a means of curbing their passions. Dr. Brown offers the surmise [2] that "it may have something to do with the custom by which parents are obliged to surrender their house and two-thirds of their property to their eldest son when he marries, and that it may have been introduced by some parent anxious to put off the evil day of his own turning out by thus placing a check on the amatory propensities of his offspring." The custom is persistent even among those who have left the hills for the valley, though its abandonment is one of the preliminary steps to entry into Hindu society. This "mutilation" is undoubtedly an initiation rite.[3]

[1] *Op. cit.* p. 39.
[2] *Op. cit.* p. 40.
[3] See p. 77.

APPENDIX II

Does totemism exist in Manipur in any of its many stages of development or decay? The question demands attention even if it cannot be answered with categorical precision, because Dr. Frazer has put forward the view that the objects which are *nāmungba* to the Meithei clans[1] may be provisionally called totems.[2] This view received support from Colonel Shakespear, who remarked in a review of the Meitheis that, "Among the surrounding cognate clans there are no signs of totemism, but there are some reasons for thinking the Manipuri 'Yek' is a totemistic division. It is exogamous and is sometimes named after animals. . . . Mr. Hodson makes no reference to totemism, and it would have been interesting to have heard his reasons for omitting to do so."[3] The evidence which in my opinion justified me in my refusal to describe the Meithei yeks as totemistic divisions was placed before Colonel Shakespear, who investigated it in Manipur, with the result that in a later article[4] he accepts my view that the Meithei yeks are not totemistic divisions. That there are tabus affecting social units both among the Meitheis and the Nāgas is a fact upon which I cannot insist too often or too strongly. In so far as Colonel Shakespear has found evidence of the origin of these tabus among the Meitheis, it is clear that the objects tabued are believed to have been proved to be dangerous to some individual member of the social unit. The sense of social solidarity is such that all the members of the social unit are constrained by custom to regard the tabued object as potentially dangerous to them and therefore to be avoided. Sometimes the tabued object is a single specific object, sometimes each and every member of a class or species of natural objects is regarded as

[1] *The Meitheis*, p. 118.
[2] *Totemism and Exogamy*, Vol. II, p. 327.
[3] *Man.*, 1908, p. 189.
[4] *Man.*, 1910, pp. 59–61.

dangerous and is tabued. Can we, then, fairly construe the belief that natural objects are dangerous to members of a particular social unit as meaning that an intimate relation exists between that social unit on the one side and the class of natural objects on the other side? If we may, are we justified in regarding this intimate relation as totemism, either in an embryonic form or in the last stage of decay? On Dr. Frazer's definition of totemism[1] the relations between social groups and species of natural objects in totemism are of friendship. But the Meithei will have none such friends. He avoids them and regards them as sources of danger, the cause of plagues, of boils and blains and such like horrors.

I have observed in Manipur many customs which elsewhere are often associated with or commonly ascribed to totemism. The social system of the Meitheis and Nāgas is based on exogamous divisions. It may well be true that some of the clan eponyms are the names of animals or of some other natural object. At the moment I can only call to mind one such instance. The word Luang is the name of one of the Meithei saleis or clans, and is also the name of a variety of fish found in hill streams. I do not know enough of the many Nāga dialects to be certain that not one of the clan names which I have recorded was or had been also the name of some species of natural object. The clan eponyms were explained to me by Nāgas as the names of the common ancestor of the clan. No other signification was attached to them. It is a matter of common knowledge that all these dialects have been subject to natural processes of change and decay.[2] They are all built up on monosyllabic bases, and homophones abound. The maxim that things that are equal to the same thing are equal to one another must be applied with caution to the linguistic evidence until the history of the progress of these dialects is better known to us. Where the pedigree of some of the monosyllabic roots now in use is known to us, it is clear that their present form is the result of consonantal detrition and vowel modification, whose laws remain to be ascertained and codified.

Food tabus such as those described above[3] may be due to the belief that "the qualities of the thing eaten pass into the eater."[4] On this view it is the quality of masculinity which accounts for the tabu observed by unmarried girls against the flesh of male animals. It may be urged that we have here a

[1] *Op. cit.*, pp. 3 and 4.
[2] Grierson, *Linguistic Survey of India*, Vol. II, p. 69.
[3] Pp. 182-4.
[4] Tylor, *Early History of Mankind*, p. 131.

faint reminiscence of a time when it was believed that there was a causal connection between food and the procreation of children. Hartland has argued[1] that the laxity which characterises the prenuptial relations of the unmarried of both sexes signifies a degree of physiological ignorance. If this be so, and if ignorance of the physical process by which men and animals reproduce their species be indeed, as Dr. Frazer is now inclined to think, the ultimate source of totemism, then there is some evidence of the existence among the Nāgas of beliefs which are explicable by the hypothesis that the Nāgas were once more ignorant on this delicate subject than they now are.

It may be that the horns and tail with which a Nāga warrior adorns himself on high days and holidays are reminiscent of totemism. Nowadays these decorations are worn without much thought of esoteric symbolism. The folktale,[2] which portrays the ancestress of the Marām Nāgas as semi-animal in form, may be totemistic; but it is at least probable that it is only a modern attempt to explain and to validate an important communal tabu. What made them think that the custom stood in need of an explanation at all? We may infer that the particular mechanism of the explanation was selected and the explanation itself accepted because they were in harmony with popular ideas of causation as regards social phenomena of this order. It gives us a glimpse into the minds both of those who invented the tale and of those who accepted it and adopted it as an article of faith.

What these facts seem to prove is the existence in this area not so much of totemism as of a mental attitude, a *Weltanschauung,* which in other parts of the world have permitted totemism to flourish and prosper.

[1] *Op. cit.*, Vol. II, Chap. VII.
[2] Above, p. 13.

INDEX

PLACE NAMES.

The rectification of the frontier line at the north-east corner of the State has resulted in the transfer to the jurisdiction of the Nāga Hills District of a number of the northern Tangkhul villages which were for years administered as subject to Manipur. They were included in Manipur at the time of the last census and are shown above accordingly.

R. CLAY AND SONS, LTD. BREAD ST. HILL, E.C., AND BUNGAY, SUFFOLK.